STUDIES IN SOCIAL POWER

STUDIES IN SOCIAL POWER

Edited by

DORWIN CARTWRIGHT

RESEARCH CENTER FOR GROUP DYNAMICS
INSTITUTE FOR SOCIAL RESEARCH
THE UNIVERSITY OF MICHIGAN, ANN ARBOR

1959

ISR Code No. 1413

Library of Congress Catalog Card No. 59-63036
ISBN 0-87944-025-2 paperbound

Published by the Institute for Social Research
The University of Michigan, Ann Arbor, Michigan 48106

First Published 1959
Fourth Printing 1974

PREFACE

The chapters of this book have been written by eleven people and report work done over a period of seven or eight years. All are concerned with some aspect of social power. The various contributions represent a common point of view, or identifiable approach, but they do not report the product of an integrated program of research. Instead, they reflect the convergence of interest among a number of people working on various research problems, to whom it became evident that social power had to be better understood if these other problems were to be solved.

As a result of the different directions from which the problem of power was approached, rather diverse aspects have been studied. No single theoretical formulation has served to guide the research. Indeed, no two investigations have used precisely the same definition of power. For this reason the findings of the several studies do not produce a tightly knit theoretical fabric. Nevertheless, the different investigations all do point to roughly the same range of phenomena. One study deals with the ability of one person to influence the attitudes and behavior of another; a second focuses on the ability of individuals to influence the decisions of a group; a third is concerned with the ability of a person to make decisions for others; and a fourth examines the ability of one person to determine whether or not another reaches his goal. Throughout, power is viewed as the ability of one person (or group) to influence or control some aspect of another person (or group).

It is possible to view any social variable both as independent and dependent, as cause and effect. Power is no exception. Some of the studies reported here are directed toward answering such questions as: How does power influence communication? What does the possession of power do to one's personal relations with others? Is power always threatening to those over whom it might be exercised? Other studies focus on the determinants of power: What are the sources of power? What characteristics of personality affect the development of a group's power structure? Under what conditions is the possession of power converted into the exercise of power? None of the studies attempts to view power simultaneously as both an independent and dependent variable.

Empirical research on power has been hampered by the fact that the usual tools of research and the populations customarily studied by social psychologists do not lend themselves readily to investigation of the "harder" aspects of power. In the research reported in this book several different techniques have been employed: an interview survey of a sample of three interacting professional groups; a field study employing systematic observations of behavior in two summer camps; a laboratory experiment, conducted in a business office, in which the formal structure of the organization was used to create experimental variables; and the more customary laboratory experiment with student volunteers. While each of these techniques contributed to the total research, it is clear that more methodological ingenuity will be required before power becomes fully susceptible to empirical investigation.

Each chapter of this book has been written so that it can be read without reference to any of the others. At the same time, chapters have been arranged so as to facilitate an orderly study of the problems of social power. The sequence is designed to present a natural development of data and concepts for the reader who starts at the beginning and reads consecutively.

The first chapter develops the thesis that social power has been neglected by researchers and theorists in the field of social psychology. It attempts to show in some detail why the classic problems of social psychology cannot be solved without devoting greater attention to power.

The next three chapters take power as an independent variable and examine some of the consequences for persons who find themselves under the power of others. Major attention is directed to the threatening aspects of power and to how people respond to these disturbing features of power systems.

The next two chapters concentrate on the ways in which power relations become established. The first compares the development of power structures among groups of boys who differ in level of personal adjustment. The second reports an attempt to generate power relations in the laboratory and to document microscopically the processes leading to stable power relationships. The following two chapters examine the determinants of power in natural groups —the family and the military work-group.

The last three chapters are concerned with theory. First is a discussion of "types of power" and of sources of power in groups and institutions. Then a model, employing mathematics, is described which permits rigorous derivation of several theorems concerning influences on opinions and attitudes among members of a group. The last chapter outlines a formal system of concepts by which it is hoped that the construct *power* may be placed unambiguously in a more general theory of human behavior. An effort is also made to specify the conceptual properties of power which must be considered explicitly in designing empirical research and in theorizing about power.

The authors of the various chapters were all members of the staff of the Research Center for Group Dynamics at the University of Michigan at the time the work reported was undertaken. Since several have moved to other institutions in the meantime, the present location of each author is listed here: Arthur R. Cohen, Yale University; George Levinger, Bryn Mawr College; Bertram Raven, University of California at Los Angeles; Sidney Rosen, Marquette University; Richard Snyder, Human Research Unit #2, Ford Ord, California; Ezra Stotland, University of Washington; and Dorwin Cartwright, John R. P. French, Jr., Frank Harary, Donald M. Wolfe, and Alvin Zander, University of Michigan.

Many persons in addition to the authors made significant contributions to the work reported here. Specific reference is made in each chapter to those who contributed most directly to the particular study. It is an unfortunate feature of collaborative research, however, that all who contribute cannot be properly recognized in print. We hereby express our appreciation to all our colleagues, present and past, who helped make this book possible.

DORWIN CARTWRIGHT

November 26, 1958

CONTENTS

1

POWER: A NEGLECTED VARIABLE IN SOCIAL PSYCHOLOGY [1]

Dorwin Cartwright

Twentieth century social psychology can be traced back to the earliest philosophers, but its complexion is largely determined by developments in this century. Prior to World War I social psychology had failed by and large to meet those requirements of an abstract, positive science which Comte had laid down about the middle of the nineteenth century. Today, in sharp contrast, the spirit of positivism holds sway, and the only problems deemed worthy of attention are those susceptible to objective observation and, preferably, quantification. But this gain has not been made without cost, for scientific status has been achieved by neglecting any phenomena which do not lend themselves readily to the operations of science.

In his review of the history of social psychology, Allport (2) points out that writers in its metaphysical epoch mapped out many of the phenomena which a developed scientific social psychology must handle. Advances in our present era will largely consist, then, in devising ways for treating by scientific techniques (empirical and conceptual) the many phenomena identified by the early theorists.

Power is such a phenomenon. This topic received considerable attention in the metaphysical era of social psychology. The classic reference is Hobbes (14) who in 1651 analyzed the motivation for power and some of its social consequences. More recent discussions, still in the metaphysical era, are those of Nietzsche (27) and Adler (1). Many other philosophical and speculative treatments could, of course, be cited.

At the present time questions about power are more commonly raised by men of practical affairs than by social psychologists. How does one best organize a group so that the activities of its members are coordinated? Why do so many people react to leaders by displaying either dependence or defiance? Is it possible for groups to be effective without concentrating power in

---

[1] This chapter is based on the presidential address delivered at the 1953 annual meeting of the Society for the Psychological Study of Social Issues.

the hands of a very few people? How can one keep a group from destroying the individuality and personal freedom of its members? Must strong groups always exploit weaker ones? Questions of this sort are concerned with the influence exerted by some people over others, or, in short, with power.

Both early social psychology and modern society recognize the importance of power. If, however, we examine social psychology since the beginning of its scientific epoch, we search in vain for any concentrated attack on the problem. Surely this constitutes a weakness of modern social psychology. We can only conclude that twentieth century social psychologists have been "soft" on power. Direct investigation has been evaded in many ways. One mode of evasion has been to study power in safe or weak populations—witness the classical stature of research on pecking order among chickens and on dominance among children. Another has been to convert the problem of power into one of attitudes, expectations, and perceptions. Thus, there is more interest in authoritarianism than authority; expectations are made the critical element in the notion of role rather than behavioral restrictions or compulsions; prestige is studied because it can be investigated apart from any specific situation of interpersonal interaction and influence.

It is not here suggested that social psychologists have been cowardly; the fact is that the softer aspects of power have been more accessible to investigation. Nor is it implied that these softer aspects are irrelevant or psychologically uninteresting. The complaint is, rather, that power is often seen as essentially not a psychological problem. When asked about power the social psychologist has typically referred the question to the political scientist, sociologist, or economist; or, worse, he has given answers based upon purely personal values. In any case, the social psychologist has not seen how the central body of his knowledge could be brought to bear on such problems. But surely inability to deal with power within traditional theories does not mean that the problem should be ignored in the future.

The point may be stated differently: it simply is not possible to deal adequately with data which are clearly social psychological without getting involved with matters of power.

SOME ILLUSTRATIVE PROBLEMS INVOLVING POWER

To document the point it is necessary to show how power is inevitably a part of the accepted phenomena of social psychology. This task is made difficult by the fact that there is considerable ambiguity concerning the boundaries of the field. Nevertheless, it is possible to identify certain phenomena (problem areas) as essentially social psychological in nature. Allport (2) has provided a list of these, not intended to be exhaustive, which contains the following: leadership, public opinion, rumor, propaganda, prejudice, attitude change, morale, communications, race relations, and conflicts of value. We shall attempt to show that phenomena of this sort cannot be adequately understood without the concept of power.

Leadership and Social Roles

Empirical research has progressively forced a restatement of the problem of leadership from that of identifying personal traits of the leader to one of determining the causes and consequences of leadership behavior. In this analysis concepts like "social situation," "position," "function," and "role" have come to the fore. As long as leadership was viewed only as a particular combination of personality traits, properties of the social system could easily be ignored. A major advance in the study of leadership therefore came with the abandonment of this narrow point of view, mistakenly labeled "psychological."

Some of the features of the new approach may be illustrated by brief reference to a study of the relation between supervisory practices and employee satisfaction. In this investigation, carried out by the University of Michigan Survey Research Center, Pelz (28) analyzed data from a large manufacturing company to determine whether employee satisfactions were related to certain supervisory practices which could be classified along a continuum from employee goal facilitation to hindrance. His results proved to be inconclusive until he separated the supervisors into two classes: those with high influence in their department at large and those with little influence. The results then formed a consistent pattern. Considering only high-influence supervisors and their subordinates, 19 of 28 correlations between supervisory practices and employee attitudes were positive (goal facilitative behavior of the supervisor being associated with employee satisfaction). For the low-influence supervisors, 20 out of the 28 correlations were zero or negative. The significance of these results is clear: a supervisor who is helpful in form only is not appreciated or even resented, and a spiteful supervisor who cannot carry out his malevolent designs offers no real threat.

The implications of such findings as these have been explored with regard to leadership training in an excellent study by Fleishman, Harris, and Burtt (12). Their careful evaluation of a foreman training program operated by a large industrial concern revealed that there is often a discrepancy between the behavior taught in the program and that expected by the foreman's supervisor. They conclude that "when what is taught in the School is at variance with what is practiced in the plant, the latter is generally the more powerful influence." (p. 58) They show, moreover, that trained foremen who are returned to a setting whose leadership climate is at odds with the style of leadership advocated by the School display signs of conflict.

The gradually accumulating evidence from studies such as these fosters a dim view of supervisory training schemes which ignore the power structure of the organization; any theory of leadership which ignores power cannot be viewed more favorably.

If we turn our attention to the general theory of role, we are forced to conclude that here too power is inevitably involved. Since recent work on role, especially that of Newcomb (26), has broadened the scope of social psychology and increased its ability to deal with important phenomena in an integrated fashion, the significance of this conclusion is far-reaching.

Perhaps the best way to communicate the qualitative flavor of the phenomena of role is to quote some anthropological reports made by Campbell (8) from his participant-observing among the tribe Social-Researcher. Here is his account of the role of research administrator.

"The researcher who assumes the position of administrator is likely to be slower in recognizing his new role than are the people whom he directs. . . . The people who now report to him know immediately that he has become the 'gatekeeper' on a variety of critical decisions. They see him almost at once in his new role and they quickly develop expectations for appropriate administrative behaviors for him.

"This change of roles may be difficult for the new executive to accept. He has to learn to modify his behavior in many subtle ways. He has to guard against casual thoughtless remarks that might be interpreted as criticism and to be wary of hopeful observations that may be recalled later as promises. He must not indicate undue uncertainty about future appropriations or appointments for fear of setting disquieting rumors spreading through his staff. He learns not to make light of salary levels in his organization or of other perquisites which his staff may feel they deserve.

". . . He cannot escape the basic fact that as the director he has the ultimate word on many questions of great personal importance to his associates, and that he is universally seen by these people as having this power." (p. 225)

Certain features of this description deserve emphasis. (a) The occupant of the position of research administrator (and this may be generalized to other positions in society) can determine whether or not certain other people are able to satisfy their important needs. The occupant of this position also has a decisive voice in group action, so that when others engage in behavior relevant to the group they must relate their behavior to his. (b) The occupant of even a powerful position is not personally free to do certain things and not to do others. (c) If we consider the same person when he is located inside and outside a given position, we find that others behave toward him in drastically different ways under the two conditions. (d) Any communications originating from the occupant of a powerful position are likely to be highly authoritative, that is, have pronounced effects on others.

Strodtbeck (**31, 32**) has devised an ingenious experimental method for determining the relative influence of roles. He has used this method to study the roles of husband, wife, and son in different cultures. The procedure is to place members of a family in a situation where they will have a difference of opinion and then to record the ensuing events. He finds, for example, that among Navahos the wife wins 46 arguments to the husband's 34. But among Mormons it is husband 42 to 29! The son seldom wins except by forming coalitions. This research of Strodtbeck and that of others makes it clear that even in groups having no formal table of organization the power of one person to influence another depends upon the role he occupies.

The program of investigations by Shartle, Stogdill, Hemphill and others in the Ohio State Leadership Studies (**30**) is providing important documentation for our theories of role. In their work the concept of responsibility is assuming fundamental importance; each member of an organization is responsible for the performance of certain activities and is responsible to certain other individuals. Positions in an organization can be described in terms of these two aspects of responsibility. What people in the organization do, with whom they interact, whom they like, from whom they receive recognition, and so forth—all these factors depend to a high degree upon the nature of the responsibility structure. Members of the organization may vary in the extent to which they accept this structure, but if a member does accept it, his behavior is then guided by certain other people and organizational requirements. Stated differently, the whole organizational structure acquires power over the member and consequently certain other people have power over him, the specific persons depending upon his position in the organization.

This raises the ancient sociological problem which Jaques (**20**) has analyzed in some detail and has referred to as the "sanctioning of authority." It seems that a group member cannot simply proclaim a new position of power with himself as the occupant. The authority of a position must be sanctioned by others if it is to possess power. In one of the earliest experiments upon the process of interpersonal influence, Frank (13) found that when students agreed to be subjects they automatically gave such authority to the role of experimenter that he could not get them to resist his efforts to have them perform very disagreeable tasks. He finally had to instruct them to resist before he could measure the relative effectiveness of his different techniques of pressure! In a study on changing mothers' behavior toward their children, Brim (7) found that mothers were more likely to try out advice given by a doctor the more they attributed high prestige to the role of doctor. Much of the research on the effects of prestige and credibility, it would seem, can best be interpreted in terms of the sanctioning of the authority of certain roles.

This line of theorizing raises an important question: what determines whether a person accepts the authority of a position occupied by others (or even by himself)? Although there is no research which answers this question directly, the work relating group cohesiveness to strength of group standards (discussed below) suggests that if the authority structure of a group is functionally equivalent to the standards of a group, then the more strongly members are attracted to the group the more will they accept its authority structure. This hypothesis could readily be tested.

The personality characteristics of individuals may also be expected to influence their readiness to sanction the authority of a role. Much of the work on authoritarianism can be interpreted as dealing with this problem. Another provocative approach is represented by the research of Jeanne and Jack Block (6) who, though not investigating directly the sanctioning of authority of a role, do show how the amount of influence exerted by a role on a person is related to certain of his personality characteristics. In this experiment they asked subjects to do a monotonous and repetitive task until satiated. When the subjects stopped, the experimenter (assumed to be an authority figure) asked, "Don't you want to do some more?" Subjects either continued or not. Certain personality variables of all subjects had previously been evaluated, and relations between these variables and compliance with the experimenter's request were examined. The results show compliance to be related to (a) a trichotomy on "ego control" into over-controllers, appropriate controllers, and under-controllers; (b) scores on the California test of ethnocentrism; and (c) speed of establishing norms in an experiment on autokinetic movement. The Blocks propose that conforming to a suggestion from an authority is the expression of a more general "structuring" approach to an unpredictable environment. This predisposition, in turn, may be viewed as part of a larger syndrome of ego control which they term "over-control." The results of this one study do not, of course, tell us whether these over-controllers tend to accept the authority of all roles which might claim authority or whether they are inclined to give sanction only to certain sorts of potentially authoritative roles.

An experiment by Hoffman (15) should also be mentioned in this connection. He, too, related behavior in an experimental setting to personality variables. In his study, subjects were dichotomized into conformers and nonconformers on the basis of conformity to an announced group average of judgments of perceived distance. His results show that the conformers scored significantly higher on such measures as parental dominance, inability to tolerate impulses, overconcern for the well-being of parents, and strict moralism. Whether submitting to an authority figure is psychodynamically the same as conforming to the norms of a group and how "ego control" relates to Hoffman's personality measures need to be known before the results of these two studies can be put together. In any case it appears that we may soon be able to isolate relatively enduring attributes which predispose people to give sanction to certain roles and to the norms of certain groups.

This brief overview of research on role raises doubt that such soft properties as expectations and perceptions adequately characterize the actual phenomena of role. The harder properties of power are inextricably a part of the phenomena referred to by the concept of role.

Communication

If we turn to research on communication, we find that power must be recognized here, too. In fact, it is the power aspect of communication which gives the concept such a central place in current social psychological theory. Communication is the mechanism by which interpersonal influence is exerted. Without communication there would be no group norms, group goals, or organized group action. Let us examine the evidence for these conclusions.

First, it is perfectly obvious as soon as one bothers to raise the question that all communications are not equally influential. This, of course, has been known for a long time, and there is a respectable literature on the effectiveness of different kinds of content in communications. We are not so well supplied, however, with findings concerning the way in which the relations between communicator and recipient influence the effectiveness of communication. The work of Hovland and Weiss (16) and Kelman and Hovland (23) on source credibility dramatizes the importance of treating separately the content of a communication and its source. They have shown that the so-called "sleeper effect" depends upon the more rapid decay over time of the effects of the source than of the content. Future work in this productive program might well examine sources of communication more integrally related to the groups to which people belong to see whether the effectiveness of source decays over time when source and recipient maintain a concrete relationship.

A program of research conducted at the Research Center for Group Dynamics adds further insight into the nature of communication. First, Festinger, Schachter, and Back (11) and Back (4) show that a communication between people in a group to which they are strongly attracted is more effective than a similar communication between people in a less attractive group. To account for such findings, Festinger has developed the concept of the "internal power of a group." The upshot of this work supports the view outlined by Barnard (5) that all communications carry some degree of authoritativeness and that a person, role, or group capable of giving authority to communications possesses power. Thus, we start out to study communication but are soon asking questions about the determinants of power.

Second, the direction and content of the flow of communication in an organized group or community are not indifferent to the social position of the people involved. Orders, for example, seldom flow up a power hierarchy, but certain other types of communication are quite likely to do so. The studies by Hurwitz, Zander, and Hymovitch (18), Jackson (19), Kelley (22), and others are beginning to reveal how upward communication may serve an individual as a substitute for upward locomotion in a power hierarchy, how a person may use communication as a device for minimizing the dangers of hostile actions by those in higher positions, and how a person of superior power may tailor the content and direction of his communications to maintain the belief among others that his superior behavior justifies his position. Thus, we must specify the power relations among people to understand either the frequency and content of communications passing among them or the authority of such communications.

Third, even the study of rumor cannot safely ignore the power situation. This conclusion dramatically arose from the experience of an action-research project in a community where the project leaders unexpectedly became the target of a hostile rumor (10). As a result of the project's stimulation of several new community activities, such as a cooperative nursery school and a softball league, new leaders began to emerge to replace the old ones. Suddenly, when everything seemed to be moving along well, the new activities came to a halt. A rumor was sweeping the community that the project leaders and the new local leaders were taking orders from Moscow. If we try to understand what happened, it seems especially significant that the content of the rumor was about power (namely, who was controlling people's behavior), that it was initiated and spread by those losing power, and that it was credible to those who believed it because they did not in fact know why these new activities were being undertaken in their community. (In a desire not to contaminate the experiment the community had not been given this information.) A general hypothesis is suggested that rumors are especially likely to flourish among people who see that their fates are in other people's hands.

If communication is to be a basic concept of social psychology, so too is power.

Interpersonal and Intergroup Relations

Let us turn now from abstract concepts like role and communication to more concrete social problems. One such problem which has long interested social psychologists deals with the kinds of things referred to by the phrase "human relations." What are the causes of harmony and conflict among people? Although systematic theories have been slow to emerge from efforts to answer this question, a sizable body of empirical data has accumulated. From this wealth of material we cite only a few specific findings to illustrate the critical place of power in shaping human relations.

A few years ago the Research Center for Group Dynamics was asked by a group of junior high school teachers to help them understand better the sources of conflict and irritation in the relations among teachers, parents, and students. A project was organized by Jenkins and Lippitt (21) which included interviews with a sample of each of these populations. Respondents were asked to indicate what they believed were the things that each group did that each other group liked (for example, "What are the things that parents do that teachers like?"). They were also asked parallel questions to indicate disliked behavior.

Consider, first, the teacher-student relationship. Of all categories of teacher behavior, the one having most significance for students is that the teacher be fair. This seems to imply that the teacher is a sort of judge who hands down decisions of importance, thus making fairness a matter of real concern. When we examine the other side of the relationship and consider the responses of teachers, we get further confirmation of the teacher's power over students. Seventy-three per cent of the teachers mention as important student behavior "being respectful" and "accepting the teacher as authority." Forty-two per cent mention "obedience."

The relations between parents and students turn out to be much the same, but with different realms of behavior coming under the control of parents. Complaints about parents consist of a long list of things "they won't let us do" and of other things "they make us do." Though parents tend not to mention the importance of obedience and respect as much as teachers, the students nonetheless report that parents do place major emphasis upon compliance to parental authority.

More subtle is the finding concerning teacher-parent relations. Here it is clear that teachers have strong needs for friendship with adults and for acceptance as members of the community. Parents chiefly control the fate of teachers in this respect; they can give or withhold gratification of these needs. This relation is, moreover, one way; there is no indication that parents would feel deprived without the friendship, recognition, or acceptance of teachers. Knowledge of this asymmetrical power relation is essential for understanding the behavior, attitudes, and feelings of teachers and parents.

Experience with intergroup discrimination and prejudice points the same lesson. Can we really hope to explain these phenomena or to build programs of social action solely with such variables as authoritarianism, ethnocentrism, displaced aggression, and attitude? How do these concepts help to understand the substantial improvement of conditions for Negroes in the automobile industry following certain union policy-decisions or the presence of a non-segregated dining room at Montgomery, Alabama—on the Air Force Base? Kurt Lewin (24) recognized the importance of power in intergroup relations when he asserted that "discrimination against minorities will not be changed as long as forces are not changed which determine the decisions of the gatekeepers." (p. 186) With such a perspective social psychologists will take more than passing notice of such findings as that of Hunter (17) in his study of the power structure of Regional City—a medium sized city with a Negro population of nearly one-third the total. Through various devices he was able to construct a list of 40 people who could safely be called the city's most powerful; the approval of these people is required for the success of any community project. Those who wish to better intergroup relations in this city might be well advised to work with this group. They should know, however, that not a single Negro is on this list of influential people. (Only 3 could be considered even nominees on a list of 175.)

Whether one's objective is social action or understanding human behavior, one should examine the possibilities of reducing discrimination and prejudice through the *fait accompli*, legal action, and administrative order. It is interesting in this connection to note the conclusion reached by Deutsch and

Collins (9) from their study of the effects upon interracial attitudes of different patterns of interracial public housing.

"We are, in effect, rejecting the notion that has characterized much of sociological thinking in the field of race relations: the notion, originating with William S. Summer, that 'stateways cannot change folkways.' The evidence of our study is that official policy, executed without equivocation, can result in large changes in beliefs and feelings despite initial resistance to the policy. Thus, it is clear from our data that although most of the white housewives in the integrated projects we studied did not, upon moving into the projects, like the idea of living in the same buildings with Negro families (and certainly the community as a whole did not favor it), a considerable change in attitudes and 'folkways' has taken place as a consequence of their experiences resulting from a 'stateway.' " (p. 127)

Unfortunately there is as yet insufficient systematic knowledge about the social psychology of power for us to specify with much conviction the conditions under which administrative orders and legal action will carry along attitudinal changes or will stimulate heightened resistance.

Social Determinants of Emotional Adjustment

The importance of the concept of power for social psychology may be illustrated with respect to one other social problem. What determines the mental health or illness of individuals? While it is clear that physiological determinants are important, it is now known that social situations differ significantly in their impact upon the emotional adjustment of all those involved in them. Perhaps one of the clearest demonstrations of such influences was provided by the experiment of Lewin, Lippitt, and White (25) on different styles of leadership. Here it was found that the aggressiveness of a given child depended upon the style of leadership provided by the adult in charge of the group. Although the different styles of leadership studied in this experiment differed from one another in a number of ways, it appears that the most critical aspects of leadership were the size of the space of free movement allowed the children and whether the leader's power was used to support or obstruct the behavior of the children. The leader's use of power basically affected the emotional climate of the group.

In any social situation, and especially in hierarchical ones, certain people have power to help or hinder the goal-directed behavior of others. Emotional security depends rather directly upon the magnitude of this power and upon the benevolence of its use.

Experiments by Arsenian (3) and Wright (33) have examined this conception in greater detail. They propose that a person's feeling of security is determined by the relative magnitude of two sets of factors which may be expressed as a ratio. The numerator is the person's perception of the magnitude of his own power plus all friendly or supportive power he can count upon from other sources; the denominator is the person's perception of the magnitude of all hostile power that may be mobilized against him. In the Arsenian experiment the emotionality of young children was measured when they were left alone in a strange room and when put there in the presence of a friendly (but passive) adult. Consistent with the formulation of the determinants of security proposed, Arsenian found less emotional disturbance when the supportive power of the adult was present. The experiment by Wright may be interpreted in similar terms. He compared the reactions to frustration of pairs of children varying in the strength of their friendship and found that strong friends displayed less reduction in constructiveness of play, less negative emotionality, more cooperation between themselves, and more aggression against the experimenter than did weak friends. The power of each of the strong friends was supportive to the other.

Consistent with this general conception of the relation between security and power are the findings of a rather different sort of experiment conducted by Pepitone (29). He placed boys in a situation where the achievement of an attractive object was under the control of a panel of three judges. After a standardized interaction between the boy and the panel, each boy was asked to rate the relative power and relative benevolence of each member of the panel. In this setting Pepitone found perceptual distortions designed, as it were, to minimize the threatening power of the panel members—if a member was rated as powerful, his benevolence was rated higher; and if he was rated as malevolent, his power was rated lower.

From the findings of research of the sort reported here it seems clear that the impact of social situations upon emotional adjustment will be adequately understood only if power is explicitly recognized.

SUMMARY

This brief overview of the field of social psychology leads to four conclusions:

1. A major deficiency of the theories of social psychology is that they have been soft on power.

2. The important social problems which demand our attention raise questions about power—questions which our systematic knowledge cannot answer.

3. Quite apart from any practical considerations, a social psychological theory without the concept of power (or its equivalent) is incomplete. Such concepts as communication, role, attitude, expectation, and norm cannot by themselves account realistically for the processes of influence to which they refer, nor can they deal effectively with social change and resistance to change.

4. A concerted attack on the problem of power should produce a major advance in the field of social psychology. Such an advance will consist of an improved understanding of the proper subject-matter of social psychology and a reorganization of its conceptual systems.

REFERENCES

1. Adler, A. A study of organ inferiority and its psychic compensations. *Trans. Nerv. ment. Dis. Monogr. Ser.,* 1917, **24.**

2. Allport, G. W. The historical background of modern social psychology. In G. Lindzey (Ed.), *Handbook of social psychology.* Cambridge: Addison-Wesley, 1954, 3-56.

3. Arsenian, J. M. Young children in an insecure situation. *J. abnorm. soc. Psychol.,* 1943, **38,** 225-249.

4. Back, K. W. Influence through social communication. *J. abnorm. soc. Psychol.,* 1951, **46,** 9-23.

5. Barnard, C. I. *The functions of the executive.* Cambridge: Harvard Univer. Press, 1938.

6. Block, J., & Block, J. An interpersonal experiment on reactions to authority. *Hum. Relat.,* 1952, **5,** 91-98.

7. Brim, O. G., Jr. The acceptance of new behavior in child-rearing. *Hum. Relat.,* 1954, **7,** 473-491.

8. Campbell, A. Administering research organizations. *Amer. Psychol.,* 1953, **8,** 225-230.

9. Deutsch, M., & Collins, M. E. *Interracial housing: A psychological evaluation of a social experiment.* Minneapolis: Univer. Minnesota Press, 1951.

10. Festinger, L., Cartwright, D., et al. A study of a rumor: Its origin and spread. *Hum. Relat.,* 1948, **1,** 464-486.

11. Festinger, L., Schachter, S., & Back, K. W. *Social pressures in informal groups.* New York: Harper, 1950.

12. Fleishman, E. A., Harris, E. F., & Burtt, H. E. *Leadership and supervision in industry: An evaluation of a supervisory training program.* Columbus: Ohio State University Bureau of Educational Research, 1955.

13. Frank, J. D. Experimental study of personal pressures and resistance: I. Experimental production of resistance. *J. gen. Psychol.,* 1944, **30,** 23-41.

14. Hobbes, T. *Leviathan.* Reprint of 1st (1651) Ed., Cambridge: Univer. Press, 1904.

15. Hoffman, M. L. Some psychodynamic factors in compulsive conformity. *J. abnorm. soc. Psychol.,* 1953, **48,** 383-393.

16. Hovland, C. I., & Weiss, W. The influence of source credibility on communication effectiveness. *Pub. Opin. Quart.,* 1952, **15,** 635-650.

17. Hunter, F. *Community power structure.* Chapel Hill: Univer. North Carolina Press, 1953.

18. Hurwitz, J. I., Zander, A. F., & Hymovitch, B. Some effects of power on the relations among group members. In D. Cartwright & A. Zander (Eds.), *Group Dynamics: Research and theory.* Evanston: Row, Peterson, 1953, pp. 483-492.

19. Jackson, J. M. Analysis of interpersonal relations in a formal organization. Unpublished doctor's dissertation, Univer. Michigan, 1952.

20. Jaques, E. *The changing culture of a factory.* London: Tavistock, 1951.

21. Jenkins, D., & Lippitt, R. *Interpersonal perceptions of teachers, students and parents.* Washington: Nat. Train. Labor. Group Devel., 1951.

22. Kelley, H. H. Communication in experimentally created hierarchies. *Hum. Relat.,* 1951, **4,** 39-56.

23. Kelman, H. C., & Hovland, C. I. "Reinstatement" of the communicator in delayed measurement of opinion change. *J. abnorm. soc. Psychol.,* 1953, **48,** 327-335.

24. Lewin, K. *Field theory in social science.* New York: Harper, 1951.

25. Lewin, K., Lippitt, R., & White, R. K. Patterns of aggressive behavior in experimentally created "social climates." *J. soc. Psychol.,* 1939, **10,** 271-299.

26. Newcomb, T. *Social psychology.* New York: Dryden, 1950.

27. Nietzsche, F. *Der Wille zur Macht.* Book 3, sec. 702. In Nietzsche's complete *Werke,* vol. **16.** Leipzig: Alfred Kröner, 1912.

28. Pelz, D. C. Influence: A key to effective leadership in the first line supervisor. *Personnel,* 1952, **3,** 3-11.

29. Pepitone, A. Motivational effects in social perception. *Hum. Relat.,* 1950, **3,** 57-76.

30. Stogdill, R. M. Leadership, membership and organization. *Psychol. Bull.,* 1950, **47,** 1-14.

31. Strodtbeck, F. L. Husband-wife interaction over revealed differences. *Amer. sociol. Rev.,* 1951, **16,** 468-473.

32. Strodtbeck, F. L. The family as a three-person group. *Amer. sociol. Rev.,* 1954, **19,** 23-29.

33. Wright, M. E. The influence of frustration on the social relations of young children. *Charact. Pers.,* 1943, **12,** 111-122.

2

POWER AND THE RELATIONS AMONG PROFESSIONS [1]

ALVIN ZANDER, ARTHUR R. COHEN, AND EZRA STOTLAND

Cooperation among professional people is at once the easiest and most difficult of relationships. It is the easiest because service to others is a common standard in professional bodies, and members place great value upon it. For this reason, it is easy for people from different professions to join hands in a shared purpose. But cooperation is also difficult because it requires that there be trust and understanding among those who would work together. The members of various professions bring their own points of view, social positions, and skills to the collaborative relation. Differences among them may hinder the development of confidence and mutual agreement.

Why is it that the feelings among members of some professional groups are strongly favorable, while those among others are unfavorable? The research reported here is an attempt to answer this question. It is primarily concerned with the beliefs which members of three different occupations have about one another and the way in which these beliefs are determined by an individual member's role and power. This report contains data from a larger study of the relations among psychiatrists, clinical psychologists, and psychiatric social workers (1). A variety of determinants of professional interaction were studied there, but here we are concerned only with one central factor—power relations.

An examination of the writings by members of these professions about their role relations and the results of pilot interviews made us aware that the mental health team composed of psychiatrists, clinical psychologists, and psychiatric social workers is an ideal subject for the study of power and its effects on interpersonal relations. Certain conditions among these professions make it important to know who has the right to determine what is done and who does it. Most important are: the frequent unclarity in the definition

[1] This investigation was supported by a grant-in-aid (M-325 (C)) from the Institute of Mental Health of the National Institutes of Health, Public Health Service. We wish to thank Bernard Hymovitch and Otto Riedl who participated in certain stages of the research.

of roles, the rapid changes in functions and skills in all three professions, the overlapping of functions among these groups, the recent arrival of clinical psychologists upon the scene, the high value placed upon mutual interdependence, and the reported ease and comfort in some places contrasted with strain and discomfort in others. In addition, social workers are becoming more and more professionally self-conscious, while psychiatrists tend to perceive a wider use of their services in varied agencies in the community and are placing more value on the help of the ancillary professions. The relations among these three groups, then, are typified by unclarity and professional aspirations in which some are seeking to expand their activities while others are attempting to maintain their professional stature.

THEORETICAL RATIONALE

In our effort to deal conceptually with these phenomena we employ certain terms referring to social structure and others which describe properties of individuals. Our basic assumption is that a person's power relations with members of another group will have important consequences for the perceptions and behaviors he directs toward them, primarily because the amount of power he possesses helps to determine the degree of security he feels when interacting with them. We define *security* as that state of the individual in which he believes that his professional needs and other more personal needs which are linked to them can or will be satisfied in a given relationship with others. Many of the attitudes and actions that a person directs toward members of other groups may be predicted, once one understands that these attitudes and actions stem from the person's insecurity and his efforts to provide greater security for himself.

It should be noted, however, that this process operates in a social system and is conditioned by it. A person's profession specifies his role. In its most general sense a role is a set of behaviors which a person is expected to perform. A role specifies certain functions or duties as well as the amount of authority others have over him and the accountability he has to them. It is thus possible, if one knows the title of the role (profession) of a given individual to anticipate the sorts of duties he will typically perform as well as the nature of the interactions he will have with those around him. Eventually these relationships become stabilized, both with respect to individuals in other professions and at a more abstract level with other professions as a whole. The concept "structure" indicates that the interrole relations have become more or less regularized. In a well structured situation there may be a great variety of regularized relations among professional groups, involving such matters as contact, knowledge and skills, and power.

An individual's behavior on his job is also influenced by the norms and values of his professional group. Psychologists aspire toward increased usefulness and recognition as a profession; social workers have similar though less strong goals; and psychiatrists seek to maintain their superior professional status and to make better use of the services provided by the adjunct professions. These aspirations concerning the standing of his profession, along with interprofessional power relations, affect each individual's security in his interactions with members of another profession. Aspirations provide an atmosphere, or environment, within which power relations have effects.

Let us now attempt to define our concepts more precisely and specify more clearly the relationships between power, security, and professional interactions.

Perceived Relative Power

Perceived relative power is the ability of P to influence O or to determine O's fate indirectly, as P perceives the situation. Person P may also feel that O has some power over him. Thus the resultant amount of power that P attributes to himself in relations with O is the degree to which he believes he can successfully influence O, less the amount he believes O can influence him.

Some individuals will perceive that their power is great in relations with certain people, while others will feel that it is relatively small. Those who believe that their power is great will feel that they can determine what the others think and do. Those who see that their power is small will feel that they can have few such effects on more powerful people. For the sake of brevity, the simpler term *power* will be used hereafter. It should be understood, however, that it refers to perceived relative power.

The origin of a person's perception concerning his power may stem from a number of sources. The most general of these are the status differentials implied or explicitly defined by society, the nature and value of the functions included within his role, and the responsibility he has to others or that they have to him. Thus, if he regularly carries out activities in which he is assisting another person, his power in relation to the other person will be seen as low, but if he routinely supervises or instructs others, his position will be one of more influence. It is possible that a person may have more power as a result of engaging in some functions than others. For example, psychologists may feel that they are more effective in influencing psychiatrists while conducting research or in interpreting psychometric tests than in suggesting therapeutic procedures. The nature of the power relations may shift, depending upon which function is being performed. It is important, therefore, to know interprofessional power relations within each class of functions.

Taking all these considerations into account, it can be said that one profession has, in general, more power than another. A profession for which power in many areas is a traditional prerogative may view itself as being more influential as a group than another one with which it interacts and which it supervises or instructs.

Within any one profession, however, members will vary in the amount of power they attribute to themselves relative to the members of another group, for no two persons in the same profession will regard their roles in exactly the same way. In a specific working situation, a particular clinic or hospital, role prescriptions may be influenced by local conditions, and the way a particular member of one profession in that setting relates to a particular member of another profession will be affected. As an illustration, even though the professional role of psychiatrist has superior status to that of social worker, the prescribed working relations in a given setting may be de-determined by the fact that the social worker is a highly experienced supervisor while the psychiatrist is a young, lower-status member of the staff.

Effects of Power on Security

Each profession has its own goals which motivate members to realize their fullest professional capacities. Goals differ from one profession to another in content and in their relevance to interprofessional relations. Usually the needs of an individual member of these professions, insofar as his career aspirations are concerned, are highly similar to those of his colleagues. All members, in short, place high value upon their group's goals.

A person may perceive that his professional needs, like any others, are being gratified or frustrated. A person is secure if he perceives that he is able to satisfy important needs and he is insecure if he is blocked, or believes that he will be blocked, in the achievement of these aspirations.

A person with high perceived power will attribute to himself a greater probability of fulfilling his aspirations than one who has little power. He has greater control over his own fate through his ability to influence others, and, therefore, a stronger likelihood of ensuring that events will occur as he wishes. Thus he is secure in his relations with members of the other profession. In contrast, a person who is low in power is likely to be subject to the impulses and wishes of more powerful persons. He will assign a lower probability to the possibility of fulfilling his aspirations and will be less secure in his relations with those in other professions.

Attempts to Maximize Security

In order for a person to increase the possibilities of professional need gratification he must act (at some level of awareness) upon the source of deprivation. It is not easy for him to increase his power, though he may attempt to do so, because it is difficult for him to change the social factors which define his power. What is more feasible is to try to increase the effectiveness of those influences favorable to, or to decrease the effectiveness of those detrimental to, need gratification. He may act upon his environment, including other persons, or seek to convince himself of others' favor toward him, in order to improve the perceived chances of achieving his needs. He will be most secure when he views relations with others as facilitative to need satisfaction.

Typical behaviors which may be used in order to maximize security are:

1. Perceive others as facilitative to need satisfaction; see no conflict of interests, see them as helpful advisors, attribute helpful stereotypes to them.

2. Seek to increase the effectiveness of need facilitating behavior from others; attribute friendly stereotypes to them, praise them, seek advice from them, desire many contacts with them, value their help, communicate in a way to protect good relations.

3. Perceive others as weak in their attempts to hinder need satisfaction; see them as troubled by conflict of interests, see them as incompetent, see them as not respected, attribute negative stereotypes to them.

4. Seek to decrease the effectiveness of hindering behavior from others; encroach upon their prerogatives, avoid contact with them, prefer own group to theirs, freely communicate hostile feelings.

Average Interrole Feelings and Behavior

In the light of the discussion thus far, how will each of these professional groups feel toward the other two?

We expect to find that psychiatrists are more secure in any relationship between their profession and the ancillary groups. They are more secure because when in a relationship with subordinates, their role prescriptions tend to give them relatively greater freedom to meet their professional aspirations. The psychiatrist's task-functions are such that the adjunct groups contribute to them, and their responsibility relations generally require that the adjunct groups be subordinate. Because they are more secure, psychiatrists will perceive that they have the support and admiration of the other two professions and will feel friendly toward them.

Psychologists and social workers, in contrast, are less secure in any relationship between their professions and psychiatrists. They are less secure because their role prescriptions make them dependent upon psychiatrists for gratifying their professional ambitions. Their task-functions and responsibility relations make it highly probable that, when interacting with psychiatrists, they cannot easily move toward satisfaction of professional aspirations without the help or permission of psychiatrists.

Because of these conditions, members of the ancillary professions will be eager to win good will from psychiatrists so that they will use their authority in a helpful fashion. They will be more inclined to accept and admire psychiatrists than to reject them because this will increase the probability that psychiatrists will develop positive feelings toward the adjunct professions.

Effects of an Individual's Relative Power

Among the members of each of these professions there will be differences in the amount of relative power they assign to themselves. Those who are high in power within any one profession may be expected to have different interrole attitudes and behavior from those who are low in power.

A psychiatrist who attributes high power to himself (and is thereby secure) is likely to perceive that the members of the ancillary groups respect him, like him, and seek to make a good impression in his eyes. He will be ready and willing to associate with members of the adjunct profession since when he does so he is usually in a superior position; frequent contacts satisfy rather than threaten his desires.

In contrast, a psychiatrist who sees himself as low in power will feel that he is in a relationship which is unusual for psychiatrists and threatening for him. He will show his feelings by believing that the members of the ancillary groups do not respect or admire him and by fearing that the other professions are attempting to perform functions ordinarily reserved for psychiatrists alone. Furthermore, he will be eager to avoid members of the adjunct professions and will be less ready to communicate with them; by avoiding interactions he will maintain his professional stature.

An individual in one of the ancillary roles who finds himself relatively higher than his colleagues with respect to influence on psychiatrists will be eager to maintain this power so that he may continue to move toward his professional aspirations. An efficient way for him to do this is to avoid contacts with psychiatrists so that he cannot be placed in an assistant position and thus lose his power. We may expect, therefore, that the person in an ancillary profession who sees himself as being relatively high in power, for a member of his profession, will want few contacts with psychiatrists and will have little desire to talk with them. His desire for independence and autonomy will be further apparent in his greater attachment to, and positive evaluation of, his own profession rather than psychiatry. The assurance he obtains from his relatively high power will also cause him to have little concern about winning the good will of psychiatrists or making a good impression upon them.

An individual in either of the assisting professions who attributes relatively low power to himself may be expected to be insecure. Since his power position provides him with little freedom to meet his own needs, he must depend upon developing good relations with psychiatrists in order to do so. Thus, the ancillary professional member with low power will be concerned about being liked and respected by those with greater power. He will seek to make a favorable impression on psychiatrists in order that the greater power possessed by them will be used in a supporting and rewarding manner rather than a punishing or depriving one. And he will want frequent interaction with those of higher power in order to have ample opportunity to win from them protective and rewarding actions.

What about the interrole attitudes between persons in groups at a peer level? Clinical psychologists and psychiatric social workers have strong professional needs. Neither, however, can be of much help or hindrance to the other in fulfilling these desires because of the prescribed equality and the lack of interdependence of their activities. We may anticipate, then, that a person who perceives himself as high in power in his relations with the members of the other ancillary group will act very little differently toward them than a person low in power.

METHODS

A theory concerned with the effects of power can best be tested by concentrating upon people who spend some proportion of their time working in institutional settings where formal power relationships and lines of authority exist. Accordingly, a sample of individuals in these professions was drawn from eight different kinds of institutions: private hospitals, school systems, clinics, universities, Veterans Administration installations, state hospitals, mental health agencies, welfare institutions, and psychiatric or psychoanalytic institutes. With this diversity of institutional setting we believe that the results may be generalized to a wide range of situations in which the members of these three professions collaborate.

It was decided to limit selection of interviewees to people in six widely separated cities of the United States. This decision was based upon the fact that relatively few psychiatrists are found outside the large centers of population. A probability sample of the twelve largest metropolitan areas in the nation was made and from this sample six cities were chosen: New York, Boston, Pittsburgh, Los Angeles, St. Louis and Chicago.

Within these cities, the persons to be interviewed were selected from complete lists of all members of the three professions living there. Those considered potentially available for interviewing were required to fulfill certain minimal criteria. The psychiatrists had all completed their psychiatric residency and were members of the American Psychiatric Association. The clinical psychologists had earned a Ph.D. degree and were members of the American Psychological Association. The psychiatric social workers had been working in clinics or other agencies for an appreciable time and were members of the American Association of Psychiatric Social Workers. The sample consisted of 156 psychiatrists, 165 psychologists, and 159 psychiatric social workers. We assumed that almost all of these people would be connected with institutions where those in the other relevant professions participated. This assumption was borne out; 88 per cent of the psychiatrists, 90 per cent of the psychologists, and 98 per cent of the social workers interviewed were working in settings in which members of the other two professions were also employed.

The interview situation, because of the nature of the population, required sophisticated interviewers. The interviews were therefore conducted by the field supervisors of the University of Michigan Survey Research Center who were located in the designated metropolitan areas. The interviews, on the average, lasted about two hours.

The questionnaire was highly structured, frequently asking for quantitative judgments in response to specific questions. Before the questioning began, the respondents were handed a sheet containing a series of graphic rating scales. They were then asked to reply to the questions in terms of these pre-established scales. Open-ended questions were also used in conjunction with some of the scalar items in order to give qualitative meaning to the item and to allow an elaboration or explanation of a given rating.

Measurement of Power

To obtain a measure of his power to influence, each respondent was asked to describe the nature of his authority in relation with the members of another specified profession. To illustrate, the psychologists were asked:

> "To what extent, if at all, do you have the authority to determine with what cases any psychiatrist does psychotherapy? Please choose your reply from scale number —."

Each respondent was also asked, within the same framework, to describe his perception of the amount of authority the others had to determine the nature of the work he did. Since the amount of power a person has in relation to others may vary according to the professional activity, a series of questions was posed concerning the respondent's perception of his authority in varied functions such as therapy, diagnosis, case-history writing, and community contacts.

In order to determine the respondent's power relations with members of a given professional group in each of these functional areas, a discrepancy score was obtained between the respondent's perception of his own authority and the amount of influence which he attributed to the members of the other group. This procedure is in accord with the relational conception of power. The size of this discrepancy was considered to be the amount of power the respondent had in relation to members of the other profession. With the aid of such data all the respondents in one profession were ordered in comparison to others in the same group, according to their degree of power in relations with the other groups.

When the power of a group appeared to be generalized across all the functions the scores from the different areas were combined into a single index of power; where there seemed to be disparate areas of power, they were kept separate. These combinations were made when there was both statistical and theoretical reasonableness for them.

Measurement of Interrole Attitudes and Behavior

Several separate measurements of dependent variables were made during the interview. There were no direct measures of security as such. In the scheme represented here, security is viewed as a hypothetical construct upon which predictions are based. It serves to explain the relationships between power and the dependent reactions. These may be grouped into seven areas.

1. *Attitudes of admiration and esteem for others.* Both direct and indirect questions were used to reveal the degree to which the respondent liked and respected members of the other groups. Respondents were asked directly about their affective reactions: how well they would get along with others on a hypothetical interprofessional committee; how they would evaluate their own and others' potential contributions to such a group; how they felt about leisure-time contacts; and how they would characterize members of the other occupations.

2. *Desire for admiration and esteem from others.* Several direct queries were made to determine the degree to which each person wished to be liked

and respected by members of the other groups and by those in his own profession.

3. *Amount of admiration and esteem received from others.* Indications were sought of the degree to which the respondent perceived he was liked and respected by members of the other groups.

4. *Attitudes indicating use or receipt of solicitous behavior.* We were concerned with the frequency of attempts on the part of the respondent to win favor for himself or the respondent's perception that he is the target of such attempts. Direct questions concerning the necessity for flattery or solicitousness, the attribution of "apple-polishing," the selection of certain communication topics, and indirect questions concerning the reasons for contacts with those in other professions were all viewed as relevant indicators.

5. *Attitudes indicating use or receipt of encroachment and hostility.* Both direct and indirect questions were used to measure the respondents' efforts to decrease the influence of those in other professions over them, the energy put into competing with others, and the degree to which they aspire to take over others' functions. Questions were also asked about the perception of others' behavior in this regard.

6. *Stereotypes about other groups.* The respondents judged their own and the other groups on a series of thirteen characteristics such as "striving," "threatening," and "clinical insight."

7. *Willingness to communicate to others.* Each respondent was asked about his readiness to communicate to members of his own and the other professions concerning eleven different topics such as own failures, own group's positive attributes, interpersonal conflicts, and professional successes. Readiness rather than actual communication was measured in the belief that it would better reflect a respondent's attitudes toward others and allow for the projection of friendliness or hostility.

Data Concerning Social Structure

Certain questions were included to provide objective information about type and size of institution in which the person was employed, the formal authority structure of the organization, the professions of those at various points in the hierarchy of the institutions, the numbers of people from various professions employed there, income, and professional training. The value of this material is that it makes clear who works with whom, for whom, and where. It also provides a reality base-line which may be kept in mind while considering the perceptions that the members of these roles have concerning one another.

RESULTS

How well were our assumptions about the nature of the power hierarchy supported by the reports of the members of the three groups?

Table 1 shows the proportion of members of each profession who attribute various degrees of power to themselves in the different functional areas. It is evident that the psychiatrists are certain of their superior power in each of the functional areas examined. The members of the other two groups agree that it is the psychiatrists who have power, though they do not attribute as much power to the psychiatrists as the psychiatrists do. The psychologists and social workers indicate a perceived equality of power between the two groups. Consistent with these data is one additional finding: nearly all respondents report that a psychiatrist is the chief executive of the organization in which they work.

TABLE 1

REPORTED RELATIVE DEGREE OF POWER AMONG THREE PROFESSIONAL GROUPS

	Reported Degree of Power		
	Psychiatrists have more	Both equal	Social Workers have more
Social Workers Responding:			
In diagnosis and therapy...............	55%	24%	21%
In social histories and community contacts.	61%	32%	7%
Psychiatrists Responding:			
In diagnosis, therapy, social histories, and community contacts	80%	19%	1%
	Psychiatrists have more	Both equal	Psychologists have more
Psychologists Responding:			
In diagnosis, therapy, and case assignments.	51%	29%	20%
Psychiatrists Responding:			
In diagnosis, therapy, and case assignments.	85%	14%	1%
	Psychologists have more	Both equal	Social Workers have more
Psychologists Responding:			
In diagnosis and therapy...............	9%	81%	10%
Social Workers Responding:			
In diagnosis and therapy...............	4%	54%	42%
In community contacts.................	8%	80%	12%

Average Reactions of Each Profession

The data provide several indications that psychiatry holds a position of higher status and value than do the ancillary professions. When asked about the careers they would choose, assuming they were able to begin their training anew, 100 per cent of the psychiatrists say that their first choice would be psychiatry and not psychology or social work. However, 42 per cent of the psychologists and 39 per cent of the social workers indicate a preference for psychiatry. When asked to rank professions according to the quality of their contribution to a committee concerned with mental health problems in the community, psychiatrists were given a mean rank of 3.10 by psychologists and 2.84 by social workers whereas psychiatrists gave a rank of 5.84 to psychologists and 3.78 to social workers. The significance of the differences between the ranks given and received by psychiatrists is beyond the .001 level.

Another indication of the lower status and value assigned the adjunct groups is the fact that all three groups believe that psychologists' and social workers' incomes should be smaller than those of psychiatrists. Ninety-one per cent of the social workers feel that their incomes should be less than a psychiatrist's, and an equal proportion of psychiatrists agree. Forty-five per cent of the psychologists assert that their incomes should be less than those of psychiatrists, and 85 per cent of psychiatrists agree. It is noteworthy, however, that 53 per cent of the psychologists believe that they should earn as much as psychiatrists.

A basic assumption of this study was that members of a profession with low power are likely to be more insecure than members of a profession with high power and that interrole perceptions and feelings reflect an individual's attempt to maximize his security. Consistent with these expectations is the finding that both social workers and psychologists are more likely to feel threatened by psychiatrists than are the psychiatrists by them. Each respondent was asked to indicate the degree to which certain stereotypes are typical of members of the other professions. On the stereotype "threatening," social workers rate psychiatrists higher than psychiatrists rate them (2.18 to 1.45, different at .05 level of significance), and psychologists rate psychiatrists higher than psychiatrists rate them (3.39 to 1.86, significant at .001 level).

At the same time, psychologists and social workers express a greater desire for supportive relations with psychiatrists than do the psychiatrists with them. As seen in Table 2, the ratings of psychologists and social workers are higher than those of psychiatrists in the desire to be respected and liked by the other group and in the wish to have professional and leisure-time contacts with them. In addition, psychologists predict that they would get along

TABLE 2

MEAN RATING OF DESIRE FOR SUPPORTIVE RELATIONS *

| | Rating made by | | | |
Nature of Desire	Psychiatrists re Psychologists	Psychologists re Psychiatrists	Psychiatrists re Social Workers	Social Workers re Psychiatrists
To be respected	3.79	4.44	3.99	4.28
Professional contacts	4.66	5.05	4.82	5.31
To be liked	2.72	3.60	2.90	3.38
Leisure-time contacts	3.27	3.76	3.04	3.72

* The higher the mean value, the greater the desire. Differences between contrasted pairs of means are significant at the .05 level or less.

better on a committee with psychiatrists than do psychiatrists with respect to psychologists. It seems reasonable to view all of these reactions as a form of defensiveness since the ancillary workers are often dependent upon the psychiatrist's power for satisfaction of their professional needs.

This interest in the good will of the more powerful profession is also shown in the nature of the topics members of each profession choose to talk about with the others. The data in Tables 3 and 4 indicate that psychologists and social workers are more ready to communicate about their own personal and professional strengths or weaknesses to psychiatrists than are psychiatrists in return. In contrast, psychiatrists are more ready to communicate complaints about the other professions' behavior. Thus, these communication patterns reveal a greater desire on the part of psychiatrists either to protect their superiority or to use their greater authority in correcting situations of which they

TABLE 3

MEAN RATING OF DESIRE FOR COMMUNICATION AS STATED BY PSYCHIATRISTS AND SOCIAL WORKERS

| | Mean readiness to talk shown by * | | |
Topic	Psychiatrists to Social Workers	Social Workers to Psychiatrists	Significance of difference
My profession's inadequacies...........	2.74	2.46	.01
My personal successes.................	2.77	2.41	.01
My personal failures.................	2.70	2.13	.01
Complaints about the other profession's behavior	2.95	3.22	.02

* The lower the mean value, the greater the willingness to discuss the topic.

TABLE 4

MEAN RATING OF DESIRE FOR COMMUNICATION AS STATED BY PSYCHIATRISTS AND
PSYCHOLOGISTS

Topic	Mean readiness to talk shown by *		
	Psychiatrists to Psychologists	Psychologists to Psychiatrists	Significance of difference
My profession's inadequacies.......... 2.35		1.92	.05
My profession's positive characteristics... 2.92		2.26	.01
My personal successes................ 2.88		2.39	.01
Complaints about the other profession's behavior 2.61		3.08	.02

* The lower the mean value, the greater the willingness to discuss the topic.

disapprove; for both adjunct groups, communication to psychiatrists suggests a dependent relationship.

We have seen that in general the psychologists and social workers react similarly to the psychiatrists' higher status. They desire more support from the psychiatrists, are more supportive and cautious in their communication to them, place more value on psychiatry than the psychiatrists place on social work and psychology, and find the psychiatrists more threatening than the psychiatrists find them. All of these behaviors are what might be expected when the reactions of a powerful group are compared with those of a dependent group: they are attempts to win the good will of the superiors so that need satisfaction within this professional social structure can be facilitated.

While the two adjunct groups do reveal highly similar responses to the superior status of psychiatrists, psychologists appear to have a stronger desire for equality and to react more strongly to the psychiatrists' superiority. We may explore this aspect of the situation further by examining attitudes of the different professions toward the proper distribution of functions among the groups. The members of any professional group develop abilities and knowledge which are unique to that role. These are the functions usually considered as making up the role. Certain functions possessed by one group may, however, be shared by closely related professions. Undoubtedly this sharing of participation in a given function is valued in some instances and disliked in others depending upon the consequences which are foreseen in cooperation or rivalry.

In response to an open-ended question concerning what the members of each group know and what they feel they can offer to members of the other professions, both social workers and psychiatrists are in close agreement concerning the functions in which the skill of the other is superior. Both agree (i.e., there are no significant differences in the number of persons naming each skill) upon the unique skills that they and the other profession can provide; they both know what they may expect to learn from the other and what the other wants them to offer. The responses of psychologists and psychiatrists, however, are rather different. Although these two groups agree in general upon the areas in which the psychiatrists are superior, they differ considerably on what the psychologists have to offer. The psychologists wish to provide a wider array of skills to psychiatrists than psychiatrists expect from them. Psychiatrists hold that psychologists' competencies are restricted to the administration of various measuring devices; psychologists perceive themselves as being able to provide a variety of therapeutic, diagnostic, and research services. This discrepancy is pertinent to an understanding of the reactions of psychologists to the psychiatrists' superior power: psychologists may be expected to react vigorously to an insecure position because their aspirations are strong and are not accepted by psychiatrists.

Table 5 gives the mean scores on a number of questions concerning attitudes toward encroachment and role conflict between psychologists and psychiatrists. On comparable items none of the responses of psychiatrists and social workers are significantly different. It is evident that psychiatrists perceive psychologists as encroaching upon psychiatric functions, seeking to enter private practice, and envying the psychiatrist's income more than psychologists attribute these behaviors to themselves. Psychiatrists perceive psychologists as desiring to encroach upon the functions of psychiatrists more than psychologists admit. It is interesting to note that psychologists perceive that psychiatrists fear psychologists as a financial threat (a charge which the

TABLE 5

MEAN RATING BY PSYCHOLOGISTS AND PSYCHIATRISTS OF THE MOBILITY MOTIVES
AND EFFORTS OF PSYCHOLOGISTS

Topic	Rating by Psychiatrists	Rating by Psychologists	Significance of difference
Psychologists' attempt to encroach on psychiatric functions	3.93	3.04	.01
Psychologists entering into private practice	5.05	4.06	.01
Psychiatrists see psychologists as threat to psychiatrists' income	3.45	4.43	.001
Psychologists envy greater income of psychiatrists	5.46	5.06	.01
Psychologists strive to win approval of psychiatrists	4.36	3.19	.001

psychiatrists are likely to deny), and psychiatrists believe that psychologists are striving to win the approval of psychiatrists (a statement which the psychologists rate low).

Differences Within Professions

We have seen that psychiatrists view themselves, on the average, as having greater influence than the members of the other professions. Do differences among psychiatrists in the degree to which they have this power make for differences in their attitudes and behaviors toward members of the other groups? Results relevant to this question will be presented in the form of correlations between power and the dependent variables specifying attitudes and behaviors.

The data presented in Table 6 show that the more power the psychiatrist has in his relations with psychologists and social workers the more confident he is of their respect and liking. Moreover, the more power possessed by the psychiatrist the more he expresses the desire to be liked by psychologists ($r=.25$, $p=.01$). This finding probably reflects a desire on the part of the more powerful psychiatrists to maintain a state of affairs which is satisfactory to them.

The amount of power of the psychiatrist also affects the frequency of his contact with the other professions and his desire for such contact. In Table 7 it is apparent that the psychiatrist with more power in his relations with members of the other groups is likely to have more contacts with the adjunct workers and to desire a high degree of contact with them.

In summary, the psychiatrists who have more power than their fellows in their relations with psychologists and social workers are more confident of their positions, surer of recognition by members of the ancillary groups, have a higher degree of contact with them whereby they can exercise this power, and are more willing to have frequent contacts.

We turn now to the effects of power on the attitudes of social workers

TABLE 6

CORRELATIONS BETWEEN PSYCHIATRISTS' PERCEPTION OF OWN POWER TO INFLUENCE SOCIAL WORKERS OR PSYCHOLOGISTS AND CERTAIN ATTITUDES TOWARD THESE GROUPS

	r	p
The greater the power of psychiatrists:		
The more they perceive that social workers respect psychiatrists	.21	.02
The more they perceive social workers as liking psychiatrists	.29	.01
The more they perceive that psychologists respect psychiatrists	.21	.01
The more they perceive psychologists as liking psychiatrists	.18	.05

TABLE 7

CORRELATIONS BETWEEN PSYCHIATRISTS' PERCEPTION OF OWN POWER TO INFLUENCE
SOCIAL WORKERS OR PSYCHOLOGISTS AND RATE OF CONTACT WITH THEM

The greater the power of psychiatrists:	r	p
The more contact they have with psychologists.................	.27	.01
The more contact they have with social workers................	.37	.001
The more contact they desire with psychologists...............	.35	.01
The more contact they desire with social workers..............	.33	.01

and psychologists toward psychiatrists. The results show that the greater the power of the psychologists and social workers, the more they behave in a way indicative of social distance and desire for independence from psychiatrists.

This tendency to avoid psychiatrists is shown in a number of ways in the data. For the social worker, (with respect to writing social histories and making community contacts) the greater the power she attributes to herself in relation to psychiatrists, the less she tends to want professional contacts with them ($r = -.41$, $p = .001$), the less she wants leisure-time contacts with them ($r = -.22$, $p = .01$), and the less is she willing to talk to them regardless of the topic ($r = -.22$, $p = .01$). It seems quite apparent that social workers with higher power are more likely to avoid psychiatrists.

For the psychologists, the same trend can be seen. Since psychiatrists are the superior group, face-to-face interaction with them might require the psychologist to assume a subordinate position. Thus it is interesting that there is a negative relation between the psychologist's power in his relations with psychiatrists (measured in terms of his power in diagnosis and therapy) and the frequency of professional contact with psychiatrists ($r = -.47$, $p = .001$). Furthermore, the amount of power held by the psychologists affects their professional identifications. Those psychologists with greater power in their relations with psychiatrists are more attracted to the profession of psychology, whereas the less powerful psychologists are more attracted to psychiatry as a profession (by chi square, $p = .001$).

Clearly, then, power is closely associated with feelings of professional autonomy and independence for both social workers and psychologists. Does this mean that those with little power feel dependent upon the psychiatrist's good will while those with considerable influence do not? The results show that this is probably the case. The more power the social worker has, the less she expresses a desire to be liked by psychiatrists ($r = -.26$, $p = .01$). The same is true for psychologists. For example, those psychologists who have more power tend to see themselves as less likely to curry favor with psychiatrists ($r = -.22$, $p = .02$), as making few attempts to strive for the psychiatrists' recognition ($r = -.29$, $p = .01$), as less likely to "get along" well with psychiatrists should they both be members of the same committee ($r = -.27$, $p = .01$), and as more able to speak frankly to psychiatrists concerning the behavior of a psychiatrist which psychologists consider unpleasant ($r = .21$, $p = .01$). In general, then, it seems that the more potent psychologists are less concerned with what psychiatrists think about them and are less hesitant about threatening psychiatrists via direct and personal remarks. In passing, it is interesting to note that the more powerful psychologists think of themselves as above social workers. When asked about the degree to which they feel that they are in competition with social workers for the psychiatrists' recognition, they reject this imputation of equality or rivalry ($r = -.27$, $p = .01$).

To summarize, the large majority in all groups agree that the power of the psychiatrists is much higher than that of the other two groups. High power, however, causes different reactions from psychiatrists and members of the adjunct groups. When the psychiatrist is aware that his power is relatively high, he feels close to the others and wants more professional contact with them. He is confident of his position and of their respect. The members of the less powerful groups, on the other hand, behave quite differently when they have power. They want fewer contacts, are more independent, and have less desire for the psychiatrists' good will. For them psychiatrists are not so threatening and they have less need to protect themselves in their relations with psychiatrists.

SUMMARY AND CONCLUSION

We have examined the interrole perceptions of three professions in the field of mental health. These professions were viewed as existing within a framework set by a hierarchical social structure. It was initially assumed that each of these professions would have aspirations either to increase their areas of professional responsibility or to maintain their present status. It was also assumed that members of these professions would be secure or insecure depending upon whether or not they expect to continue, or soon to begin, to satisfy their professional aspirations in their relations with one another. The state of security or insecurity was expected to influence the interpersonal behavior and perception directed toward members of the other professions.

The effects of security or insecurity were predicted to occur as a function of the position of each group in relation to the others. The more powerful groups, it was reasoned, should be more secure and therefore less threat-oriented in their reactions to the others, while the less powerful groups, by seeing smaller possibility of meeting their needs, should be more threat-oriented. Similar effects were expected when variations in the power among members of the same group were examined.

These assumptions were tested by data from a sample of psychiatrists, psychologists and social workers located in six large cities throughout the United States. These people were questioned concerning their power relations with those in the other groups, their attitudes and behaviors toward others, and the nature of the professional environment within which they worked. The major independent variable, power, was measured by asking the respondent about the degree to which he could determine the work of the members of another group in a number of functional areas, and the degree to which those others could determine his work. In line with the conception of power as involving a balance between two persons' abilities to influence each other, the discrepancy between these two attributions of power was taken as fixing the person's position on the dimension of power relationship with members of that other group.

When the data were examined by comparing the average responses of the groups toward one another, the main line of reasoning was confirmed. The psychiatric profession is seen by all groups as at the top of the pyramid of power, while psychologists and social workers are seen as subordinates. The average member of an ancillary profession has a strong desire to be supported and rewarded by those in the superior profession, reflecting his view that there is small likelihood that he can fulfill his professional aspirations without the aid of psychiatrists.

The data were also analyzed to reveal the reactions of those in each profession who perceive that they have more power in their relations with the other professions than do most of their colleagues. We find that the more powerful member of the subordinate group is less concerned with the psychiatrists' good will or with their opinions about him; he values his own profession more, and avoids professional contacts with psychiatrists. All of these reactions may be viewed as efforts toward achieving or maintaining autonomy. The low-power subordinate, in contrast, wants to be liked, makes efforts to be admired, wants frequent supportive contacts with psychiatrists, and values the psychiatric profession more than his own. These actions may be viewed as efforts to gratify needs for increased security.

The average member of the superior group is less concerned with winning the good will of his subordinates than they are with winning his good will. The psychiatrist with high power feels that he is admired and respected, wishes to have frequent professional contacts with subordinates, assumes that they are interested in his good will, and thinks well of their competence. The psychiatrist with low power thinks less well of the ancillary group members, assumes that they are attempting to invade his professional prerogatives rather than win his support, and thinks poorly of their competence.

REFERENCES

1. Zander, A., Cohen, A. R., & Stotland, E. *Role relations in the mental health professions.* Ann Arbor, Mich.: Institute for Social Research, 1957.

3

SITUATIONAL STRUCTURE, SELF-ESTEEM, AND THREAT-ORIENTED REACTIONS TO POWER [1]

Arthur R. Cohen

One persistent problem in the study of human behavior is that of specifying the links between social structure and personality. The concept "power" appears to be ideally suited for this purpose. Power is essentially a structural concept, referring to certain central aspects of the functional arrangements of any social system. At the same time, it necessarily deals with the motivations of individuals. The exercise of power requires some acceptance by those who are part of the social system, and since reward and punishment are inherently involved, it has various repercussions upon the adjustment and reactions of everyone in the power relation.

The present study is concerned with some of the conditions under which power becomes a threat to the individual over whom it is exercised and some of the reactions stemming from this threat. The particular conditions investigated were selected largely because they had been found to be operative in a previous field investigation (see Chapter 2). In that study two conditions appeared to be particularly important in determining the amount of threat experienced by a low-power person in his relations with someone of high power.

The first of these concerns the individual's self-feelings. It appeared that a person's reactions to being under the power of another depends to a considerable degree upon his view of himself. Consequently, it was decided to study the variable "self-esteem" under more controlled conditions.

The second condition has to do with the structure of the role situation. In the earlier field study, it was found that persons of different occupational groups often differed in the designation of their own and others' functions and duties, that there was often overlap of functions, and that frequently the goals were unclear and the means of reaching them vague. On the basis of

[1] This investigation was supported by a grant-in-aid (M-325 (C)) from the Institute of Mental Health of the National Institutes of Health, Public Health Service.

this experience, it was decided to investigate more thoroughly the variable "structure of the situation."

The experiment to be reported here deals, then, with some of the conditions under which power becomes a threat to the individual over whom it is exercised. We have concentrated upon two conditions: individual level of self-esteem, and structure of the situation.

THEORETICAL BACKGROUND

Power may be conceived of, in most general terms, as the ability of one party of a relationship to influence the behavior of the other party. Within this general conception of power we are here interested in the situation where a person's power consists of the ability to determine whether or not another person reaches some goal which is important to him. In this type of situation, the person with power possesses the ability to control the means by which the other can reach his goal. This ability to control another's means of goal attainment undoubtedly affects the person's ability to influence the other's behavior in a wide realm of activities and thus has broad repercussions. In the presentation which follows, we shall confine ourselves to the means-control aspects of power. We may define power, for our purposes, as *the ability of one party of a relationship to determine whether or not the other party is carried toward his goals or away from them, over and above the second party's own efforts.*

Threat may have many sources varying from the most objective, such as starvation and potential death where responsibility is readily externalized, to the most subjective and personalized sources where the individual's basic mechanisms for coping with the social world are questioned. In the present experiment we are concerned with the end of the continuum where the individual's perception of the adequacy of his self to deal with the situation and to satisfy his needs is the salient factor in threat (4).

Threat, then, is *that state of the individual in which he feels inadequate to deal with a given situation and to satisfy his needs.* From these two definitions one might conclude that anyone under the power of another would automatically experience threat. Further consideration, however, prevents this conclusion. It must be emphasized that the possession of power consists of the *potential* to withhold or to permit the gratification of a need. In any actual situation it may not be used at all, or it may be used in either a friendly and supportive or a hostile and punishing manner. Thus, in the face of any power relation which contains the possibility of deprivation a person may develop a wide range of expectations concerning his own adequacy for dealing with the situation.

Despite these different possible reactions to power it is important to note that the degree of threat an individual may *potentially* experience in a social setting is related to the degree of power which can be exercised over him.

We now consider two factors which may determine to what degree a situation of potential threat is actually experienced as threatening. In discussing these factors we confine ourselves to a situation of constant power over an individual whose motivation toward need satisfaction is constant and strong.

Structure of the Situation

"Structure" refers to the degree to which a social situation provides the individual with clear and accessible cues so that he may behave in a goal-directed and need-satisfying manner.

When a stimulus situation is relatively ambiguous, a person can make only certain responses whose effects he cannot predict. Lack of prediction and control make it difficult for him to meet his needs adequately, fostering feelings of worthlessness and threatening the security of the self. A situation characterized by a high degree of structure, in contrast, is one which provides the individual with guide lines so that he has some way of influencing the situation or of behaving toward it so as to achieve adequate need satisfaction. As a result the experience is less threatening (1, 2, 5, 6, 11).

If a person is in a position where someone else determines whether or not he is to attain a goal, a clearly structured situation enables him to act better in his own behalf and improves his chances of goal attainment. It may also reduce the chances that the other person can behave arbitrarily with regard to his goal achievement. In such a situation, structure may be viewed as composed of:

1. *Degree of clarity of the paths to goals.* A person may not be certain of his course because the problem upon which he is working is vague and he cannot draw upon past experience to solve it. He is not certain of his steps because there are few cues. The result is that he is less certain as to how to satisfy his needs and he is consequently more easily threatened.

2. *Degree of consistency of the power figure's behavior.* If a person with power arbitrarily changes the rules of the game or keeps shifting the reference points, the dependent person will experience a corresponding degree of threat. Inconsistency of the power figure's behavior prevents the dependent person from understanding the other's actions and from anticipating the consequences of efforts he may make.

Self-Esteem

By "self-esteem" we mean the evaluation that a person places on whatever aspects of his self are relevant to him at a given time. It is dependent upon his success and failure in the past. An individual with high self-esteem may be expected to show behavior that is more organized, effective, realistic, consistent, and meaningful than that of a person with low self-esteem (12). He should, therefore, feel more able to deal with a given task and be less threatened when confronting another person who has potential control over his need satisfaction. In contrast, a person with low self-esteem should feel less confident of reaching his goal, more readily anticipate failure, and experience threat in any situation where someone else has the power to determine his goal achievement.

On the basis of the foregoing, the following hypotheses may be generated:

1. The more ambiguous a situation in which power is being exercised over an individual who is highly motivated toward need satisfaction, the more threat he will experience.

2. The lower the self-esteem of an individual who is highly motivated in a situation in which power is being exercised over him, the more threat he will experience.

3. When both self-esteem and structure are varied simultaneously, the strongest effects on threat should be observed. Thus, the person with high self-esteem in a clearly structured situation should experience far less threat than the person with low self-esteem when confronted with ambiguity.

These hypotheses are stated in the most general fashion. Threat can be viewed as a mediating construct which may be identified only in terms of its manifestations, both direct and indirect. The following specifications of the general hypotheses are stated in terms of the effects of the two major variables on different manifestations of threat. Thus, compared to those of high self-esteem and clear structure, conditions of low self-esteem and ambiguity will produce the following characteristics: [2]

(a) *Less attraction experienced by the individual toward the interpersonal situation.* A person will be more attracted to interpersonal situations which

---

[2] All of the dependent variables and their experimental manifestations are expected to go in the same direction. It is anticipated, of course, that reactions will vary with the nature of the persons involved and the situation within which they behave. While some people might show more aggression, for example, than others in a threatening situation and the latter might show more anxiety than the former, still, as a group, both should show more of both aggression and anxiety than a group of people exposed to an experimental condition with no threat.

are supportive than to ones which are threatening. Lack of structure with its consequent lack of supportive frames of reference and relative inability of the low self-esteem individual to manipulate the situation will bring out more threat and result in less attraction.

(b) *Less social support (social validity or security) experienced by the individual in the interpersonal situation.* Feelings of social support are based upon feelings of assurance, safety, or certainty and are related to the person's experiences in social situations which are relevant for him (7, 8, 9). When the situation is one which lacks structure, these feelings of social validity for one's opinions, attitudes, beliefs, and behaviors tend to disappear since it is more difficult to perceive the power figure as one who shares the same outlook. In addition, the individual with low self-esteem is less predisposed to experience social support.

(c) *Greater anxiety experienced by the individual in the interpersonal situation.* Threat can manifest itself in attempts at leaving the field, heightened somatic reactions, and feelings such as helplessness. These reactions are presumed to characterize anxiety. The individual's relative inability to meet his needs in a situation where his tried concepts and values do not prove effective leads him to feel inadequate and to deny the value of the interpersonal experience as a defensive and self-protective reaction.

(d) *More negative evaluation and perception of the power figure by the individual.* A person of low self-esteem in an ambiguous situation will make negative attributions to the power figure, the source of reward and punishment and the gatekeeper to his goal attainment. He will tend to perceive the power figure as malicious and punishing. By blaming the power figure, he maintains the structure of the self against attack.

(e) *More negative perception and evaluation by the individual of himself in the interpersonal situation.* A person with low self-esteem, when confronted with ambiguity, will have few standards by which to judge his performance. He is also predisposed not to value highly his own performance. He will thus tend to see himself as having failed and having made a bad impression on the power figure.

(f) *Less motivation in the interpersonal situation as a result of experiences in that situation.* One response to this type of situation is to withdraw involvement. This is a defensive reaction which protects the individual against loss of self-enhancement and threat. When he feels that he is not really being evaluated, that the situation contains no control over his goal attainment, or when he is not motivated to strive for need satisfaction, he experiences less threat.

(g) *More aggression exhibited by the individual in the interpersonal situation.* Since an unstructured situation involves arbitrariness of the power figure and less chance to perceive his own behavior as constructive, there should be greater frustration and consequent aggression. Furthermore, the person with low self-esteem may characteristically show more generalized frustration. Of course, the person does not have to aggress outwardly against the power figure. Depending upon his characteristic ways of handling frustration, he may internalize his aggression, suppress it, identify with the power figure, withdraw from the situation, or change his frame of reference for evaluating the situation. Nevertheless, the conditions of ambiguity and low self-esteem may be expected to produce more frustration and consequent aggression, on the average, than conditions of structure and high self-esteem.

(h) *More time required to complete an assigned task.* It is expected that the threat engendered for the person of low self-esteem will immobilize him to some degree. This may prevent him from completing an assigned task as quickly as someone less threatened.

METHOD

Research Design

Two variables are examined as determinants of threat: (1) degree of structure of the situation, and (2) level of self-esteem. Structure may be broken down into the dimensions of clarity of paths and consistency of the power figure's behavior. This permits the creation of a condition of structure by combining clarity of the goal with consistency of the power figure's behavior and the creation of an ambiguous condition by combining unclarity of the goal with inconsistency of the power figure's behavior. The intermediate conditions which permit specification of the interaction of the factors making up the structure variable (i.e., clarity-inconsistency and unclarity-consistency) were also studied in order to help determine the differential contribution of these factors to threat reactions. The variable of self-esteem may conveniently be divided into three levels of high, medium, and low self-esteem.

This classification makes possible a 4 x 3 factorial design with four degrees of structure and three degrees of self-esteem. The experiment was in fact run according to this design, but for convenience of analysis, the extreme structure condition and the extreme ambiguity condition were taken as the structure variations, and high and low self-esteem were used as the self-esteem variations.[3] For analysis, then, a 2 x 2 design was employed con-

[3] For a discussion of the analysis of the different aspects of structure and of the middle self-esteem groups see the full report of this research (3).

sisting of four conditions: structure, high self-esteem; structure, low self-esteem; ambiguity, high self-esteem; and ambiguity, low self-esteem. Each of the four cells represents a different experimental treatment. Twenty-two subjects were placed in each treatment, making a total of 88 subjects.

A laboratory experiment was conducted to test the hypotheses. The experimental setting consisted of two-person groups, one of the persons being a power figure and the other the experimental subject. In order to maximize the comparability of different experimental treatments and of different groups within each treatment and to control for difference in interpersonal interaction, a trained assistant was used as the power figure. Thus, one subject was needed for each group to function as the person of low power. The subjects for the experiment were female employees of a public utility company. The experiment was designed so that it would fit into the power structure of the company in that the authority person was to be seen as coming from the supervisory level immediately above that of the subject. This imparted to the study a degree of realism often difficult to achieve in laboratory experimentation.

The company supplied a supervisor who was not known in the office where the experiment was run. The subjects were taken directly from their work and asked to go to the experimental room to participate in a "survey" which the University of Michigan was conducting. The instructions appeared to occasion no conflicts or negative expectation, being in a setting where similar procedures were not uncommon.

General Experimental Setting

In all conditions it was necessary to create a consistent perception by the subjects that the supervisor had a high degree of power. The situation had also to be realistic and interesting so that a high level of motivation would be produced. The instructions to create power and motivation were given by the experimenter. The specific conditions of each experimental variation were set for the subject by the trained assistant.

As the subject came into the room she was greeted by the experimenter and shown to a seat at the side of the table at which the supervisor was seated, busily looking over some papers. In all experimental conditions the supervisor attempted to convey an impression of "cool impersonality."

In order to create high motivation, the subject was told that both the University and the Company were interested in how well she was able to do the task with the supervisor. She was urged a number of times to do as well as she could since the University was interested in studying the relationship between a person's ability, sensitivity, and intelligence. She was told that problems like these are sometimes used in intelligence tests and entrance examinations and that they would be an indication of her ability to observe while working with others and to use correctly any suggestions or aids she was given.

The power of the supervisor was established by telling the subject that how well she did on the problems would be decided by the supervisor and by her alone. She was told that the supervisor was very familiar with such problems, would be working with her, and would be continually observing her so as to judge her competence, ability, and success or failure. Before the experimenter left the room he stressed again the fact that the subject's success or failure would rest entirely with the supervisor.

The supervisor then continued with the experiment by behaving in the way appropriate to each condition. Her behavior will be described below.

When the subject had completed the task, the supervisor called the experimenter back into the room without giving the subject any explicit statement of her evaluation of the subject. The experimenter then asked the subject for her reactions to the session. These reactions were obtained by a questionnaire which measured the dependent variables. The subject filled out the questionnaire privately, sealing it up, when through, in a large envelope conspicuously stamped "University of Michigan."

The experimenter then chatted with the subject about her experiences in the experiment. All subjects were told that they had done "quite well," "very well," or "as well as could be expected since even people at the University don't understand these tasks," and so on. Most subjects were readily made comfortable and all left with some degree of positive feelings. In addition, they were emphatically assured that only people at the University would see their results and that their job would in no way be affected by their participation in the experiment.

Creation of Specific Conditions

1. *Self-esteem.* Two weeks before the actual conduct of the experiment all subjects were given a self-esteem questionnaire of a modified Q-sort type. On the basis of these questionnaires, three self-esteem groups (high, medium, and low) were formed. Subjects were then assigned to appropriate conditions of structure to achieve the required number of subjects in each of the experimental conditions.

The measure of self-esteem used in this study involves a sequence of judgments concerning the subject's self ideal and her self percept. Each subject received a series of behavioral statements grouped around such general needs as autonomy, affiliation, achievement, and recognition. She was instructed to check, within each set of statements, the one most and the one least descriptive of her self ideal and to do the same thing as regards her self percept. The level of self-esteem was taken as the discrepancy between the self ideal and the self percept attributions; the larger the discrepancy between one's ideals for oneself and the attributed location of one's self, the lower the self-esteem. The complete questionnaire may be found in the full report of this experiment (3). The rationale for the scoring system is described elsewhere (10).

2. *Structure of the situation.* The clarity-unclarity aspect of the situation was created by the kind of problems handed the subject. The consistency-inconsistency aspect was established by the supervisor through the way she supervised the problem and presented suggestions to the subject.

The problems had been previously established as being "objectively" clear or unclear. They were word-symbol matching tests in which the subject was asked to match a given word with one of several pictures. In the clear condition, familiar pictures and commonly understood words were presented a few at a time. In the unclear condition, vague and unfamiliar pictures and uncommon words were presented in large groups. Prior to this experiment a sample of 110 college students had been given the problems, and an index of agreement computed for both sets. For the clear set the agreement index was over 80 per cent, for the unclear set it was less than 35 per cent. It was thus concluded that the sets were sufficiently different to establish the clarity-unclarity aspect of structure.

By suggesting cues to the subject, the supervisor created a given degree of consistency. To be consistent, she gave the subject a single cue which would presumably aid her to match words and pictures, repeating this cue a number of times. To be inconsistent, she presented a variety of cues in no particular order, switching from cue to cue in a seemingly arbitrary fashion.

Measurement

All of the dependent variables except "time spent on the task" and "aggression" were measured by use of a questionnaire. Most of the measures involve ratings by the subjects on a series of eight-point a priori scales. Several measures were made for some dependent variables, since it was desirable to avoid making assumptions about the effects of the experimental situation on any one facet of any given variable. Where several measures were used, an index was created, consisting of the cumulation of the responses on the different measures. The dependent variables and the different measures making them up were as follows:

1. *Attraction:* An index of the subject's attraction to the power figure, to

the task and to the prestige derived from the experience of participation in the research.

2. *Social support:* A measure of the degree to which the subject felt that she was receiving validity for her opinions, beliefs, and attitudes from the other person.

3. *Anxiety:* An index of the subject's subjective anxiety experience, her worry about the situation, her desire to avoid such experiences in the future, and her feelings about how valuable she perceived the "test" to be.

4. *Perception of the power figure:* An index of the subject's perception of the power figure's approval, intent toward the subject, competence, and self-centeredness.

5. *Self-perception:* An index of the subject's perception of the quality of her performance, and the impression she made upon the power figure.

6. *Motivation:* A measure of the subject's desire to do well toward the end of the experimental situation.

7. *Aggression:* A measure of the subject's generalized aggression in the situation. The subjects were presented with a checklist of ambiguous frustrating situations which specified no reasons for the frustrations. They were then asked to respond to these hypothetical situations by indicating whether they would or would not be angry. The number of anger responses projected by the subject was taken as an indication of her generalized aggressive feelings as a result of the experimental situation.

8. *Time spent on the task:* This was a simple measure taken by the trained assistant (power figure) of the time it took the subject to complete the "task."

FINDINGS

Effectiveness of the Experimental Inductions

Let us first check on the validity of the theoretical assumptions. Two minimal conditions for the experiment required that the subject perceive the superior as having power over her and that the subject maintain strong motivation to achieve success and avoid failure. On both of these scores, the inductions were effective. No matter what the experimental condition, all subjects perceived the power figure as having a great deal of power over them and all rated their motivation prior to the session as very strong. The means were close to the upper limits of these scales, and both analyses of variance and tests for homogeneity of variance failed to disclose any real differences among the various treatments.

A third factor, degree of company identification, also had to be controlled if measures obtained in the various experimental conditions were to be interpreted unambiguously. Analysis of a number of measures, such as the importance of getting ahead, the importance of being liked by management and supervisors, and satisfaction with job, revealed no differences among experimental conditions. We may conclude, then, that the basic assumptions underpinning the experiment are valid.

Tests of the Hypotheses

The data bearing on the hypotheses can be seen in Table 1. In this table, the smaller the mean, the less the assumed threat. It can be seen by examin-

TABLE 1

MEAN EFFECTS OF STRUCTURE AND SELF-ESTEEM ON VARIOUS THREAT-ORIENTED BEHAVIORS (N = 88)

1. Attraction

	Hi SE	Lo SE	Total	
Structure ...	7.91	9.00	8.46 }	$p < .001$
Ambiguity ..	10.77	10.69	10.73 }	
Total	9.34	9.89		

n.s.

5. Self-Perception

	Hi SE	Lo SE	Total	
Structure ...	5.00	5.03	5.01 }	$p < .02$
Ambiguity ..	6.05	5.55	5.80 }	
Total	5.52	5.29		

n.s.

2. Social Support

	Hi SE	Lo SE	Total	
Structure ...	6.34	8.41	7.43 }	$p < .01$
Ambiguity ..	9.00	9.54	9.27 }	
Total	7.78	8.98		

$p < .05$

6. Resultant Motivation

	Hi SE	Lo SE	Total	
Structure ...	1.22	1.50	1.36 }	$p < .10$
Ambiguity ..	1.64	1.54	1.62 }	
Total	1.43	1.55		

n.s.

3. Anxiety

	Hi SE	Lo SE	Total	
Structure ...	11.14	11.14	11.14 }	$p < .01$
Ambiguity ..	13.14	13.68	13.41 }	
Total	12.14	12.26		

n.s.

7. Aggression (% of group)

	Hi SE	Lo SE	Total	
Structure ...	36.3%	59.1%	47.8% }	$p < .01$
Ambiguity ..	68.2%	81.8%	75 % }	
Total	52.3%	75 %		

$p < .10$

4. Perception of the Power Figure

	Hi SE	Lo SE	Total	
Structure ...	8.00	8.95	8.48 }	n.s.
Ambiguity ..	8.64	9.50	9.07 }	
Total	8.23	9.23		

n.s.

8. Time on Task

	Hi SE	Lo SE	Total	
Structure ...	8.19	8.41	8.30 }	$p < .001$
Ambiguity ..	13.50	11.48	12.49 }	
Total	10.85	9.95		

n.s.

ing the structure marginals that on all dependent manifestations of threat, the differences between the structure conditions are in the expected direction, and on at least six measures, these differences are at highly acceptable levels of confidence.[4] We may thus conclude that variation in the structure of a power situation does affect the degree to which the person over whom power is exercised experiences threat. These results provide confirmation for Hypothesis 1.

The same table provides data bearing on Hypothesis 2. It appears that the hypothesis concerning the effects of variations in self-esteem is less well supported. Though the differences between the high and low self-esteem marginals are in the expected direction in six cases, only in two cases, social support and aggression, do they approach statistical significance.

The assumption in Hypothesis 3 is that the effects of self-esteem and structure are cumulative, that the conditions combining structure with high self-esteem and ambiguity with low self-esteem will differ most from each other. In all cases, the differences between the two extreme cells are significant at the .01 level or beyond. Support is thus provided for the assumption that both variables working together are strong determinants of threat-oriented reactions to a power-laden situation.

It should not be concluded, however, that variations in self-esteem make no difference in the amount of experienced threat. In Table 1 it can be seen that within the structure condition primarily, and to some degree within the ambiguity condition, differences in experienced threat appear between the high and low self-esteem groups. In several cases the differences in the expected direction between high and low self-esteem persons in the structure condition are quite striking. Under conditions of ambiguity, the differences are less pronounced and in some cases are the reverse of the predictions. Table 2 illustrates these trends more precisely. In this table is specified the interaction between the structure conditions and the self-esteem conditions in producing threat. The hypothesis tested is that within structure, the low self-esteem subjects will show more threat than the high self-esteem subjects and that this difference will be greater than in the ambiguity condition.

It can be seen in Table 2 that in most cases (a number of them reaching or approaching significance) differences in amount of threat experienced by persons with low and high self-esteem are greater in the structure condition than in the ambiguity condition. This result appears to be due to the higher degree of threat with which the low self-esteem subjects enter a structured situation. The similarity among the different self-esteem persons in the

[4] All statistical tests in this report are two-tailed tests.

TABLE 2

INTERACTION DIFFERENCES BETWEEN HIGH AND LOW SELF-ESTEEM WITHIN
STRUCTURE AND WITHIN AMBIGUITY

($+$ = more threat for Low SE, less threat for Hi SE;
$-$ = less threat for Low SE, more threat for Hi SE)

Dependent Variable	Within Structure	Within Ambiguity	Interaction Differences	p-value of Interaction
1. Attraction	+1.09	− .08	1.18	<.05
2. Social Support	+1.96	+ .54	1.42	<.02
3. Anxiety	0	+ .54	−.54	n.s.
4. Perception of the Power Figure	+ .95	+ .80	.15	n.s.
5. Self-Perception	+ .03	− .50	.53	n.s.
6. Resultant Motivation	+ .28	− .09	.37	<.10
7. Aggression (% of group)	+ 23%	+ 13%	10%	n.s.
8. Time on Task	+ .22	−2.02	2.24	<.01

ambiguity condition seems, in many cases, to be due to the increase in threat for high self-esteem subjects as they "move" from a condition of structure to one of ambiguity.

DISCUSSION

Taken together, the findings strongly support the hypothesis concerning the effects of variations in structure on threat-oriented reactions to power. In all cases the differences between the structure and ambiguity conditions were in the predicted direction, and for all but a few were highly significant. Those subjects in the ambiguity condition, in comparison to the subjects in the structure condition, demonstrated more threat by being less attracted to the interpersonal situation, to the power figure, and to the task. They were less secure, showed more anxiety, tended to perceive the power figure more negatively, and felt that they had made a bad impression. They were less motivated to do well towards the end of the session, had more generalized aggression, and spent more time on the task.

We may say, then, that the exercise of power in an ambiguous situation can provide a great deal of threat for the person who is attempting to reach some sort of need satisfaction. The question may be asked, however, concerning the differential effect of the two specified sources of the structure variation, consistency-inconsistency and clarity-unclarity. In a further analysis, the interaction between these two variables was examined in an effort to determine which appeared to be more potent in producing variations in threat. The results of this analysis showed that though variations in the power figure's consistency led to predictable variations in threat experienced by the subjects, variation in the clarity of the task is a more important determinant of the degree to which threat-reactions to power will be produced. Thus, while in the data presented, the effects of both variables have been cumulated in an effort to produce the widest variations in degree of structure, it should be realized that most of the effect found was due to the clarity-unclarity manipulation.

In the present situation, the subjects were instructed to do their very best and were led to assume that the task was a method by which their ability and intelligence could be assessed. This strong motivational induction may have been partly responsible for the greater importance of the clarity variable. It is more likely, however, that the clarity variation was a more reliable one; evidence from post-experimental interviews indicates that the subjects concentrated so much upon their performance that they were sometimes unaware of cues provided by the power-figure.

In this connection, another issue may be raised. One could alternatively interpret the differences between structure conditions, which depended mostly on differences in clarity, as due solely to the increased difficulty of the unclear tasks. It is, of course, true that difficulty of goal-directed behavior is an important element in any kind of ambiguity, but such an explanation might tend to make the major hypothesis somewhat less compelling. An analysis was undertaken to check on this point. On the basis of a measure of perceived difficulty of the task, the subjects were broken down into those who saw the task as relatively more difficult and those who saw it as less difficult. As might be expected, more of the former fall in the ambiguity condition whereas more of the latter are in the structure condition, but within each of the two difficulty groups the relationship between degree of structure and threat was examined. The absolute levels of threat are somewhat different, but the data show that though there is a lessened effect of the structure variations for low self-esteem subjects who saw the task as easy, on the whole, the assumption is supported that differences in structure produce differences in threat-oriented reactions to power.

Hypothesis 2, which specified the effects of variations in self-esteem, was less well supported. Hypothesis 3, which dealt with the operation of both self-esteem and structure, was confirmed; it illustrates the effect of both factors together in producing threat. When each of the main factors operates alone, its effect may not be as strong or pervasive as when both factors operate together in complementary fashion either to lend support to the individual or to deny him support. Nevertheless, the strong effects of the structure variation alone were apparent: on the whole and within each level of self-esteem, ambiguity tended to produce more threat than structure. This was more pronounced, though, for high self-esteem people than for low self-esteem people. Ambiguity may trigger off the reaction of the highs to the experimental situation, while the lows, who are more threat-oriented to begin with, may not be so affected by additional threat which takes the form of few situational supports.

The effects of self-esteem alone appeared to be least predictable. However, it was seen in the interaction data that low self-esteem subjects did experience more threat than the highs within the structure condition. This difference between self-esteem groups was greater in the structure than in the ambiguity condition. The original hypothesis about the effects of self-esteem was expected to hold true within any degree of structure, on the assumption that people of low self-esteem are in general more threatened than those of high self-esteem. But the hypothesis is better supported in highly structured situations where the individual seems to bring the threat into the situation with him. This finding is consistent with the original assumptions. However, in ambiguous situations where the situational push is pervasive, the high self-esteem people appear to be as threatened as the lows.

The difference between these two types of people, then, may reside not in the amount of threat they experience in an ambiguous situation, but rather in the mechanisms by which they attempt to handle threat. In the data from the specific measures within the indices, there are some tendencies for the highs to repudiate and depersonalize the situation to save face, and for the lows to be more dependent upon the situation and to be more vulnerable to imposition from external events. The highs tend to deny the value of the task, to withdraw their motivation, to be less attracted to the situation, to feel the power figure could have improved the way she conducted it, but yet to spend more time on the task. They appear to be concerned with keeping up a good front under threat. The lows, on the other hand, tend to be more dependent upon the power figure and more concerned with the power figure's behavior. They tend to find it more difficult to reject the situation, to be more willing to say the task is difficult, and to say that one worries about such things and avoids them if possible. Their major concern, then, tends to be with the way they are treated by the power figure.

These findings necessitate a modification of our original theory. Though structure and self-esteem, operating together, permitted the specification of degrees of threat, self-esteem by itself did not so effectively. It may no longer be said flatly that people of high self-esteem find a challenging power situation less threatening than people of low self-esteem. The difference between them, rather, may be that the highs tend to handle threat by maintaining their selves intact, while the lows tend to be more vulnerable to outside influence.

In the light of these findings we should re-examine the measure used to classify people according to self-esteem. It will be recalled that we took the discrepancy between self ideal and self percept as the index of self-esteem. Those individuals with large discrepancies between their self ideal and self percept were classified as low, and those with small discrepancies were classified as high. It appears, then, that people became classed as high because they were not so ready to admit inconsistencies in their self picture, whereas lows became lows because they were more willing to see and publicly admit these inconsistencies.

In order to explore this possibility, a special study was conducted on another small sample of people. Here personality measures derived from the Blacky test were related to our ideal-real self-esteem index. The results provide some support for the above conjectures. Except for a number of high self-esteem people characterized by absence of conflict, most of those with high self-esteem revealed rigidity and self-protectiveness. Those with low self-esteem, on the other hand, appeared to have greater need for structure and to be more dependent upon situational supports. These data are consistent with the interpretations advanced to explain the behavior of the different self-esteem groups.

These differences between the self-esteem groups within each condition of structure and the differences between structure variations within self-esteem are clearly outlined by the interaction analysis. There is, however, a more general point which can be made as a result of this analysis. It seems that when the power situation is ambiguous, such a personality variable as self-esteem may make little difference in the amount of threat experienced by the person. A strong and pervasive power situation which is threatening may affect everyone regardless of variations in their personality make-up, though people may possibly differ in the mechanisms by which they handle threat. On the other hand, when the situational push is minimal because the power is exercised in a highly structured and secure environment, then the self-selective factor of different personality predispositions may operate to create differences between people in their threat-oriented behavior. In other words, when the stimulus situation is potent in its ability to evoke threat (ambiguity), then persons of all degrees of predisposition to be threatened are affected. However, when the stimulus situation is "weaker" (structure), then only the strongest predispositions (low self-esteem) are cued off. It would thus seem that there are some·conditions for the exercise of power within which personality variations remain poor predictors of threat-oriented behavior. Within other conditions, however, it may be very important to specify personality variations in order to predict behavioral effects accurately.

SUMMARY AND CONCLUSIONS

This experiment was designed to investigate some of the conditions under which power exercised over an individual becomes a threat. The two conditions explored were level of self-esteem and structure of the situation. Although there are presumably many conditions under which power may become more or less of a threat, these two were selected for study because they had been suggested by a prior field investigation and because knowledge about their nature might advance our understanding of the relations between social structure and personality.

A theoretical model was used which relates power to threat and interposes the factors of self-esteem and structure between these. The theory assumes that power may lead to threat, but that the actual threat present is dependent upon self-esteem and structure. It assumes that the individual will be more or less able to cope with a situation in which he is strongly motivated to reach a goal, depending upon the degree to which self-esteem and structure are present. Little structure affords few guide lines and cues for behavior. A person of low self-esteem has an unsure grasp of the world and an anticipation of failure and punishment. When a person of low self-esteem is in a situation of little structure he is unable to act effectively in his own behalf in the fact of power exercised over him; since action is necessary for need satisfaction, he experiences a great deal of threat. Thus, when the power-laden situation provides no support and when he has low self-esteem, the person is more likely to see the situation as threatening, since the exercise of power involves control over his goal attainment.

The major hypothesis specified that the exercise of power in an ambiguous situation would produce more threat for the person over whom it is exercised than in a structured situation, and that persons with low self-esteem would experience more threat than those with high self-esteem. It was also expected that when both factors were varied in a complementary fashion, more threat would be produced: the ambiguity–low self-esteem condition would be more threatening than the structure–high self-esteem condition. These hypotheses were tested in a laboratory situation, the data on threat and insecurity being gathered by means of a post-experimental questionnaire aimed at measuring a range of concomitants and effects of threat. These factors were: attraction, perception of social support, anxiety, perception of the power figure, self-perception, resultant motivation, aggression, and time spent on the task.

The hypothesis which specified the complementary effects of structure and self-esteem was completely confirmed. The effects of structure alone are strong in the predicted direction, but less so. The self-esteem variable appeared not to have been a strong determinant of threat in this situation. Thus, the two variables operating together created stronger and more demonstrable effects than either operating alone. However, there is some evidence to suggest that the measure of self-esteem was not entirely satisfactory.

Further research may well concern itself with the relationship between modes of reacting to threatening power-laden situations and modes of self-evaluation. Research in this area would serve to delineate some of the articulation points between interpersonal relations in the experimental situation and general ways of presenting one's self to the world in order to maintain and enhance the self. In this connection knowledge of the person's characteristic ego defenses and their relation to his self-evaluation would be extremely helpful.

Future research might also take up the general question of the social conditions within which personality variations make for behavioral differences and the social conditions under which they make for little difference for behavior. Such research would help to specify some of the links between social structure and personality.

REFERENCES

1. Allport, G. W. & Postman, L. *The psychology of rumor.* New York: Holt, 1947.
2. Cantril, H. *The psychology of social movements.* New York: Wiley, 1941.
3. Cohen, A. R. The effects of situational structure and individual self-esteem on threat-oriented reactions to power. Unpublished doctor's dissertation, University of Michigan, 1953.
4. Hogan, R. A. A theory of threat and defense. *J. consult. Psychol.,* 1952, **16,** 417-424.
5. Krech, D. & Crutchfield, R. S. *Theory and problems of social psychology.* New York: McGraw-Hill, 1948.
6. Lippitt, R. An experimental study of authoritarian and democratic group atmospheres. *University of Iowa Studies in Child Welfare,* 1940, **16,** No. 3, 45-195.
7. McClelland, D. *Personality.* New York: Sloane, 1951.
8. Murphy, G. *Personality.* New York: Harper, 1948.
9. Newcomb, T. M. *Social psychology.* New York: Dryden, 1950.
10. Shapiro, D. Psychological factors in friendship choice and rejection. Unpublished doctor's dissertation, University of Michigan, 1952.
11. Sherif, M. & Cantril, H. *The psychology of ego-involvements.* New York: Wiley, 1947.
12. Symonds, P. *The ego and the self.* New York: Appleton-Century-Crofts, 1951.

4

PEER GROUPS AND REACTIONS TO POWER FIGURES [1]

EZRA STOTLAND

Multiple group membership is a phenomenon found in every aspect of life. One important type of multiple group membership arises in groupings of peers at the same level in a power hierarchy. Each individual is a member of two groups, the group of peers and the group consisting of himself and those above or below him in the power hierarchy. A common example would be an informal group of workers in a factory, each of whom also is a member of a group consisting of himself and his foreman. The problem then arises, What is the relationship between a person's memberships in these two groups? This problem may be narrowed to a study of the effects of membership in a group of peers (subjected to similar power) on behavior in the hierarchical power group. Or, it may be narrowed to the effects of the hierarchical group on behavior in the peer group. In the present study, the first focus of the problem will be the primary but not only concern. Also, the problem will be limited to groups of low-power people.

The literature on this problem is not extensive. Wright (5) and Thibaut (4) studied reactions of people with little power to those with high power under conditions where the former acted or could have acted as a whole group. These studies, however, did not examine in detail the ways in which relations in one group affect, and are affected by, relations in the other. The work of Kelley (3) on communication in hierarchies provides a closer approach to this problem. In this study each low-status person was paired with only one high-status person and could not act in concert with other low-status people. Kelley found that the low-status people tended to be more attracted to each other than were people in a control group. From these findings, it is not unreason-

[1] This report is based upon a dissertation submitted to the University of Michigan in partial fulfillment of the requirements for the degree of Doctor of Philosophy. The author is deeply indebted to Dr. Alvin F. Zander, who directed the dissertation, for his many valuable suggestions and criticisms. This investigation was supported by a grant-in-aid (M-325 (C)) from the Institute of Mental Health of the National Institutes of Health, Public Health Service.

able to derive the hypothesis that lower-status people will tend to be more attracted to each other than people not in a hierarchical situation at all. Finally, Gerard (2) studied both attempts to influence the opinion of another group member and resistance to attempted influence as a function of the anchoring of opinion in another group. He found that the number of attempts to influence was a function of the degree of agreement in the other group, but only for those highly attracted to the other group. These highly attracted people also changed their opinion less often in the second group. Although this experiment does not deal with power relations among individuals, it does show that the strength of a person's opinions in one group may be a function of his attraction to another group and the degree of social reality attained in it.

The conclusion of Kelley's and Gerard's experiments can be combined as follows. If low-status people are attracted to each other, it is not unlikely that they will form a group. They might then reach some degree of agreement on the ways of relating to high-status people, since attractive groups tend to produce agreement on relevant matters. To the extent that this process is carried out, they would be expected to react to the higher-status people in the ways agreed upon by the groups of low-status people. This derivation will be elaborated below.

THEORY

For the purposes of this study, power is defined as the authority that one person has to prevent another from reaching his goal. This definition excludes power which derives from personal characteristics, power which is helpful, and power which aims to set up own forces in the other person. In addition, the power studied here is exercised rather than latent or potential. The conclusions of this study should then be limited to this restricted type of power.

The exercise of the obstructive characteristics of this type of power makes it a threat to those subjected to it. In other words, the power is actually used to prevent a person's reaching his goal and therefore threatens him. By threat is meant the state of a person in which he feels that he has lost, is losing, or clearly may lose his ability to reach his goals. Power is thus threatening, since those subjected to it cannot move toward their goals.

Three possible reactions to threatening power are postulated: withdrawal, cooperation, and aggression. In withdrawal, the person gives up his own goals, and thus cannot be threatened. In aggression, the person tries to decrease the ability of the source of threat (i.e. power) to obstruct attainment of the goal by weakening it, asserting independence of it, or eliminating it.

In cooperation, the person attempts to attain the goal only to the extent that the threatening person permits or in the form that he allows.

Among the determinants of an individual's choice of reaction to threatening power is his membership in groups consisting of others in a similarly threatened position. The first way in which these effects can take place is through the supportiveness of the groups. By support is meant the agreement that a person receives for his ideas and perceptions relevant to his interactions with the power figure. This support can be expressed either by direct agreement with a member's perceptions and ideas or by means of group norms in which there would be uniformity of perception and ideas.

As indicated by Gerard's experiment, such support tends to strengthen the person's ideas and perceptions against change due to contact with conflicting ideas and perceptions. Threatening power figures obviously present such conflicts to the person. Therefore, a person who has received support from a group will be better able to resist giving up his own ideas and perceptions than one who has not received support. Among such ideas and perceptions are the person's own ways of achieving his goals and of setting them. Therefore, the following hypothesis can be stated:

Hypothesis 1. The greater the supportiveness of peer groups, the more will the members tend to persist toward a goal despite the obstructiveness of the power figure.

This persistence toward the goal is a special case of aggressive reactions to power figures and is a result of support in conflicts with the power figure. Another special case of aggressive reactions to power figures is hostility expressed directly toward the power figure. In distinction from Hypothesis 1, aggression takes on the meaning of personal hostility. (Hypotheses 1 and 2 are limited to groups whose norms do not prescribe submissive reactions to power figures.) Thus the following hypothesis can be stated:

Hypothesis 2. The greater the supportiveness of peer groups, the more will the members show overt, direct hostility against the power figure.

From the above, it follows that support will lead to less need to find substitute ways of expressing hostility toward the power figure, for it will be directly manifested. In addition, aggressive reactions may tend to minimize frustration, since there is probably more chance of reaching own goals. Thus there will be less hostility to express as a function of such frustration. Both these factors then lead to the following hypothesis:

Hypothesis 3. The greater the supportiveness of peer groups, the less will there be expressions of hostility (directed at substitute objects or at symbols of the power figure) outside the face-to-face relationship with the power figure.

The implication of the above discussion is that, with no support to facilitate aggressive reactions, cooperation and withdrawing reactions will increase. Such reactions lead to greater dependency on the power figure, and
thus to attempts to secure his good will. Moreover, these reactions might increase the probability of accepting the goals of the power figure, since own
goals are given up. In that way, the person will become more attracted to the
power figure's goals and to the power figure himself. These tendencies can be
summarized in the following hypothesis:

Hypothesis 4. The greater the supportiveness of peer groups, the more
will the members be rejecting of the power figure and his goals.

In the statement of the hypotheses, it has been implicitly assumed that
peer groups will tend to develop supportive characteristics, and will do so
to varying degrees. The reasonableness of this assumption can be shown by
an examination of the needs that members try to satisfy in these groups and
their manner of satisfying them. In trying to agree with the threatening
power figure, the person tends to develop needs for support to reassure him
as to the correctiveness of his reactions to the power figure. Several people
in a similar situation of being threatened by a power figure are in essence faced
with a similar ambiguous or unstructured situation, with no social reality to
guide their reactions. This condition is an ideal one for the development of
group norms, which serve to dictate the correct reactions to the power figure
and thus support them. However, in the evaluation of norms, there is a process
of presenting individual ideas and feelings which are then accepted, rejected,
or integrated. Through this process of giving and taking, the members receive
support even before the norm arises. In either case, the members receive
support. However, groups will vary in the amount of this support because
of the personalities of the members, how they interact, and the accidents of
the communication process. In short, it is assumed that groups will develop
supportive qualities and do so to varying degrees.

METHOD

The hypotheses stated above were tested in a laboratory experiment. The
general design of the experiment involved the placement of each subject alone
in a position subordinate to a single power figure, while working on a task.
The subject's reactions to the supervision and to the supervisor were observed,
while the degree of relationship he had with his subordinates was allowed to
vary. In one condition, the so-called *alone* condition, he did not meet or
know about any other subjects besides the supervisor. In the *membership*
condition each subject was allowed to have two meetings with another sub-

ordinate person who was being given similar treatment by another supervisor in an adjoining room. The types of data were observations of behavior directed toward the supervisor, recordings of the meetings of the two subordinates in the membership condition, and a final questionnaire about reactions to many aspects of the experience. The subjects were male undergraduates at the University of Michigan. There were 36 subjects in the alone condition and 72 subjects in 36 groups in the membership condition.

Alone Condition

The experimenter began by telling the subjects and a paid assistant who pretended to be a subject that they would be working on a common task of designing a layout of a city using wooden models. These models, representing various buildings and structures of a city, were to be placed in a representation of a landscape (see picture, facing). The subjects were then told that one of them would make the placements and the other would exercise veto power over the placements. The choice was made ostensibly by a chance drawing of cards, but the cards were stacked so that the paid assistant always became the supervisor or person with veto power. The experimenter then explained that the supervisor would have a free choice of moves to disapprove or approve, and that he could give reasons for his opinions, but did not have to.

The reasons for selecting this task were: (1) its involving qualities, thus establishing the subject's own goals as required by the definition; (2) its lack of complete structure, permitting presumably rational criticism of any move; and (3) the possibility of an interaction between the two people with every placement. The choice was made by "chance" to prevent the attribution of expertness to the supervisor, and evaluation of his ability as a town-planner was prevented by not having him suggest any moves, nor give any reasons for his disapprovals.

During the course of the experiment, the supervisor acted in an impersonal, yet not hostile way, to prevent a personal relationship from contaminating the experiment. The supervisors disapproved of a fixed proportion of the placements, but the proportion was not so great as to completely discourage the subjects. Since the subjects worked at variable speeds, some of them had more placements disapproved than others. The order of the moves disapproved was the same for all subjects, and complicated enough so as to prevent prediction of the approval or disapproval of a particular move. The supervisor's response to any query or action on the subject's part followed a script.

The general tone of the answers was to justify the supervisor's behavior by referring back to the instructions.

In the alone condition, the supervisor and subject worked for a period of seven minutes from the beginning of the experiment, but were then interrupted and told to take a recess of a few minutes by reading a magazine in an adjacent cubicle. The subject and supervisor went to separate cubicles during the recess. They were called back to work after two minutes, allowed to work for four minutes more and then took another two-minute rest. After another four-minute work period, the experiment was called to a halt. The purpose of these two interruptions was to keep the working time and the breaks the same for the alone and membership conditions, for in the latter the breaks were used for meetings between the subordinates. The task was long enough to keep all subjects working for the whole period.

Membership Condition

The procedure in the membership condition was basically the same as in the alone, with the following variations. When two subjects came to the laboratory at the same time, each would go to a different, but adjoining experimental room. Each room had similar town-planning equipment, a paid assistant assigned to it, and an experimenter. Two experiments were then started simultaneously. The instructions were the same as for the alone condition, with the addition that each subject had a chance to observe briefly the other experimental setup through a one-way mirror before starting to plan. This mutual observation facilitated later meetings.

After seven minutes of work, the subjects from both experiments were brought together in a separate room, while the supervisors waited in cubicles. The subjects were not given any instructions as to topics of conversation, but were merely told that each had the same job in their experiments and that they would have a few minutes to talk. Thus, the subjects could structure their meetings as they pleased. After two minutes they resumed work but were told that they would meet again, thereby increasing their feelings of belonging to this group. The second two-minute meetings occurred after four minutes of work, and were followed by a final four-minute work period.

Data

Observation. The subjects' behavior toward the supervisor was recorded according to the Bales Interaction Process Analysis Scheme (1). In addition, a recording was made of the supervisors' disapprovals. The observation was done through one-way observation mirrors by the two experimenters, one for each room during the membership condition. The reliability of observation was tested by joint observation of the same three subjects, and no significant differences between observers were found.

Tape recordings of meetings. The conversations of the subjects during their meetings in the membership condition were recorded on tape with a hidden microphone. The tapes were then coded according to the Bales scheme, with the addition that a special category was set up for praise of another subject's ideas about the town. Also, the content of the conversations was classified into two classes relevant to the town design and relevant to the supervisor's behavior and reactions to it.

Questionnaires. (Fixed alternative and scale items.) A post-experimental questionnaire was administered. It contained items designed to measure the following variables: (a) feelings of frustration, (b) ego-involvement in the experiment, (c) evaluation of the supervisor's personality, (d) attraction to the supervisor, (e) evaluation of supervisor's fairness and reasonableness during the experiment, and (f) interest in task. In the membership condition, additional items were designed to measure: (a) attraction to the other subject, (b) perception of mutual influence in behavior of the subjects, and (c) interest in the experiences of the other subject.

Questionnaires. (Open-ended items.) The following items were included: (a) perception of purpose of experiment, (b) description of manner of reacting to supervisor early in the experiment, (c) description of manner of reacting to supervisor later in the experiment, and (d) description of supervisor's behavior. These items were content analyzed, each subject's response being coded simply according to the presence or absence of the quality described by the category. Thus, a response could be coded for the presence of several different qualities. The reliability of the categories used was checked by a check coder on 25 per cent of the subjects. The percentage of agreement of the coders ranged from 75 per cent to 100 per cent, with the bulk of discrepancies being under-codings by the coder where data were used. Thus, the reliability of the coding can be assumed. The specific categories will be treated in the section on results.

RESULTS

Observations of Meetings of Subjects

The observations of the meetings of the subjects provided a means for checking the assumption made in formulating the hypotheses that the meeting would be supportive. However, technical difficulties in making the recordings of the meetings reduced the number of coded meetings from 72 to 48, so that only a limited analysis was possible. The results will, therefore, only be summarized.

The assumption that the meetings would tend to be supportive is confirmed by the content of the discussion. The subjects showed a great proportion of friendly and positive acts in the meetings with little antagonism or disagreement. In addition, the majority of the comments centered around the town rather than the supervisor, probably for reasons of social propriety. Thus, the meetings tended to be supportive of the subjects' own goals or sub-goals in designing the town. There is no evidence for the release of tension in the meetings or the displacement of hostility on to the other subject.

Comparison of Alone and Membership Condition

Observational data. Predictions of more aggressive and hostile behavior toward the supervisor in the membership condition was checked by comparing the data from the Bales observation system. For the total length of the working time with the supervisor (15 minutes) including the time before the first break or meeting, the membership persons showed more overt hostility toward the supervisors than did the alones. The mean for the "alones" was .11 expressions of hostility, for the "memberships" .61, the critical ratio of the difference being significant at the .05 level. Considering only the work periods after the first meeting (8 minute total), the "memberships" show more overt hostility, their mean being .61, the "alones" being .06, the critical ratio of the difference being significant at the .001 level. Finally in the period after the first meeting, the "memberships" disagree with the supervisors more often. Their mean number of disagreements is .80, that for the "alones" .22, the critical ratio of the difference being significant at .001. In short, these data confirm the predictions of more aggressive and hostile reactions and overt hostility among the membership persons.

Open-ended items on questionnaires. One question concerned the subjects' percept of the purpose of the experiment. The responses were content analyzed to measure the degree of frustration felt during the experiment, but no differences were found between the conditions.

The next open-ended questions were, "How did you try to deal with the supervisor's disapprovals of your moves early in the experiment? Answer as fully as possible" and "Did you change your ways of dealing with the supervisor's disapproval later in the experiment? If so, how and why?" In order to

test the hypotheses of more persistive reactions among the membership individuals, the categories used in content analyzing the responses were grouped
into three classes in terms of the three postulated responses to threat: withdrawal, cooperation, and aggression (i.e., persistive reactions). The categories which are included in each class are treated in Table 1, as are the
frequencies of these categories for the early and later parts of the experiment.
Also, the overlap in the answers within each class was eliminated so that chi-
square tests could be performed to compare the frequencies within each class
of responses.

In the early part of the experiment there are no significant differences between the conditions. However, in describing the behavior they employed
toward the end of the experiment, the "memberships" were significantly
more persistive and less cooperative than the "alones." Since the difference
appears only toward the end of the experiment, we may assume that the
meetings were the cause of the differential aggressiveness.

The importance of the meetings is further demonstrated by the much
greater change of answers in the membership condition than in the alone. In
the membership condition, there is a decrease of seven in the number of withdrawing responses, while there is an increase of one for the alones. There is
a drop of eleven in the number of cooperators in the membership condition,
and a drop of only two in the alone. In the membership condition, the number
of aggressors increases by six, but does not change in the alone. This shift
away from withdrawing and cooperativeness to greater aggressive persistence
is presumably the result of the meetings, which have already been described
as supportive in nature. Thus, the predicted relationship between supportiveness and aggression is verified by the subjects' own perceptions, as well as
by direct observation of their behavior. The behavioral and perception data
are mutually supporting.

It is also interesting that the only significant difference between the groups
in a particular category is in that of explaining own ideas. It seems that the
members of the group gained a better understanding of their own ideas or a
greater willingness to defend them. Thus the effectiveness of the meetings
in stimulating aggressiveness operated partly through the postulated mechanism of supporting the member's ideas or feelings. It may also have operated
through obtaining a better frame of reference for evaluating ideas gained
through the stimulation of the discussions in the meetings. In either case, it
is clear that the meetings had the effect of making the subjects more aware
of the degree of rationality of their own behavior.

Another question was, "How did the supervisor behave toward you and why do you think he behaved that way?" The purpose of this question was to obtain some measure of the amount of hostility felt toward the supervisor after the experiment (and to determine how many subjects detected that the supervisor had been a collaborator).

Table 2 shows that the membership condition produced more negative reactions toward the supervisor and the alone condition produced relatively more positive reactions. These findings indicate that the "alones" did not have any great need to express hostility. Indeed, they seem to have rationalized their acceptance of the dominance of the supervisor by attributing good qualities to him. The "memberships," on the contrary, apparently received support in their meetings for their aggressive and hostile approach to the supervisor. Thus, it seems that the meetings served to provide support to the

TABLE 1

SUBJECTS' PERCEPTIONS OF THEIR REACTIONS TO THE SUPERVISOR EARLY AND LATE IN THE EXPERIMENT FOR THE ALONE AND MEMBERSHIP CONDITIONS

	Early Reactions		Late Reactions			
	Member-ship N = 72 *	Alone N = 36 *	Member-ship N = 72 *	Alone N = 36 *	Chi^2 **	p
Withdrawing Reactions						
Satisfying supervisor	21	7	18	7		
Withdrawal of own ideas.....	8	2	5	5		
Positive evaluation of supervisor's ideas	8	4	4	3		
Total withdrawing with overlap eliminated	35	13	28	14		
Cooperative or Neutral Reactions						
Discovering supervisor's ideas..	20	13	15	10		
Finding alternative moves.....	16	7	15	8		
Compromising	5	7	4	6		
Total cooperation with overlap eliminated	38	24	27	22	8.32	.01
Persistive Reactions						
Explaining own moves........	18	4	21	3	4.81	.05
Negatively evaluating supervisor's criticisms	4	2	7	1		
Ignoring supervisor	2	0	2	1		
Bypassing supervisor	1	1	2	1		
Total aggressive with overlap eliminated	24	6	30	6	6.59	.02

* It should be noted that the N's for the alone and membership conditions are in the ratio of one to two.
** All open cells indicate that the Chi^2 is not significant. This applies to all subsequent tables.

subjects' resistance rather than to supply an opportunity for the expression of substitute hostility. The meetings had the effect of increasing hostility, not reducing it.

The only category which by itself is significantly different for the two conditions refers to the rationality of the behavior of the supervisor. In the membership condition the subjects express dissatisfaction with the supervisor's failure to give reasons for his behavior. This finding should be interpreted together with the finding (Table 1) that the subjects in the membership condition are more concerned with explaining their own behavior to the supervisor. It would seem that one of the functions of the meetings was to develop a frame of reference for the evaluation of behavior in the experiment, although it is possible that this concern with rationality may be simply a way of expressing hostility.

Questionnaire items. No differences inexplicable by chance were found

TABLE 2

PERCEPTIONS OF SUPERVISOR'S BEHAVIOR FOR THE ALONE AND MEMBERSHIP CONDITIONS

	Condition			
	Alone N = 36	Membership N = 72	Chi^2	p
Negative				
Unfriendly	2	6		
Failed to present reasons for criticisms or suggestions	7	30	5.30	.05
Poor ideas about town	1	2		
Supervisor lost his power because of inadequacies	0	8		
Total without overlap	8	38	9.24	.01
Neutral				
Role-player	5	9		
Indifferent to situation	2	0		
Total without overlap	7	9		
Positive				
Friendly	15	13	7.04	.01
Cooperative	10	11		
Reasoning	7	10		
Total without overlap	25	29	8.23	.01
Collaborator				
Possibly a collaborator	1	7		
Certainly a collaborator	2	7		
Total without overlap	3	14		

between the alone and membership conditions on the scalar and fixed-alternative items of the questionnaire. Since significant differences were found among responses to the open-ended questions, it appears likely that the failure of these items to discriminate between the two conditions is due to defects in these measures.

Felt Relationship between Subjects and Reactions to Supervisor

The discussion thus far has centered mainly on a comparison of the alone and membership conditions. In this section only the membership condition will be examined to determine the differential effects of degree of perceived or felt relationship between the two subjects who came together in the meetings. Three indices of felt relationship will be discussed.

Attraction between subjects. An index of the degree of attraction between the subjects was constructed by adding their scores on questionnaire items regarding the desire to have the other subject as a friend and as a working partner. No significant relations were found between this index and the subject's behavior toward his supervisor. There is evidence, however, to indicate that attraction to the other subject is part of a larger syndrome of attraction to the total experiment. Thus attraction to the other subordinate correlates .70 ($p=.001$) with desirability of the supervisor as a friend, .47 ($p=.01$) with his desirability as a co-worker in a cooperative situation, and .54 ($p=.001$) with interest in the task. Since the attraction index appears to be tapping a global, undifferentiated reaction to the total experiment, it is not useful as an indicator of the specific reactions to the other subject.

Normativeness. Normativeness is defined as the degree to which the members perceived that they influenced each other. An index of normativeness was constructed from responses to four items concerning (a) evaluation of the other subordinate's ideas about city plan, (b) perception of influence on other subordinate's city plan, (c) perception of influence of meetings on own behavior toward supervisor, and (d) perception of influence of meetings on own city plan. Although the interrelations among these items is sufficient to suggest that they are measuring some characteristic in common, the index is not significantly related to the subjects' behavior toward their supervisors or to other items on the questionnaire.

Interest in other subject. An effort was made to get an indication of the subject's interest in the experience of the other subject while separated from him. Such an interest implies that the subject regards himself and the other subject as having something in common, as falling into the same general class (i.e., lower-status subjects in a town-planning activity). It would seem also to imply a willingness to provide sympathetic support for the other subject who is in a similar, unfavorable position. One might assume, then, that a subject who displays high interest in the other subject is reacting to a *group* (either a reference or membership group) of subordinates.

An index of interest was constructed from two items which measured the degree of interest in the behavior of the other subordinate's supervisor and in the resemblance between the subject's and the other subordinate's reactions to the supervisor. The correlation between these items is .69 ($p = .001$). Together these two items may be taken as a measure of interest in the other subject's (similar) experience.

Further light is shed on the meaning of this interest by a correlation of .69 ($p = .001$) between the indexes of interest and normativeness, the only significant correlation among the three indexes of felt relationship. This correlation suggests that the kind of interaction in the meetings which causes mutual influence also leads to real interest in the experiences of the other person. Thus, interest seems to be an index of the development of a supportive group in which experiences are shared or exchanged and in which there is a feeling of group identity.

To assess the effects of interest, the subjects were divided approximately equally into "high" and "low" interest categories. Comparing these two, it was found that the high-interest subjects reacted more aggressively (persistently) to the threat of the supervisor's power. It can be seen in Table 3 that the high-interest subjects maintained throughout the experiment approximately the same level of requests for the supervisor's opinion, while the lows increased their requests as the experiment progressed, thus becoming more dependent upon the supervisor.

Additional evidence for the same conclusion is provided by examining the correlations between the number of requests for opinion from the supervisor with the number of agreements with him. One should expect these to be

TABLE 3

EFFECT OF INTEREST IN OTHER SUBJECT ON CHANGE AFTER FIRST MEETING IN THE NUMBER OF REQUESTS FOR SUPERVISOR'S OPINION

	Interest in Other Subject	
	High	Low
Increased requests	12	20
No change	9	4
Decreased requests	17	8

$Chi^2 = 6.8$ $p = .05$

TABLE 4

CORRELATIONS BETWEEN RATINGS OF HURT PRIDE AND INDICATORS OF FRUSTRATION
AMONG HIGH- AND LOW-INTEREST SUBJECTS

	Interference from emotions	Pleasantness	Avoidance of laboratory	Angry reactions to frustration
High interest	+.36	—.08	+.19	+.17
Low interest	+.19	—.09	—.06	+.03

positively correlated, but the important question here is whether the magnitude of the correlations changes differently for the high- and low-interest subjects as the experiment progressed. Among the highs there was no significant change (a correlation of .28 before the first meeting and .41 afterwards). In other words, there was no significant tendency to agree more with opinions requested of the supervisor after the meeting had taken place. Among the low-interest subjects, the results are quite different: before the first meeting the correlation was .51 and afterwards .92. Low-interest subjects tended increasingly to agree with the opinions they requested from the supervisor. (The critical ratio of z scores comparing the two correlations within the low-interest group is 4.16, and that between high and lows after the first meeting is 4.45—$p=.001$ for both.)

Another effect of high interest in the other subordinate is increased involvement and tension in the relationship with the supervisor. This greater tension is indicated by a .36 correlation ($p=.01$) between interest and tension in the work situation after the first meeting and by a .42 correlation ($p=.01$) between interest and the subject's perception of interference in designing the town from his own emotional reactions. (The latter variable was measured by a semi-projective scalar item on the questionnaire.) Further evidence is the differential reaction of the subjects with high and low interest to having their pride hurt by the supervisor. The figures shown in Table 4 indicate that wounds to the pride made the high-interest subjects feel more emotional, angry, and desirous of escaping the situation (as measured by scales on the questionnaire), while they produced generally less pronounced reactions in the low-interest subjects. It would seem that the increased sensitivity and tension among the subjects having high interest in the other subordinate was due to their greater conflict with the supervisor.

DISCUSSION

The results of this experiment are consistent with the hypotheses that supportive peer groups serve to heighten persistence toward own goals and aggressiveness in the face of a threatening power. They also indicate that membership in these peer groups leads to more expression of direct, overt hostility to the threatening power figure. It seems, however, that this reaction is more than a bolstering of courage in the face of a tough opponent, for there is evidence that the individual's total reaction to the threat of power may be affected. Without the support of the peer groups, the individual accepts the power figure much more as a person. In the setting of this experiment the "alones" were more positive in their private evaluation of the supervisor's behavior, attributing more cooperativeness and reasonableness to him than did the "memberships." Although this finding contradicts the hypothesis that there should be more residual hostility in the alone condition, it is congruent with other indications of greater aggressiveness and rejection of the supervisor in the membership condition.

The data also indicate that the primary function of the meetings between the subjects was to provide support rather than a chance to release tension or to displace hostility. The subjects came to the meetings with a need to gain support in the face of the threat of the power figure, and they were able to support each other. This is evidenced by the positive interchange of ideas that typically took place in the meetings. The effects of support received from the other subject are shown by the increased aggressive reactions to the power figure, and the prevention of a complete acceptance of the person and ideas of the power figure. By establishing a positive relationship with one person, the subject was protected from having to establish a similar relationship with another, less satisfactory person.

Thus, the general line of reasoning followed in developing the hypotheses seems to have been confirmed. There are pressures to form supportive groups of peers on the same level in a power hierarchy and these groups do influence the person's reactions in the groups in which he is subordinated.

A closer examination of the membership condition gives additional insight into the reasons for the effectiveness of the meetings. First, attraction to the other subject seemed to be a part of an undifferentiated attitude toward the total experiment. Secondly, the perception of support or mutual influence did not have any direct effects on behavior toward the power figure, but did provide a necessary condition for the development of another factor which did affect reactions to the power figure. This factor was interest in the experiences of the other subject. Subjects in the membership condition who were high in such interest showed more resistance to the power figure and showed more involvement in the work relationship with him. The support they received led them to try harder to achieve their own goals despite the power figure and therefore made the relationship more emotional and sensitive.

If the supportiveness of groups were the only factor necessary to produce the effects of membership in the groups, it would be expected that the perception of mutual support or influence in the groups would also have been related to the subjects' reactions to the power figures. Since this relationship was not found, some other factor in group membership would seem to be necessary. This factor apparently is "interest" in the fate of the other group member, since it correlated with reactions to the power figure.

A problem is thus raised as to the origin and meaning of interest in another subject. A clue as to its origin is given by the correlation of interest with normativeness or the perception of mutual support and influence. This interchange of support and influence among the members may then have led to the greater integration of the two subjects into a group. They may then have taken an interest in each other's welfare or fate as members of the same group. Another interpretation of interest stated earlier was that high interest is predicated on the subject's perception of his similarity to the other subordinate town-planner. Similarity to the other person becomes the basis of the formation of a group consisting of the two subordinates. Thus, a group may have been formed because of the mutual influence or the similarity of the subjects.

The question then arises as to why membership in the group and its manifestation in high interest should be related to greater independence of the power figure. One possible answer is that the subject perceived himself to be a member of a group of subordinates like himself while he was in face-to-face contact with the power figure. He could then behave as a representative of this group, and therefore be more independent of a threatening power figure. This interpretation in terms of self-perception as a member of a group of subordinates points to the problem of a perceptual aspect of group membership. This perceptual aspect may prove to be independent of, and different in effects from, attraction to the group, as was found in the present study.

REFERENCES

1. Bales, R. F. *Interaction process analysis.* Cambridge: Addison-Wesley, 1950.

2. Gerard, H. B. The anchorage of opinion in face-to-face groups. *Hum. Relat.,* 1954, **7**, 313-325.

3. Kelley, H. H. Communication in experimentally created hierarchies. *Hum. Relat.,* 1951, **4**, 39-56.

4. Thibaut, J. An experimental study of underprivileged groups. *Hum. Relat.,* 1950, **3**, 251-278.

5. Wright, M. E. The influence of frustration on the social relations of young children. *Character & Person.,* 1943, **12**, 111-122.

5

EFFECTS OF ADJUSTMENT ON THE PERCEPTION AND EXERTION OF SOCIAL POWER [1]

SIDNEY ROSEN

The concept "power" has been treated by both social theorists (5, 6, 14, 16, 18) and students of personality (1, 2, 9, 11, 13, 14, 20). But, despite a growing body of empirical research on power (2, 6—pp. 428-92, 7, 15), very few investigators have attempted systematically to link the group-relevant aspects of power with those involving personality dynamics.

A typical approach to the study of power is illustrated by personality theorists who have interested themselves in the psychopathology of power. These writers have generally associated intense power needs with interpersonal maladjustment, both of which are essentially attributes of personality. A broader analysis would require an examination of the relations between personality and social structure. Is there, for example, any relation between the intensity of an individual's power needs and his position in a power system or between personal maladjustment and the possession of power?

The present study focuses upon the latter relation. How does a person's degree of adjustment affect his actual power in social groups? In order to answer this question it is necessary to look more closely at the nature of "adjustment" and "power." It may be assumed that one characteristic of a person who is persistently maladjusted in his interpersonal relations is that he has failed to develop adequate perceptual and behavioral skills for dealing with others. More specifically, a maladjusted person is deficient in his ability to

[1] This paper is based primarily on a dissertation submitted in partial fulfillment of the doctoral requirements in the Program of Social Psychology at the University of Michigan. This writer is indebted to Drs. Ronald Lippitt, Dorwin Cartwright, Roger W. Heyns, William C. Morse, Harold L. Rausch, and Guy E. Swanson, for guidance received.

The investigation was initiated within the context of a broad program of studies concerning the dynamics of power among children's groups. The program, which began in 1948 and ended in 1951, was supported by grants from the National Institute of Mental Health of the U. S. Public Health Service. The principal investigators were Drs. Ronald Lippitt and Fritz Redl. Project directors, successively, were Dr. Norman Polansky, and this writer.

perceive his relations with others and to behave appropriately with regard to them. This deficiency, in turn, serves to reduce his capacity for influencing others. Since the achievement of many goals is made possible through influencing others (1, 16), inability to influence is a major personal liability.

Examination of the concept "power" reveals that it refers to the relative ability of people to influence each other,[2] and the existence of a power structure implies that the members of a group have established enduring patterns of potential influence. From the point of view of an individual member, this structure serves as a part of the objective social world in which he must behave; it determines how effective his perceptual and behavioral skills can actually be.

There is a well known tendency for formal and informal groups to differentiate into power hierarchies (6, 15, 17). Such power hierarchies greatly influence the magnitude and direction of communications (4, 6, 10) because they set limits upon the effectiveness of one person's attempt to influence another. To the extent that a person realistically appraises his power relative to that of others, he will select as targets for influence those whose power position assures him some reasonable probability of success. Maladjustment, however, implies a deficiency in the ability to make realistic appraisals of power and thus also in the ability to select targets appropriately.

In keeping with this line of thought, certain hypotheses may be advanced. It is proposed that, when relatively adjusted individuals are introduced into a new group setting, they will show, in comparison with less adjusted peers: (a) greater accuracy in the perception of their own positions, (b) greater consensus among themselves in their perceptions of the relative power of other group members, and (c) greater accuracy in these perceptions of others. In behavior, these relatively adjusted individuals will: (d) show a greater tendency to select as targets for influencing those who have a power position close to their own, (e) achieve greater success in influencing others, and (f) be perceived by other group members as having greater ability to influence others.

METHODS OF ANALYSIS

It was possible to test these hypotheses by conducting special analyses of data obtained from a larger study of the dynamics of power in four-week summer camps for preadolescent and young adolescent boys (15). In this study detailed data were collected concerning the perception of power and

---

[2] Social power has been defined as "the potentiality for inducing forces in other persons toward acting or changing in a given direction" (15).

the exercise of influence in two widely differing camps. Children sent to one of these camps, the University of Michigan Fresh Air Camp (M-camp), were social agency referrals primarily of lower socio-economic backgrounds. This camp was conducted as a therapeutic installation for maladjusted boys. Children sent to the second camp, a YMCA camp in northern Wisconsin (W-camp), came primarily from middle socio-economic backgrounds and could be assumed to be relatively well adjusted.[3] Comparisons of data from these two camps would reveal some of the effects of previous maladjustment upon the power relations among boys.

It should be noted, of course, that these two populations differed also with respect to socio-economic level. The author knows of no systematic evidence to indicate that the results which are to be reported could be attributed primarily to the class differences between the two populations (3, 8). However, in order to check further upon this possibility, a special analysis within the M-camp was undertaken in which class was held constant while comparing data from relatively adjusted and maladjusted boys. This analysis was accomplished by constructing a checklist to differentiate the Michigan camp boys with respect to degree of maladjustment, on the basis of case history material available on each camper prior to his arrival at camp. It was not technically possible with the available data to test all of the hypotheses listed above in both kinds of analysis. Hypotheses a, b, d, and e were tested by comparisons between the two camps, while hypotheses a, c, d, e, and f were tested by comparisons of the relatively adjusted and maladjusted boys within the M-camp.

The data for this analysis are based on sixteen cabin groups, eight in each camp. There were approximately eight boys in a cabin group, yielding a combined population of 128 boys.

One research team was assigned to each camp to observe each day a sample of the interactions of the boys in each group. Of special interest to the analysis reported here are the records of the initiation and receipt of interactions intended to influence the behavior of others. In addition, information about the perceptions and attitudes of each boy was obtained through individual interviews conducted at the end of the first and third weeks. A more detailed description of the methods of data collection, observer reliability, and the primary behavioral and perceptual indices is included in a report of the larger study (15).

[3] The author is deeply indebted to Elmer Ott, Director of Camp Manitowish, YMCA North Central Area Council, and Dr. William C. Morse, Director, University of Michigan Fresh Air Camp, for their generous cooperation and support.

BETWEEN-CAMP COMPARISONS [4]

Indices

From the interviews and observations of behavior five indices were constructed which permit comparisons between the W-camp (relatively adjusted boys) and the M-camp (relatively maladjusted boys).

Attributed power. In the interview each boy was asked to rank his cabin members, including himself, on "who is best at getting the others to do what he wants them to do." The rankings received by each member from the other group members were averaged for the two administrations in order to obtain a composite measure reflecting the state of affairs during the entire camp period. This combination seems justified since the average group *rho* between the first and second interviews was .85. These composite rankings were then ordered and the final rank of each member was designated as his attributed power position.

Accuracy in evaluating own power. All of the *self-rankings* in each camp (averaged for two interviews) were grouped relative to the attributed power position of the respective individuals. It was then possible to compute a single *eta* correlation for each camp and thus to compare camps on degree of accuracy in evaluating own power. (*Etas* computed separately for each interview showed little change over time in either camp; in absolute terms, *eta* increased slightly in W-camp and decreased slightly in M-camp.)

Group consensus about power. The average deviation of individual rankings around the composite (mean) rank of power attributed to each group member was computed. These deviations, weighted for size of group, were averaged in turn for the entire camp population. It was then possible to compare the two camps on mean average deviation in attributing power. For reasons to be discussed below, these averages were computed separately for the first and second interviews as well as together for the total period.

Position proximity in target selection. The attributed power positions of the members of each group were dichotomized as high or low with respect to that group. For each boy, averages were computed of the number of influence attempts which he made toward targets of high power and toward targets of low power. In this way it is possible to compare the two camps on the extent to which boys with high power direct their influence attempts to high-power targets and boys with low power direct their influence attempts to low-power targets.

---

[4] A more detailed description of the indices and statistical analysis may be found in the author's thesis (20).

Relative success in influencing others. The proportion of influence attempts which were successful was computed for each boy. A median (57.7 per cent) was calculated for the entire population of the two camps. The number of boys in each camp falling above and below this combined median gives an indication of the relative standing of the two camps on the general level of successful influence.

Results

Differences in these indices between the two camp populations are tentatively taken to indicate the effects of degree of prior adjustment upon the power relations among the campers. Four hypothesized effects of degree of adjustment can then be tested by comparing the camps.

Accuracy in perceiving own power. According to hypothesis *a*, we should expect to find the boys in W-camp to be more accurate in evaluating their own power positions than the boys in M-camp. Table 1 shows this hypothesis confirmed; accuracy of perception, as measured by *eta* correlations between self-ratings and others' ratings of power, is greater in W-camp than in M-camp (.81 vs. .58). A rough approximation of the significance of the difference between these correlations can be made by treating the *etas* as product-moment correlations and transforming them into z-scores. This procedure is justified since the correlation plots of the *etas* appear to be linear. So treated, a critical ratio of 2.56 is obtained, which is significant at the .02 level by two-tailed test.

Group consensus about power. Hypothesis *b* states that there should be greater group consensus concerning the power positions of the group members in W-camp than in M-camp. Table 2 presents the evidence relevant to this hypothesis. A smaller average deviation from the mean attributed power of each member indicates greater consensus. Considering the combined data from the two interviews, differences are in the predicted direction but at a low level of significance. (A two-tailed *t*-test is significant at the .14 level.) On the basis of other evidence obtained in the larger study (15), it was ex-

TABLE 1

BETWEEN-CAMP COMPARISONS OF ACCURACY IN EVALUATING OWN POWER

Camp	Eta	N	p *
W-camp	.81	65	.001
M-camp	.58	63	.001

* *Eta* was evaluated by means of *F*-test.

TABLE 2

BETWEEN-CAMP COMPARISONS OF GROUP CONSENSUS ABOUT POWER
(GREATER DEVIATION INDICATES LESS CONSENSUS)

Camp	Mean Average Deviation	N	p *
Data based on first interview only:			
W-camp	1.04	64	.01
M-camp	1.30	62	
Data based on second interview only:			
W-camp	.98	65	not significant
M-camp	.98	58	
Data based on both interviews combined:			
W-camp	1.01	64	.14
M-camp	1.13	57	

* p-levels (two-tail) are based on t-tests for independent means.

pected that the difference in favor of the W-camp would show up primarily with first interview data. This expectation was borne out when the data were analyzed separately for the two interviews. The difference in degree of consensus between the two camps at Interview 1 (end of first week) is significant by two-tailed test at the .01 level. There was no difference in degree of consensus at Interview 2 (end of third week). As might be expected there was a significant improvement in degree of consensus over time in M-camp (t-ratio = 3.82, significant at less than .001 level), but no significant change in W-camp (t-ratio = 1.19, significant at approximately the .30 level).[5] The boys of M-camp were thus slower in achieving consensus about power although they eventually came up to the level of W-camp.

Selection of targets for influencing. Hypothesis *d* calls for the boys of W-camp to show in comparison with those of M-camp a tendency to select targets for influencing whose power positions are closer to their own. Table 3 reveals that in W-camp boys with high attributed power tend to direct more influence attempts at targets of high than low power and that boys with low power tend to direct more influence at targets of low than high power. (Two-tailed tests of significance are at the .10 and .05 levels respectively.) A two-tailed *t*-test for the selection of like-status targets based on the entire W-camp yields a *t*-ratio of 2.75, significant at the .01 level. There is no significant tendency in M-camp for boys to select targets of power position

[5] Direct comparison of the two camps on change in consensus makes the obtained *t*-ratio of 2.90 (*p* .01) more difficult to interpret, for the error variances were, respectively, .50 for M-camp, and .16 for W-camp. The variance ratio is significant at the .001 level. Both *t*-ratio and variance ratio, however, support the hypothesis of greater change in M-camp.

TABLE 3

BETWEEN-CAMP COMPARISONS OF RELATIONSHIP OF ACTOR'S POWER TO POWER OF
TARGETS.* (EXPRESSED IN AVERAGE NUMBER OF INFLUENCE ATTEMPTS
DIRECTED TO HIGH-POWER AND TO LOW-POWER TARGETS)

Actor's Power	W-camp			M-camp		
	Power of Targets			Power of Targets		
	High	Low	p **	High	Low	p **
High	1.30	1.11	.10	1.91	1.71	.20
Low	.80	1.05	.05	1.25	1.23	.60

* Boys were dichotomized into those with high and those with low attributed power.
** p-levels (two-tail) are based on t-tests for related means, with N's of 31 to 33.

similar to their own. What trend there is is for both high- and low-power
boys to direct influence attempts more toward high-power targets.

Relative success in influencing others. The data presented in Table 4 support hypothesis *e,* which asserts that the boys in W-camp should be more
successful than those in M-camp at influencing each other. The percentage
of influence attempts that were successful was calculated for each boy in
both camps. When these scores are compared to the median for the two camps
taken together, it is found that significantly more of the highly successful
boys are in W-camp. This superiority of W-camp is found, moreover, to hold
for low as well as high positions of attributed power.

In summary, the boys at W-camp, in comparison with those at M-camp,
achieve better accuracy in perceiving their own power positions, display in
the early stages of group life a higher consensus concerning the power positions of group members, show a greater tendency to select targets for influencing whose power positions are close to their own, and succeed in a larger
proportion of their attempts to influence others.

TABLE 4

BETWEEN-CAMP COMPARISONS OF ACTOR'S RELATIVE SUCCESS IN INFLUENCING
OTHERS

Camp	Number of Individuals		p **
	Below Median *	Above Median *	
W-camp	25	39	.02
M-camp	38	24	

* Individuals were placed above or below the median of the two camp populations
combined in the percentage of influence attempts that were successful. The combined
median percentage of success was 57.7.
** p-level (two-tail) is based on a 2×2 *chi*-square test.

COMPARISONS WITHIN M-CAMP

Since it is known that W-camp attracts "normal" boys while M-camp is a therapeutic installation, differences between the camps in perception and exercise of power would seem to be due to the level of adjustment of the two populations. This interpretation, however, must be held tentatively because it is also known that the camps differ in other respects. It might be accepted with greater confidence if we could find similar differences within a single camp, when comparing boys with better and poorer adjustment. For this reason, a further analysis was conducted within M-camp where considerable information was available concerning the personal history of the boys.

Indices

Degree of maladjustment. M-camp had available for each boy certain questionnaires supplied by the referring social agency, the school, the parents, and a physician. These questionnaires provided information which could be used in assessing the degree of prior adjustment of each boy. An index of maladjustment was constructed by means of a check list which was applied to each set of information. The check list was designed to tap two main aspects of maladjustment—preconditions and symptoms. The investigations of Hewitt and Jenkins (12) served as a guide in designing the check list.

The "preconditions" half of the instrument was divided, in turn, into three areas (16 items): family's economic status, family's internal situation, and equipment—physical and intellectual.

The area of "family's economic status" consisted of three items: (a) poverty, chronic unemployment, or lack of income; (b) family living in depressed area; and (c) high geographic mobility.

The part dealing with "internal family situation" consisted of nine items: (a) broken home; (b) emotional instability of parent; (c) weak parental figure; (d) traumata; (e) authoritarian parent; (f) severe, punitive, hostile parent; (g) over-protective domination by parent; (h) indifferent parent; and (i) parental preference for other sibling.

Four items made up the "equipment" area: (a) evidence of intellectual deficiency in forebears; (b) IQ of 80 or less; (c) unusual physiognomy; and (d) organic deficiencies.

The "symptomatology" half of the instrument consisted of 18 items: (a) evidence of psychosomatic disorders, psychological speech difficulties, or hysterical symptoms; (b) frequent enuresis; (c) poor school performance; (d) withdrawn, fearful behavior; (e) pathological lying; (f) low popularity with peers; (g) frequent projection of blame; (h) indecisive, overdependent behavior; (i) nervous, irritable behavior; (j) aggressive, destructive acts; (k) high impulsivity; (l) pathological theft; (m) overt indications of sexual maladjustment; (n) expressions of ambivalence or hostility to adults; (o) somnambulism, frequent nightmares; (p) bullying, teasing behavior; (q) truancy; and (r) apathy, no self-confidence.

The agency questionnaire was the sole source of information concerning the first two "precondition" areas, while the school, agency, and parents' questionnaires had in common a list of behavior symptoms requiring ratings for frequency of occurrence. In addition to the cross-checks provided by having several sources of information, supplementary reports were often available which permitted further internal checks for consistency.

Check list items were dichotomously scored zero or one. A score of one was given if the item indicated clear maladjustment (e.g., "seldom popular with peers" or "very withdrawn"). Furthermore, if two or more sources of information were available, a score of one was given only when there was agreement between at least two sources. On theoretical grounds we should expect reported symptoms of maladjustment to be a better indication of actual maladjustment than a listing of environmental preconditions. The "precondition" half of the instrument was used, however, in order to permit some correction for possible over-reporting or under-reporting of symptoms by different informants. But since greater reliance was placed upon the reports of symptoms, each symptom entry was given an arbitrary weight of two and each precondition entry a weight of one. The weighted items were then summed to give a single maladjustment score for each boy (the higher the score the greater the maladjustment).[6] The range of total scores was 8-35, with a median of 20, a mean of 19.9, and an estimated standard deviation of 5.9. The distribution of scores was approximately normal.

Attributed power. The index of attributed power used in the between-camp analysis was also employed in comparing boys within M-camp.

Accuracy in evaluating own power. The difference was computed between the rank of power which each boy ascribed to himself and the mean rank attributed to him by others, and these discrepancy scores were ranked for each

[6] Each case was initially coded independently by both the author and a second coder (George Levinger to whom the author is indebted for his valuable aid). Inter-coder reliability was as follows: Item agreement based on 2,032 items was 87 per cent, while total score reliability based on 60 subjects was .76 (product-moment r). Since these results were considered satisfactory, the next objective was to arrive at a single, "corrected" score. For this purpose, both coders then made successive individual reviews of those items where initial disagreement existed until differences were reconciled.

group without regard to sign. The ranked discrepancies were simply dichotomized to indicate high or low accuracy in evaluating own power.

Accuracy in evaluating others' power. The difference was computed between the rank of power attributed to each group member by a given boy and the average rank attributed to that member by the remaining boys. These discrepancy scores were summed for each boy and ranked within each cabin group. These ranks were then dichotomized to indicate high or low accuracy in evaluating the power of others.

Position proximity in target selection. The attributed power positions of the members of each group were dichotomized as high or low with respect to that group. Similarly, the maladjustment scores of these individuals were dichotomized with respect to that group. The 23 boys having high power and low maladjustment scores were compared with the 8 high-power boys having high maladjustment scores on the number of influence attempts which they made toward targets of high and low power, respectively. The same procedure was followed for the 23 boys having low power and high maladjustment scores and the 9 low-power boys having low maladjustment scores.

Relative success in influencing others. The index of successful influence used in the between-camp analysis was again employed.

Results

Accuracy in perceiving own and others' power. According to hypotheses *a* and *c*, we should expect to find greater accuracy among the boys with lower maladjustment scores in evaluating both own power and that of other group members. Table 5 indicates a low, positive relationship between the adjustment index and the measure of accuracy in evaluating own power (significant at the .06 level), the measure of accuracy in evaluating others' power (significant at the .07 level), and accuracy in estimating both own and others' power (significant at the .05 level). It will be recalled that the boys at W-camp were more accurate in self-evaluation than those at M-camp. These data taken together lend strong support to the view that degree of adjustment is a critical variable in determining accuracy of perception of power.

Selection of targets for influencing. Hypothesis *d* calls for the better adjusted boys in M-camp to show a greater tendency to select targets for influencing whose power positions are closer to their own. When *t*-tests were run there were no significant differences, both with regard to means and to variances.

Relative success in influencing others. Hypothesis *e* asserts that the better adjusted boys should be more successful in influencing their peers. The

TABLE 5

RELATIONS BETWEEN ADJUSTMENT INDEX AND ACCURACY IN EVALUATING POWER
(WITHIN M-CAMP)

Factors Related to Adjustment	N	2 × 2 Chi-Square	p *
Accuracy in evaluating own power..................	63	3.57	.06
Accuracy in evaluating others' power...............	63	3.27	.07
Accuracy in evaluating both own and others' power...	38	3.89	.05

* Positive relationships are found between prior adjustment and accuracy in evaluating power.

data shown in Table 6 support this hypothesis; those boys with greater precamp adjustment attained a significantly larger proportion of successful influence attempts than did those with poorer adjustment (both *rho* and *chi*-square significant at .01 level). These results are consistent with the between-camp findings reported above.

Attributed power. In keeping with hypothesis *f*, the data of Table 6 reveal that the better adjusted boys were attributed by their peers to have greater power (significant by *rho* and *chi*-square at the .001 level). It is of methodological interest, too, that the total index of maladjustment is a better predictor of attributed power than either the precondition score or symptom score alone.

In summary, the better adjusted boys at M-camp, as compared to their more poorly adjusted peers, achieve greater accuracy in judging both their own power positions and those of others, are more successful in influencing others, and are judged by their peers to have more power. There are no significant differences concerning the selection of targets for influencing.

TABLE 6

RELATIONS BETWEEN ADJUSTMENT INDEX AND (A) PERCENTAGE OF SUCCESSFUL
INFLUENCE ATTEMPTS AND (B) ATTRIBUTED POWER (WITHIN M-CAMP)

Measures Related	Av. Rho	p *	2 × 2 Chi-Square	p *
Total maladjustment index vs. percentage success.	.48	.01	6.64	.01
Total maladjustment index vs. attributed power..	.52	.001	13.16	.001
Precondition score alone vs. attributed power....	**	—	4.31	.05
Symptom score alone vs. attributed power.....	**	—	6.73	.01

* Positive relationships are indicated between prior adjustment and (a) percentage of successful influence and (b) attributed power. Analysis is based on data from 60 boys in 8 groups.
** Tied ranks were too numerous to justify using *rho*'s.

DISCUSSION AND CONCLUSIONS

The results show a fairly consistent picture of relationships between previous adjustment and power. Those who are better adjusted in previous social environments are more likely, in a new group context, to perceive accurately their own relative power, to perceive accurately the power positions of others, to agree with each other about who holds what position of power in the group, to achieve greater success in influencing other group members, and to be perceived by other group members as having greater power.

The one hypothesis receiving only partial support has to do with the selection of targets for influencing. The hypothesis was confirmed in the comparison between camps since only in the camp of relatively adjusted boys was there a tendency for boys to select targets for influencing who had power positions close to their own. However, efforts to differentiate the boys in the camp for disturbed children into high- and low-maladjustment categories failed to yield any significant differences on target selection. This finding raises a number of questions of interpretation. The M-camp population may have been too homogeneous in degree of adjustment; the maladjustment index may have been too crude, the sample too small, or the behavior data too scanty to permit the proper testing of this hypothesis.

If we ignore these possible shortcomings, we could still argue that the increase which occurred in consensus about power, as time went on in M-camp, should materially have affected target selection. It is possible that predicted differences would have been found if the analysis were conducted on data collected toward the end of the camp period.

It turned out that when the data of both camps were broken down into two time periods, the tendency for selecting targets of like status for influencing was found in both periods in W-camp, but in neither period in M-camp.

We are faced with a number of important problems. Earlier we said that maladjustment implies a "deficiency in the ability to make realistic appraisals of power and thus also in the ability to select targets appropriately." If this is so, could we assert that target selection among less adjusted persons is random? There is no justification for such an assertion. Nor can we infer that power is of less importance among the disturbed; if the clinicians are correct, we should expect the contrary.

We need to determine, moreover, the nature of these deficiencies—whether they are due to lack of information or insufficient feedback from others, whether they reflect an underdeveloped cognitive apparatus, or whether there is strong motivation to see power relations in a particular light. It may be that the power structure of the typical M-camp group rests on a more precarious base, with the membership unwilling to reconcile itself overtly to the existence of a power hierarchy, and with those having greater power never sure of their position. This could account, in part, for the seeming disregard which M-camp boys show for power differentials when they select targets for influencing. If true, this state of affairs could arise from a concern with power as an end in itself.

These considerations suggest several avenues for further research: (a) The development, maintenance, and change of power structures need to be studied more systematically. This will require conceptual refinements and more adequate diagnostic tools, as well as experimental variation both of situation and of group composition. (b) Target selection is only a vaguely understood variable. Some of its possible determinants could be identified by careful exploratory interviewing. Such interviewing might consist in principle, if not in content, of the following kind of questions: "Why did you ask X to do such-and-such? Did you expect him to do it? Why or why not? Why didn't you ask Y instead? How did you feel about X's response? Would you ask him again? Does he expect you to ask him again? Under what conditions would you be more hesitant about asking X?" (c) Finally, instruments are needed to measure the degree of individual concern with power and the nature of this concern. Such instruments would be of diagnostic importance for the practitioner and would also help us to understand power behavior more clearly.

REFERENCES

1. Adler, A. *Understanding human nature.* New York: Greenberg, 1946.
2. Adorno, T. W., et al. *The authoritarian personality.* New York: Harper, 1950.
3. Auld, F., Jr. Influence of social class on personality test responses. *Psychol. Bull.,* 1952, **49,** 318-332.
4. Barnard, C. I. Functions and pathology of status systems in formal organizations. In W. F. Whyte (Ed.), *Industry and society.* New York: McGraw-Hill, 1946.
5. Bendix, R., and Lipset, S. M. (Eds.) *Class, status and power.* Glencoe, Ill.: Free Press, 1953.
6. Cartwright, D., and Zander, A. (Eds.) *Group dynamics: research and theory.* Evanston, Ill.: Row, Peterson, 1953.
7. Cohen, A. R. The effect of individual self-esteem and situational structure on threat-oriented reactions to power. Unpublished doctor's dissertation, University of Michigan, 1953.
8. Feinberg, M. R. Relation of background experience to social acceptance. *J. Abnorm. soc. Psychol.,* 1953, **48,** 206-214.
9. Fenichel, O. *The psychoanalytic theory of neurosis.* New York: Norton, 1945.
10. Festinger, L. Informal social communication. *Psychol. Rev.,* 1950, **57,** 271-282.
11. Fromm, E. *Escape from freedom.* New York: Rinehart, 1945.

12. Hewitt, L. E., and Jenkins, R. L. *Fundamental patterns of maladjustment.* State of Illinois, 1946.

13. Horney, K. *Our inner conflicts.* New York: Norton, 1945.

14. Lasswell, H. D. *Power and personality.* New York: Norton, 1948.

15. Lippitt, R., Polansky, N., and Rosen, S. The dynamics of power. *Hum. Relat.,* 1952, **5,** 37-64.

16. Parsons, T. *The social system.* Glencoe, Ill.: Free Press, 1951.

17. Parsons, T., and Shils, E. A. (Eds.) *Toward a general theory of action.* Cambridge: Harvard University Press, 1951.

18. Pfautz, H. W. The current literature on social stratification. *Amer. J. Sociol.,* 1953, **58,** 391-418.

19. Rosen, S. Social power and interpersonal adjustment. Unpublished doctor's dissertation. University of Michigan, 1953.

20. Sullivan, H. S. *Conceptions of modern psychiatry.* Washington, D. C.: W. A. White Psychiatric Foundation, 1947.

6

THE DEVELOPMENT OF PERCEPTIONS AND BEHAVIOR IN NEWLY FORMED SOCIAL POWER RELATIONSHIPS [1]

George Levinger

Empirical investigations of social power have been concerned for the most part with the description of power structures and with the sociological or psychological correlates of social power at some given point in time (6, 9, 10, Chapter 2). Attention has been directed more toward persisting characteristics than toward changes. While this work has provided considerable understanding of the distribution of power and its consequences within different kinds of groups, relatively little is known about the ways in which power relations build up and maintain themselves or suffer modifications.

The present research deals with two questions concerning the development of power relations among members of informal groups: To what extent do different kinds of interpersonal information affect a group member's power perceptions? What is the relation between his perception of other members and his behavior toward them? Before phrasing these questions as specific hypotheses relevant to a particular behavioral setting, let us consider the concepts to be used.

THEORY AND HYPOTHESES

By *social power* we shall mean an individual's potentiality for influencing one or more other persons toward acting or changing in a given direction. According to this definition, social power is the ability to exert interpersonal influence. What, then, is the basis of interpersonal influence? Such influence is established by inducing other persons to perceive that acceptance or rejection of a given influence attempt will lead either to satisfying or depriving experiences for them. In other words, interpersonal influence implies the manipulation of valences in another person's psychological environment.

[1] This report is based on a doctor's dissertation submitted to the Doctoral Program in Social Psychology at the University of Michigan. I am grateful to Dr. Ronald Lippitt for his valuable help as chairman of the doctoral committee. I am also indebted to Drs. Dorwin Cartwright and Sidney Rosen for their constructive suggestions.

The research was supported in part under grant-in-aid (M-450 (C-2)) from the National Institute of Mental Health of the Public Health Service.

In formally structured groups, the basis of such influence is grounded in the established rules of organization. In informal groups, however, the members' differing abilities to influence one another arise out of their continuing interaction. In a newly formed group of relative strangers the prospective member has no rank or status. In such a setting he brings with him merely his individual properties such as his personal characteristics; his knowledge, information, and skills; his material possessions; and his social-emotional capacities. If the prospective member's properties are relevant to the needs of other group members, these properties may become resources which he can use in his dealings with them. He can satisfy or deprive other members to the degree that his *intra*personal properties are convertible into *inter*personal resources.

The concept "resource" requires definition. A resource is any property of an individual which he makes available to persons in his environment as a means for their positive or negative need-satisfaction. This concept refers to the actualization of properties for interpersonal consumption—a consumption which may have either positive or negative utility for the consumer. In other words, a resource refers to some definite act, past or present, which has the effect of either facilitating or hindering the locomotion of other persons or the group as a whole.[2]

One other concept is important for this research. Let us use the term "resource potential" to mean those properties of the individual which are perceived by other members of the group as relevant to their goalward locomotion, but which have not as yet been demonstrated by his behavior. Thus, resource potential refers to properties which are convertible into resources at some future time.

It is proposed here that in an informal group the bases of a member's power lie in his capacity for making available and for withholding resources which are important for the need-satisfaction of other members. This proposition derives from the assumption of an underlying exchange process by which group members attain satisfaction and avoid deprivation of their needs. The more a member is perceived as controlling resources which will satisfy or deprive others' needs, the more he will be able to influence other persons' behavior. His power in the group will be enhanced particularly when his resources have relevance for furthering the group's progress toward its goal.

In order that an individual's power may become established in a group

[2] The concepts "resource" and "property" also have been used by Bales (2) in his theoretical discussion of group interaction. However, Bales does not distinguish between these terms and uses them in a less general sense.

setting, then, other group members must perceive his ability to make available and to withhold resources. This may occur through their receiving information about his potential resources or through their seeing a behavioral demonstration of his actual resources.

During the establishment of a group, how do group members come to relate to one another in terms of resources? If we consider the hypothetical individual as he enters a new group, we may assume the following process. As he begins his contact with other members he receives some initial information about them, which leads him to form his first perceptions of his relationship with them. These perceptions will determine his first action toward the others, and this action is likely to modify their perceptions of him. Their behavior in turn will be shaped according to their modified perceptions and will probably induce a readjustment in the individual's initial perceptions. In short, it is conceived that interpersonal perceptions and behavior develop as the products of the circular process of interaction, and that the individual continually generates and is fed back information concerning his own and others' social resources.

The feedback process outlined here has implications for the growth of interpersonal relations in the group. It would appear that information fed into the circuit may lead to effects which will persist much longer than the immediate instant. If such information affects the recipient's actions, it is likely to alter the consequent perceptions and behavior of the other members and thus may have an observable impact on the pattern of interaction. It is evident that not all information will have such persisting effects. First, the saliency of such information will determine its ability to modify a relationship. The less its saliency for a given dimension of social interaction, the less it will affect the relationship. Second, the consistency of the information with other available information will affect its impact. The more it is contradicted by other relevant information, the less will be its effect. Third, its priority over later information is important. During the stages of group development, the later that information is introduced, the less will be its effect.

The present study was influenced by the above theoretical considerations. We were confronted with a choice among the many possible determinants of power in developing social relationships. It seemed worth while to consider the effects of information concerning both actual and potential resources. The following two determinants were chosen: (1) the initial information concerning the individual's resource potential relative to others in the group, (2) the information received during the group's interaction concerning the relative amount of actual resources of the members. Five hypotheses were stated.

Hypothesis 1. The individual's perceptions of the magnitude of his power will be positively associated with the favorableness of the initial information concerning his relative resource potential in the group.

This hypothesis is derived from the assertions that power is founded on resources and that relevant information will have a persistent impact over the course of the group's interaction.

Hypothesis 2. The individual's perceptions of the magnitude of his power will be positively associated with the relative amount of the resources he demonstrates in comparison with others during the group's interaction.

This hypothesis has the same derivation as Hypothesis 1. Also, there should be a far stronger effect on the individual's perceptions from the information about actual than about potential resources.

Hypothesis 3. Changes in the amount of the individual's power-relevant behavior will vary positively with changes in his perception of the magnitude of his power.

Studies by Lippitt, Polansky, Redl, and Rosen (9) and by French and Snyder (see Chapter 8) have demonstrated in field settings that a person's social power is positively related to the success, the frequency, and the directiveness of his attempts to influence other persons. This hypothesis states that a person's power perception and power-relevant behavior—e.g., number of influence attempts—are sufficiently interdependent that when one is changed the other also is changed.

Hypothesis 4. The individual's power-relevant behavior will be positively associated with the favorableness of the initial information concerning his relative resource potential in the group.

Hypothesis 4 is derivable from Hypotheses 1 and 3. If the initial information has measurable effects on perception, it ought to have similar effects on behavior.

Hypothesis 5. Changes in the individual's perception of his power during the first half will exceed those during the second half of the interaction period.

Although there are likely to be continual readjustments in an individual's perceptions during social interaction, if the situation remains relatively stable these readjustments will tend to become progressively less. This hypothesis is in accordance with statements by Asch (1) and Bruner (3) that early impressions or early hypotheses tend to become resistant to change.

PROCEDURE

An experiment to test these hypotheses was designed in the following manner. The subjects were sixty-four male underclassmen at the University of Michigan who participated as members of two-person groups. Each subject was paired with a paid participant in a series of twenty-four joint decision-making trials, during which the two partners were required to reach decisions concerning a number of city planning problems. The subject was led to perceive his partner as merely another subject, who had also volunteered to help the experimenter "develop a new version of a city planning aptitude test." In reality, the partner had been trained by the experimenter, his behavior was controlled, and each trial outcome was carefully prearranged. Subjects were assigned randomly to the various experimental conditions.

Instructions. The essence of the experimental instructions was as follows— for the full instructions see (8):

A national foundation, which had developed a test for city planning aptitude, has found that the test needs revision because in its original form it neglected social factors. The foundation has given a contract to the Research Center for Group Dynamics for building the missing social factors into the test. The two group members are helping therefore to standardize a task in which the following three factors are important: "the knack of knowing where good building sites are; the ability to maintain effective discussions with other persons; and the accuracy for understanding one's relationship with other persons."

The two partners were told that they would be presented the plans of twenty-four different small towns, one after another. In each instance they would choose the "best building site" from among three possible sites for some given construction—such as a school, a fire station, or a supermarket. They were informed that in each case they would have fifteen seconds to look at the town, to indicate their preferred site on a slip of paper, and to pass the slip to the experimenter. This was "to indicate their aptitude for choosing good sites." Then they would have one-and-a-half minutes to discuss their choice with their partner and to come to a joint decision (failure to agree on a common site would penalize the group score). This part of the task was "to indicate their ability to maintain effective discussions." Finally, before each new trial, each person would estimate his relative influence as a group member and indicate this as a percentage (from 0 per cent to 100 per cent) on a slip of paper. This was "to indicate their accuracy for understanding their relationship with the other person."

Manipulations. The manipulation of the independent variables was accomplished in the following manner. The first manipulation involved differences in subjects' initial information about their partners. Half the subjects received indications that the partner had somewhat less experience relevant to the task than they (Superior information) and the other half that he had more experience (Inferior information). That is, after the instructions, and before the start of the task, the experimenter questioned the subject and the partner concerning their college major, their acquaintance with city planning, their performance in social studies and art in high school, and their degree of confidence about doing well at this task. The subject always replied first. Where the subject was made to feel "superior," the partner said he was majoring in English, that he had never even heard of city planning before, that he had been uninterested in social studies and had done poorly at art, and that he had little confidence. In the "inferior" variation, the partner said he was majoring in architecture, that in one course he had taken up city planning for several weeks, that he had done well in social studies and art, and that he was pretty confident about this task.

The second manipulation involved two different behavior patterns on the part of the partner, the "Accept" and the "Reject" patterns. It was arranged in both patterns that during the twenty-four trials the partner would *agree* in his initial choice of site exactly eight times. As for the remaining sixteen initial disagreements, in the Accept pattern the partner would bow to the subject on fourteen trials; whereas in the Reject pattern he would find suitable arguments for maintaining his initial choice in the same fourteen trials, so that on such trials the subject either had to concede or he had to *disagree* at the end of the minute-and-a-half. Thus for any given trial there were four possible outcomes: Agree, Bow, Concede, and Disagree. In the Accept pattern there were always 8 Agrees, 14 Bows, and 2 Concedes. In the Reject pattern there were always 8 Agrees, 2 Bows, and some combination of 14 Concedes and Disagrees.

In order to determine the adequacy of the second experimental manipulation, a check was made of the partner's behavior. It was found that *within* either the Accept or the Reject condition there were no significant differences in his behavior toward the subjects. However, *between* these two conditions, he made more influence attempts and he was more assertive toward subjects in the Reject condition $(p < .001)$. Thus, except for the intentional difference between the Accept and Reject conditions, it appears that the partner's behavior was satisfactorily controlled.[3]

---

[3] In addition to the two experimental manipulations reported here, a third manipulation was introduced which will not be treated in this report. At the halfway mark, between the twelfth and thirteenth trials, subjects were given differential information about their previous performance. Some subjects were informed they had done very

Measures. The dependent variables were the subjects' perceptions of own power and their behavior during the course of the interaction period. The former was indicated by the twenty-five estimates of their relative influence, which subjects reported before each trial and after the last one in the series.

Three separate indices were used for describing the subjects' power-relevant behavior: (1) influence attempts—the number of attempts the subject made to influence his partner to his own point of view; (2) resistances—the number of times he refused to concede when his partner maintained until the end his initial choice of site; (3) assertiveness—the degree of confidence he expressed when he spoke to his partner about his choice of site. In reliability checks, it was found that "number of influence attempts" was coded with an average r of .84, and "assertiveness" had an average r of .72. The index of resistance had perfect reliability, since it was always clear whether the subject had conceded or retained his initial position at the end of a trial. These reliabilities were considered sufficiently high to justify the use of a single observer for the behavior coding. Correlations among these three behavioral indices ranged from .60 to .62 ($p < .01$).

Of the sixty-four subjects, sixteen were exposed to the Accept pattern and forty-eight to the Reject pattern. In each pattern, half the subjects received Superior information initially and the other half Inferior information.

Because of the difference between the partner's behavior toward the Accept subjects and the Reject subjects as mentioned above, it was found that these two groups differed significantly in their experimental experience. According to responses on a post-experimental questionnaire, Accept subjects tended to see their partners as "yielding" and "unsure of himself," whereas the Reject subjects perceived their partners as "resistant" and "strong." On the basis of these differences, one would be disposed to test a number of hypotheses separately for the two groups. Yet for demonstrating statistical significance, the number of Accept subjects is too small for making comparisons within that group. Therefore, while Hypotheses 2 and 5 are tested by the data on all sixty-four subjects, the results concerning Hypotheses 1, 3, and 4 are confined to the data from the forty-eight Reject subjects.

---

well, others that they had done very poorly, and still others were told nothing about their performance.

This third manipulation had no essential effect on the results to be reported here. The effects of this third manipulation were briefly as follows: The half-time information significantly influenced subject's perceptions of their power. It also had a similar effect on their behavior, but not when it was contradicted by the partner's behavior (second manipulation).

RESULTS

Figure 1 illustrates the contrasting effects of the two experimental manipulations on the subjects' perceptions of their power during the course of the interaction period. Both the variation in the initial information and in the partner's behavior exerted noticeable effects on these perceptions, but the Accept-Reject variation had clearly the greater influence.

Hypothesis 1. Table 1 shows that the initial information had a significant effect on subjects' perceptions of their relative power.[4] Those subjects who were given to understand that their potentiality was superior estimated their power as higher than did those who heard it was inferior. Although the differential effects of the initial information tended to diminish over time (cf. Figure 1), these effects were still present to some degree at the end of the period.

[4] All *p*-values refer to one-tailed tests of significance, since the direction of the expected relationships was specified in the hypotheses.

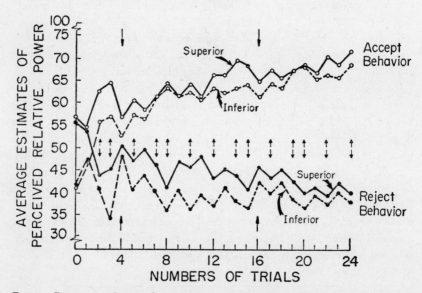

FIG. 1. EFFECTS OF INITIAL INFORMATION AND PARTNER'S BEHAVIOR ON SUBJECTS' PERCEPTIONS OF THEIR RELATIVE POWER * (64 SUBJECTS)

* The fourteen arrows pointing up for the Accept and down for the Reject condition, refer to those trials where the partner's prearranged acceptances or rejections occurred. Two other arrows, for each condition, indicate where the partner reversed his predominant behavior.

TABLE 1

EFFECTS OF INITIAL SUPERIOR AND INFERIOR INFORMATION ON SUBJECTS' AVERAGE
PERCEIVED RELATIVE POWER (48 REJECT SUBJECTS)

Initial Information	Average Perceived Power			
	Hi	Med Hi	Med Lo	Lo
Superior	10	6	5	3
Inferior	2	6	7	9

$$Chi^2 = 8.69; \quad p < .02$$

Hypothesis 2. Table 2 indicates that the two variations in the partner's behavior had strikingly different effects. All sixteen subjects whose partners demonstrated much acceptance of their ideas and suggestions developed perceptions that their power was greater than their partners'. On the other hand, those subjects whose partners showed much initiative and resisted their contributions developed perceptions that their power was less than their partners'.

Hypothesis 3. It was found in this study that subjects' perceived relative power correlated .55 with their number of influence attempts, .48 with their number of resistances, and .51 with their degree of assertiveness—all significant beyond the .01 level of confidence. These correlations between perceived power and indices of behavioral power corroborate findings by earlier investigators (9). However, in order to test Hypothesis 3, we need to compare subjects' *changes* in perceptions with their *changes* in behavior from one time to another. We must ask the question, Do perceptions and behavior show corresponding shifts from one part of the period to another?

Table 3 shows some of the data concerning subjects' changes in their perceptions and behavior from the second to the fourth quarter of the experi-

TABLE 2

EFFECTS OF PARTNER'S ACCEPT OR REJECT BEHAVIOR ON SUBJECTS' PERCEPTIONS OF
RELATIVE POWER (64 SUBJECTS)

Partner's Behavior	Subject's Perceived Power (at end of task)		
	Greater than Partner	Equal to Partner	Less than Partner
Accept	16	0	0
Reject	2	5	41

$$Chi^2 = 54.51; \quad p < .001$$

TABLE 3

RELATION BETWEEN CHANGES IN PERCEIVED POWER AND BEHAVIORAL POWER
(NUMBER OF INFLUENCE ATTEMPTS INITIATED) (48 REJECT SUBJECTS)

Changes in Number of Influence Attempts	Changes in Perceived Power (from 2nd to 4th quarter)		
	Increase (N = 17)	No Change (N = 7)	Decrease (N = 24)
Increase (N = 21)	10	3	8
No Change (N = 6)...............	4	1	1
Decrease (N = 21)	3	3	15

$Chi^2 = 8.91;\ p < .035$

mental period.[5] It is evident that there was a correspondence in direction between subjects' changes in their perceived power and their number of influence attempts from one part to another part of the period, at beyond the .035 level of confidence. This finding was even stronger for the other two indices of behavioral power. Changes in number of resistances were associated with perceptual changes at the .025 level ($Chi^2 = 10.12$; $d.f. = 4$) ; and changes in subjects' assertiveness were related at the .001 level ($Chi^2 = 20.06$; $d.f. = 4$).

The results for this hypothesis demonstrate that, comparing succeeding twelve-minute time units, over a continuous period of interaction there was a definite correspondence between persons' readjustments in their interpersonal perceptions and their interpersonal behavior.

The feedback orientation toward the process of social interaction also led to the examination of the more microscopic fluctuations of perceptions and behavior from one trial to the next. It was possible to break into the circuit and to look at the immediate effects of perceptual changes upon the immediately following behavioral changes between any given pair of successive trials, or look at the parallel effects of behavioral on perceptual changes. In this analysis it was found, contrary to expectation, that trial-to-trial changes in perceived power *did not* significantly determine parallel trial-to-trial changes in number of influence attempts or degree of assertiveness. On the other hand, trial-to-trial fluctuations in such behavior *were reflected* significantly ($p < .01$) in subjects' immediately following estimates of their perceived power. This finding seems to indicate that subjects' periodic estimates of their perceived power responded rather sensitively to their own im-

---

[5] It should be noted that the second and fourth quarters were identical with respect to the partner's behavior pattern. The first and third quarters were not used for the analysis, because of the probable confounding by the impact of the experimental information.

TABLE 4

EFFECTS OF INITIAL INFORMATION ON POWER-RELEVANT BEHAVIOR (NUMBER OF
INFLUENCE ATTEMPTS INITIATED) (48 REJECT SUBJECTS)

Initial Information	Number of Influence Attempts Initiated			
	Hi	Med Hi	Med Lo	Lo
Superior	10	5	5	4
Inferior	2	7	7	8

$Chi^2 = 7.33$; $p < .035$

mediately previous performance; while, on the other hand, their behavior
was affected mostly by a fairly global perceptual restructuring of the situation
and by the particular impact of each social episode.

Hypothesis 4. All three indices of subjects' power-relevant behavior were
significantly affected by the initial manipulation concerning the relative expertness of the partner. Table 4 gives the data regarding subjects' number of
influence attempts initiated toward their partners, showing that the initial
information about the partners' relative resource potential was an effective
determinant of this kind of behavior. The other two indices were similarly
affected: number of resistances ($Chi^2 = 7.19$) and degree of assertiveness
($Chi^2 = 7.33$) both at the .035 level of confidence with three degrees of
freedom.

Hypothesis 5. We may observe in Table 5 that, in accordance with this
hypothesis, there was a significant decrease from the early to the late stages
in subjects' trial-to-trial changes in their estimates of their relative power.
This finding confirms that the experimental task provided a rather constant
situation for the subjects. Thus, the more they became acquainted with their
partners, the less they found it necessary to make revisions in their perceptions
of the relationship.

In this experimental setting, one member of the pair was a trained participant whose behavior was influenced rather little by the subject's actions. Outside this laboratory situation, a stable relationship would probably be reached

TABLE 5

MEAN NUMBER OF CHANGES IN SUBJECTS' PERCEIVED RELATIVE POWER

First Half	Second Half	Difference Between Means	t	N	p
7.4	5.9	1.5	2.59	64	.01

sooner and to a greater degree. In that case, *both* partners would be sensitive to the social feedback and mutually would govern their behavior in order to reinforce the relationship. On the other hand, such increasing stability in social perceptions over time probably is limited to settings where a minimum of new information is introduced into the interpersonal relationship.

DISCUSSION

It was found that both experimental manipulations were significant determinants of the interaction throughout the session. Even the information introduced at the very start still had a measurable effect on the subjects at the end of the session.

It will be remembered that the first kind of information was provided by the experimental partner, who varied the amount of task-relevant properties which he attributed to himself. This initial information was given to the subject before he had any behavioral contact with his partner.

The literature on social perception abounds with studies treating of the formation of impressions concerning other people—see the review by Bruner and Tagiuri (4). All but one of these studies, however, have been confined to the impressions that individuals form after having had contact only with photographs or with verbal descriptions of other people. The one published study directed at the formation of impressions during personal contact is that by Kelley (7). Kelley informed half of his subjects that the instructor they were to meet was "warm," and the other half that he was "cold." After listening to a lecture by this instructor the two groups of subjects differed considerably in their impression of him.

The results of the present experiment give support to Kelley's findings. These subjects had considerably more opportunity for interacting with the stimulus figure than did Kelley's subjects. Even so, we find that the initial information exerted a persisting effect upon their structuring of the relationship, despite the objectively identical behavior of their partner.

However, Kelley's findings also must be qualified in an important respect. The effects of the initial information were small when compared to the effects of the second kind of information which the subject received. Regardless of whether the subject initially received "superior" or "inferior" information, the actual behavior of his partner became more important for determining his perceptions. Depending on whether his partner accepted or rejected his ideas, the average subject's perceptions of his power moved steadily up or down. In terms of our earlier discussion concerning potential versus actual resources, we may consider that the first type of information referred to the group member's comparative potential resources, whereas the second type of information gave comparative evidence about the member's actual resources. The continuous and recurring feedback of the second type of information was certainly effective in overriding the impact of the first type.

Let us now turn to the correspondence between the perceptual and the behavioral indices of the subjects' social power. Beyond the confirmation of findings in previous field studies (5, 9, 10) of the correlation between average perceived power and average behavioral output, it was demonstrated that shifts in subjects' power perceptions were related to corresponding shifts in their power-relevant behavior. This finding lends support to a general feedback assumption concerning the mutual modification and readjustment of perception and behavior during the process of social interaction.

One point of possible theoretical significance concerns the marked intercorrelations among the three behavioral indices of power. Number of influence attempts, number of resistances, and degree of assertiveness toward the partner correlated with one another in the .60's. Whereas previous studies have pointed to the positive relation between the initiation of influence attempts and the initiator's directiveness, the present indication that resistances also may betoken power warrants some comment. The explanation is simple. Usually, power is defined in terms of ability to get others to do things. This experimental setting, however, involved a somewhat competitive situation where power was measured on a relative basis. Thus, in order to enhance his own power, the individual to some extent had to resist the influence of his partner. It is probable that in situations which are less competitive, or which involve a larger number of possible areas of influence, the frequency of resistances would be a less important indicator of social power.

Finally, it was established that subjects' perceptual estimates of their power fluctuated more during the first than during the second half of the experimental session. This result is in accordance with those of other studies of social perception, notably those of Asch (1); and it is explained in terms of Bruner's assertion (3) that an individual's hypotheses become more resistant to revision the longer they are held. This finding implies that as a power relationship develops over a period of time—in an otherwise stable setting—it requires a progressively stronger input of contradictory information in order to revise the growing perceptions of the persons involved.

There may be certain methodological implications to be drawn from this study. In examining the interaction in two-person groups, the effects of subjects' exposure to various manipulations were compared by controlling the other half of the interaction pattern. This procedure of the "controlled interaction sequence" was similar to many other experiments in group dynamics (see 5). However, a further aspect of the procedure was the "breaking into the feedback circuit," through the frequent sequential measurements of the subjects' ongoing perceptions, in a fashion similar to the measures obtained in the research on level of aspiration.

This sort of technique for measuring interaction sequentially over time has possible limitations, though it may open some new paths of research. In this study, for example, it is likely that this measure made subjects perceive the power dimension more saliently than would normally have been the case. Also, it may have increased subjects' feelings of competitiveness. In this writer's opinion, these effects were not very strong, but their possible presence should be recognized in interpreting the data.

The advantages of the technique are that it makes it possible to do microscopic studies of group development. With respect to social power, one can study experimentally the changes in persons' power perceptions and behavior when transferring from one situation to another. The technique appears applicable to more controlled studies of interpersonal "schismogenesis": How do interpersonal cleavages originate? how rapidly? via what kinds of information? and in what sorts of situations? Finally, one might examine the differential predictions of the "continuity" and the "discontinuity" theories of learning in the context of human social situations: What change in social learning and behavior is the product of continuous, minor revisions in perceptions? And what change is the result of apparently discontinuous restructurings of the perceptions?

SUMMARY

This study was initiated in order to investigate a person's perceptions and behavior during the development of his power relationship with another person. A theory was outlined proposing that the individual's social power in informal groups is based largely on his ability to actualize important resources. Thus it was stated that the development of perceptions concerning the power of different group members is dependent upon the demonstration of their respective abilities to make available or to withhold resources relevant to the group's functioning.

A number of hypotheses were stated in consequence of this formulation: First, the individual's perceptions of his power will be positively associated with his initial information concerning his relative potential resources, received before the start of the interaction period. Second, these perceptions will be positively associated with the relative amount of resources he demonstrates in comparison with others during the period itself. Third, changes in the amount of the individual's power-relevant behavior—i.e., influence attempts, resistances, and assertiveness—will vary directly with changes in his perceptions of the magnitude of his power. Fourth, the individual's power-relevant behavior will be positively associated with the initial information. Fifth, changes in his perceptions of his power during the first half will exceed those during the second half of the interaction period.

A laboratory experiment was conducted to test the hypotheses. Sixty-four subjects, each paired with a trained experimental assistant, participated in a series of twenty-four joint decision-making trials. The partners were required to reach decisions regarding a number of city planning problems, ostensibly in order to help develop a new version of a city planning aptitude test. Since the behavior of the assistant was carefully prearranged, the outcomes of the trials were controlled. Data were gathered for comparing the changes in the subjects' perceptions and behavior over the entire length of the experimental session. The subjects' estimates of their relative power were obtained before and after each of the trials, and their behavior during each trial was systematically observed. Thus, it became possible to trace the various fluctuations in the subjects' perceptions and in their behavior.

The experimental manipulations consisted of variations in the information which subjects received initially about the partner's probable task ability, and in the degree of acceptance or rejection the partner gave to their ideas during the behavioral sequence.

The hypotheses received substantial support. Each of the manipulations of information concerning the two partners' relative resources exerted a significant effect on subjects' perceptions. Nevertheless, although the initial information concerning potential resources was a significant determinant of power perceptions, the continuing feedback of the partner's actual behavior acted as a much more important determinant. In this experimental situation, where it was possible to test the accuracy of information about *potential* resources by learning about *actual* resources, the partner's visible behavior provided the most important information for the subjects' periodic estimates. Further, it was found that there was a clear correspondence between changes in subjects' perceptions of their power and changes in their accompanying social influence behavior. Finally it was shown that there was a significant decrease in changes of subjects' perceptions of their power from the first to the second half of the interaction period.

REFERENCES

1. Asch, S. E. *Social psychology.* New York: Prentice-Hall, 1952.

2. Bales, R. F. *Interaction process analysis.* Cambridge: Addison-Wesley, 1950.

3. Bruner, J. S. Personality dynamics and the process of perceiving. In R. R. Blake & B. V. Ramsey (Eds.), *Perception: an approach to personality.* New York: Ronald Press, 1951.

4. Bruner, J. S., & Tagiuri, R. The perception of people. In G. Lindzey (Ed.), *Handbook of social psychology.* Cambridge: Addison-Wesley, 1954.

5. Cartwright, D., & Zander, A. (Eds.). *Group dynamics: research and theory.* Evanston: Row, Peterson, 1953.

6. Hurwitz, J. I., Zander, A., & Hymovitch, B. Some effects of power on the relations among group members. In D. Cartwright & A. Zander (Eds.). *Group dynamics: research and theory.* Evanston: Row, Peterson, 1953.

7. Kelley, H. H. The warm-cold variable in first impressions of persons. *J. Pers.,* 1950, **18**, 431-439.

8. Levinger, G. Perceptions and behavior in the development of social power relationships. Unpublished doctor's dissertation, University of Michigan, 1955.

9. Lippitt, R., Polansky, N., Redl, F., & Rosen, S. The dynamics of power. In D. Cartwright & A. Zander (Eds.), *Group dynamics: research and theory.* Evanston: Row, Peterson, 1953.

10. Polansky, N., Lippitt, R., & Redl, F. An investigation of behavioral contagion in groups. *Hum. Relat.,* 1950, **3**, 319-348.

7

POWER AND AUTHORITY IN THE FAMILY [1]

Donald M. Wolfe

The purpose of this study is to investigate several possible sources of power in the husband-wife relationship and their effects on the family authority structure. This report is divided into four sections. The first offers a conceptual analysis of power and authority in general, and suggests ways in which these concepts may be used in the study of the family. The second presents a diagrammatic model by which to compare various family authority structures. The third section describes procedures employed in an empirical study of family authority structure. The fourth presents the results of that study.

THEORETICAL APPROACH

The theoretical orientation upon which this analysis is based is primarily the group dynamics enlargement upon the Lewinian conceptualization of social power (1, 6, 7), and the development of the concept "authority" by Dubin (2).

Definition 1: Power is the potential ability of one person, O, to induce forces on another person, P, toward (or against) movement or change in a given direction, within a given behavior region, at a given time.

In general, O and P may be either persons or groups, but here we shall be concerned only with persons, i.e., the husband and wife in the nuclear family. Implicit in this definition is that this potential—power of O over P— is made up of the maximum forces O can induce on P, over and above the maximum forces P can exert in resistance to O's inductions. In the family setting, the husband may be able to influence his wife with respect to caring

[1] The data for this study were provided by the Detroit Area Study survey of 1954-1955. The Detroit Area Study is an ongoing research program of the Department of Sociology and the Survey Research Center, University of Michigan. Grateful acknowledgment is given to its director, Dr. Harry P. Sharp, for making the data available and for facilitating its analysis. The author also wishes to express his appreciation to Drs. Dorwin Cartwright, Alvin Zander, and Robert O. Blood for their helpful suggestions and criticisms and for editorial assistance.

for his clothes and use of the car, but she may be better able to influence him with respect to shopping or the use of leisure time. Thus, power is a concept of potential behavior in a social relationship, and allows for variation from one behavioral region to another from time to time.

Inherent in this approach is the fact that the power of O over P and the power of P over O are conceptually independent of each other. Both O and P may have considerable power over each other in the same region, or the power of one may be greater than the power of the other in some regions and vice versa in other regions. Or, in some power relationships, the power of O over P and the power of P over O may be small in all regions. In a single power relationship, the power of O over P may differ in magnitude from region to region and from time to time within the same region.

Since power is defined as a social relationship, and not a personal attribute, we should expect the source or basis for this power to be found in both entities or in the interaction between them. Levinger (see Chapter 6) presents a theoretical model which complies with this expectation. (A similar approach is taken by Rosen, Lippitt, and Levinger (7) with slightly different terminology.)

A number of assumptions are made about the nature of the individual and of interpersonal relations: (a) Every individual is continually attempting to satisfy his needs and desires and to attain his goals. (b) Most of the individual's needs are satisfied and goals attained through social interaction with other persons or groups. (c) During this interaction, there is a continual exchange of "resources" which contribute to the satisfaction of individual needs and to the attainment of individual or group goals.

These resources are personal properties or attributes of the individual which may be physical, intellectual, or emotional in nature (e.g., physical strength, personal appearance, knowledge or skills, or "capacities" for giving and receiving love) ; or they may be material possessions or status distinctions (intrinsically valuable or instrumental objects, or rights and privileges concomitant with holding a special social position—perhaps an office).

Definition 2: A *resource* is a property of a person or group which can be made available to others as instrumental to the satisfaction of their needs or the attainment of their goals.

A resource then is a property of one person which can be utilized by others and transferred socially to others. The more resources one person has under his control, the more he can contribute to the need-gratification or goal-attainment of others. Implicit in this definition is the idea that a resource may be instrumental negatively as well as positively, i.e., a resource may also contribute to a deprivation of needs or may act as a barrier to the attainment of goals. Thus a person who is very strong is capable of inflicting bodily injury on others, depriving them of their need for safety from harm. If a person, O, actually makes his resources available to P, then O is said to be "actualizing" his resources. If P uses O's resources to satisfy his own needs, then P is "utilizing" O's resources.

Two conditions are necessary for O to have power over P: (a) P must have needs or goals which he feels can be satisfied or attained with the help of another's resources but not without such help, and (b) P must perceive O as having resources which might be made available to him. O's power over P is based on potential rewards when P perceives that O has resources that P needs, desires, or values, or which have a positive utility for P. It is based on potential punishments when P perceives that O might actualize resources which are negatively valent for P, or which have a negative utility with respect to P's needs, desires, or goals.

We now come to the question of resources which may be a source of power for the husband or wife in the family. The assumption is made that people participate in a marriage relationship in order to satisfy certain needs and desires and to attain certain goals, not necessarily selfish in nature. In this relationship a number of common goals develop (e.g., procreation and socialization of offspring) but these are based on the needs and values of the individual members. So power may be based on resources of the husband or the wife which contribute to movement toward joint goals as well as toward individual goals. These resources may be skills, competence, or knowledge with respect to regions of common goal-directed behavior. No doubt some of the increased power of the wife in American families in recent years is based on the increase of education for the wife in various regions of behavior.

Actually, any conceivable property which can be utilized by other persons may be a source of power. It must be noted, however, that this theoretical approach to power in the family views it as being based on an exchange of needed or desired resources, and not just as a fulfillment of social norms. Norms may enter the picture, however, with respect to the values and needs of the husband and wife. Family goals may be based on a culturally derived value system, and certain resources, especially expertness in certain regions or capacities for love and affection, may be derived from the culture through a socialization process.

Power and authority are similar concepts in that they both deal with the ability of one social entity to influence or affect the behavior of another. However, authority is a special case having to do with the decision-making process in social groups.

Definition 3: Authority is the ability of one person (or group), O, to make decisions which guide the behavior of another person, P, in a given behavioral region at a given time, where both O and P perceive this ability as O's right.

Authority, as power, is a concept of potential ability involving two social entities, and is limited to a specific region and time. There are two aspects of this conception which need to be stressed. First, it pertains to the making of decisions which have interpersonal implications, and second, it involves the perception of legitimacy and propriety. The term *decision* is taken to mean a process whereby a person considers a set of alternative courses of action in a given situation and selects one of them as the course of action to be followed. In the exercise of authority, O selects a course of action which P is to follow, and communicates this to P. That is, P's behavior is determined by a decision made by O.

In an authority relationship, not only can O make decisions concerning P's behavior, but both P and O perceive that O has a legitimate right to do so and that P has an obligation to comply with these decisions. The subordinate, P, "holds in abeyance his own critical faculties for choosing between (behavioral) alternatives and uses the formal criterion of the receipt of a command or signal as his basis for choice" (8, p. 189). The concept of authority as used here is very nearly the same as one which French and Raven call "legitimate power." "Legitimate power of O/P is defined as that power which stems from internalized values in P which dictate that O has a legitimate right to influence P and that P has an obligation to accept this influence." (See Chapter 9, p. 159.) They conceive of legitimate power as being (a) culturally derived, (b) situationally required, (c) determined by social structure, or (d) designated by a legitimizing agent.

Power is seen here as an aspect of an informal social relationship based on the ability of one person to contribute to the gratification or deprivation of another's needs. But authority is an aspect of the formal structure of a group based on the role prescriptions and founded in the norm system of the group.

In some families a certain pattern of authority may be based on the mores of the society. It is "traditional" for the husband to make decisions in certain areas. In other families the wife may be more competent to move the family toward its goals, and therefore both she and her husband feel that she should make the decisions in the regions pertinent to those goals; thus her authority is legitimized by family standards or norms. Still other families may set up an authority relationship which they feel is legitimized by the state in giving a marriage license or by the church official who married them. It seems likely that when a couple first marries, societal norms will dictate which of them will make decisions in which regions. That is, there are certain pressures toward establishing a pattern of authority similar to an "ideal pattern" for that society.

From one family to another, roles and (internal) norms may differ, and even within the same family the norms may change and role prescriptions may be altered. For example, the goals and values of the family may change from the time of marriage to the time the children are grown and leave home. With these changes may come a change in the authority relationship of the husband and wife, but at any one time the authority relationship is supported by the family's own set of norms—the family "sees" the authority pattern as being "right."

Power, on the other hand, is seen as being independent of roles. Anyone may have needs or goals or may have resources valued by others regardless of his roles. However, the norms of the family may set some limits as to the kinds of influence attempts which are acceptable.

The traditional cultural norms may prescribe that the husband shall make most of the decisions in most family regions and that the wife shall behave in accordance with these decisions, and such a pattern may at first be established in the family. However, it may be that the husband has certain strong needs for which the wife has resources for gratification, thus giving her increased power. For example, the husband may be seen as the one who should make the final decisions with respect to expenditures for major purchases for the family, yet because of his insecurity in financial matters and because of her greater competence (derived from training or experience) she may be better able to advance the family toward its financial goals and she may derive more power than he in this region where he has the authority.

In order to maintain authority in an ongoing group, the authority figure must have a certain minimum of power with which to enforce conformity with his decisions—i.e., he must control certain resources which are necessary to need-gratification of those under him. In most formal organizations, such resources are made available to persons in positions of authority so that they will have power to back up their decisions. In the modern American family there is considerable variation in role structure and a high degree of ambiguity regarding the norms of authority relationships. Adequate rationale is readily available to support nearly any pattern of authority between husband and wife. Therefore we shall assume that if either the wife or the husband has a high degree of power over the other, the power figure will become accepted as the decision-maker in his regions of power and will achieve dominance in the authority relationship. Thus, various sources of power may become bases of authority if the family norms regulating the authority structure change.

TYPES OF FAMILY AUTHORITY RELATIONSHIP

In the family behavioral field, the husband has a range of authority, the wife has a range of authority, and a range of authority is shared. There may also be regions in which neither the husband nor the wife has authority over the other. Authority relationships may differ from family to family in at least two respects: the extent of the ranges of authority of the husband and wife, and the extent of the shared range of authority. The husband's range of authority may be larger than, equal to, or smaller than the wife's range.

Definition 4: The *relative authority* (RA) of husband and wife is the ratio of the wife's range of authority to the husband's range of authority.

If the wife's range of authority is larger than her husband's, she has more relative authority than he. If his range is larger, he has more relative authority. If the two ranges are of equal size, there is a balance of authority in the family.

Definition 5: The *degree of shared authority* (DS) in the family is the proportion of behavioral regions of the family field which are in the shared range of authority.

DS may vary from zero to unity—no regions of the family field in the shared range to all regions in the shared range.

Diagram 1 offers a graphic model of the possible distribution of authority relationships on these two dimensions. The ordinate represents the possible RA values, with wife dominant in all regions at the top, and husband dominant in all regions at the bottom. At the center, the wife's and husband's ranges of authority are of equal size. The abscissa indicates the degree of shared authority, with shared authority in all regions on the left extreme, and with the right extreme indicating no shared range of authority. Any point within Diagram 1 represents an authority relationship with a given RA and a given DS.

The triangular shape of the diagram has theoretical significance. A family field in which all regions are in the husband's range of authority must, by definition, have no regions in a shared range. The same is true of a family in which the wife is dominant in all regions. These two cases are represented by the lower right and upper right corners of the triangle, respectively. In like manner, the family field in which all regions are in a shared range of authority must have a balance of relative authority between husband and wife, and in Diagram 1 would be placed at the left extreme of the DS dimension.

The dotted lines arbitrarily divide the distribution of authority relationships into four types: (a) Wife Dominant is made up of those families in which the wife's range of authority is considerably larger than her husband's.

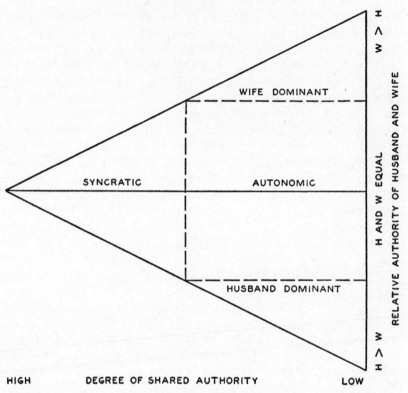

Diagram 1: Theoretical distribution of husband-wife authority relationships. The higher the degree of shared authority the more equal the relative authority of the husband and wife. The broken lines divide the distribution into four authority types: Wife Dominant, Syncratic, Autonomic, and Husband Dominant.

(b) The Syncratic type is made up of families in which there is nearly a balance of relative authority and the shared range is equal to or greater than the combined ranges of the husband and wife. (c) The Autonomic type also has nearly a balance of RA but the husband's and wife's ranges together are greater than the shared range. (d) The Husband Dominant type is an authority relationship in which his range of authority is considerably larger than his wife's.

METHOD

The data used in this study are based on personal interviews with wives in Metropolitan Detroit as part of the Detroit Area Study of the University of

Michigan for 1954-1955. Interviews were taken with 731 wives who are living with their husbands, and thus belong to ongoing family groups. This represents a multi-stage probability sample of dwelling units in Wayne, Oakland, and Macomb counties. Each interview took approximately one hour and was conducted in the home of the respondent by a trained interviewer, either a graduate student in the Department of Sociology or a member of the staff of the Survey Research Center of the Institute for Social Research.

The dimensions or variables making up Diagram 1 were measured by the use of eight questions concerning who makes the final decision about a variety of problems in various family activities. (See Appendix.) These are in no sense exhaustive of all activity regions in any one family. The eight questions, however, were thought to be pertinent to almost all urban families and sufficiently representative to give an indication of the relative authority of the husband and wife and the degree of shared authority in the family.

The relative authority index (RA) is based on the sum of the numerical codes across the eight questions on decision-making; the lower the RA score, the greater the husband's range; the higher the RA score the greater the wife's range of authority.

The Degree of Shared Authority index (DS) is based on the number of regions in which husband and wife share the authority—scores are determined by the number of questions in the decision set which are answered "husband and wife exactly the same." A DS score of 8 would indicate complete sharing of authority in all regions—completely syncratic. The lower the DS score, the more autocratic or autonomic the authority relationship.

The RA and DS indices together determine the Authority Type. The Wife Dominant group includes all families with an RA score of 29 or more (where the range is from 8 to 40); those in the Husband Dominant group have an RA score of 19 or less. The Syncratic group is made up of all families having an RA score from 20 to 28 inclusive and a DS score of 4 to 8; the Autonomic group have RA scores from 20 to 28 and DS scores of 3 or less.

Note that these are types only in the statistical sense, and are not meant to be "ideal types" in the sense of configurations of behavior. They are determined by the two variables which define the triangular model, and no other variables are inherent in them. The purpose of this research is to explore the relations between this conceptualization and other variables which may be pertinent to family structure and interaction.[2]

---

[2] This approach differs from that of Herbst (3, 4) in that authority as used here is based only on questions of "who makes decisions" and not on "who carries them out" as well. The considerable influence of the Herbst studies on the present analysis is obvious and deeply appreciated.

RESULTS AND DISCUSSION

Several possible sources of authority for the husband or wife and some of the effects of different authority relationships have been explored and will be discussed in the following sections: (a) authority and demographic characteristics of the husband, (b) the effects of the wife's employment on the authority relationship, (c) control of family money and bills, (d) emotional factors in family authority structure, (e) age of wife and authority structure, and (f) authority and marital satisfaction.

Authority and Some Demographic Characteristics of the Husband

A man who is successful in the business world must have resources for goal attainment, some of which could presumably be utilized in the home as well. His wife is more likely to perceive him as a person who is generally competent and who has resources for need-satisfaction and goal-attainment which he can readily actualize within the home as well as elsewhere. Thus she will attribute more power to him and will accept his influence attempts. In families in which the husband is not so successful, the wife is apt to perceive him as being less competent; she will feel that he is less capable of helping the family move toward its goals, and she will therefore attribute less power to him. There are of course many circumstances under which this would not be true; for example, when the wife's needs are very strong, when she perceives success and competence somewhat differently than most, or when the husband has and actualizes resources with respect to his wife but not when away from home. Other things being equal, however, we should expect that husbands who have resources of value in the business world probably control resources of value to the home and will have more power in the home than will less successful husbands.

There are three variables—income, occupational level, and general social status—which are estimates of "success" of the husband in society at large and which probably influence his wife's perception of his general competence. A person with a large income not only has financial resources which may be sources of power but also prove that he is a capable person in general. Occupational level and income are certainly related, but being high in the occupational scale is also evidence of general competence. Professional and managerial workers are generally thought of as being quite capable of handling their affairs—they probably have intellectual and skill resources of high utility for locomotion toward individual and group goals. At least it is likely that their wives so perceive them. If so, these husbands should have relatively high power, and, in turn, considerable authority in the home.

Hypothesis 1: Husbands who are generally successful and prestigeful will have more power and will therefore derive more authority in the home than husbands who are less successful.

Table 1 shows the mean annual income and percentage of families having high (above median) social status for each authority type. The average income ($6437) for Husband Dominant families is significantly higher than the total mean income for all others ($t=3.1$, $p<.001$), and the Wife Dominant mean income ($4692) is lower than the mean for all other groups combined, just missing the .05 criterion of significance ($t=1.5$, $p<.07$).

Turning now to occupational level, we find that nearly a third of the husbands in Husband Dominant families are classified as professional, technical, or kindred workers, or as managers, officials and proprietors, a disproportionately high number when the total sample contains less than a quarter in these occupational classes. This goes along with the finding above with respect to income and lends general support to Hypothesis 1. Oddly enough, the husbands in Wife Dominant families have more than the expected number in the managers, officials, and proprietors class. They tend, however, to be self-employed and to have lower incomes and thus perhaps do not contribute to a perception of general competence.

The social status index is an indicator of the husband's position on a general prestige dimension. It is a composite of his position (based on percentile rankings) on four variables—education, occupation, income, and ethnic background. Social status in an upward mobile society is certainly an important factor in the perception of one's general competence. In a sense, high social status and "success" are almost synonymous. Table 1 gives the percentage of families in each authority group who are above the median

TABLE 1

MEAN ANNUAL INCOME AND SOCIAL STATUS BY AUTHORITY TYPE

Authority Type	Mean Income	Percentage High Social Status *	N
Husband Dominant	$6437	58%	166
Syncratic	5490	49	201
Autonomic	5378	46	267
Wife Dominant	4692	36	22
Total Sample	5646	50	656

* Families have High Social Status if their index score is above the median for the total sample (see text).

for social status. The Husband Dominant group is significantly higher than expected by chance, and only 36 per cent of the Wife Dominant families have social status scores above the median for the Detroit Area population. Thus, higher-status husbands tend to have more authority in their homes than lower-status husbands.

The results of this analysis of income and social status strongly support Hypothesis 1, and there is a tendency in that direction with respect to occupational level. Husbands who are successful in the business world do tend to have more power and authority in the home than do less successful men.

The Effects of the Wife's Employment on Family Authority Relationship

The wife gains in power in at least two ways when she works outside the home. First, she develops resources (financial, intellectual, skill, etc.) which usually are not readily developed in the home. Second, she becomes less dependent upon her husband for the satisfaction of her needs. The contacts she makes outside the home provide resources for satisfying some of her affiliational need, her own success and prestige are less contingent upon those of her husband, and she becomes aware of other sources of aid for her goal-attainment. The husband also finds that his wife now controls many resources which he could utilize for his need-satisfaction and goal-attainment, and he will attribute more power to her. In many homes, the right to make decisions is almost an aspect of the role of provider. "He who pays the piper calls the tune."

Hypothesis 2: Wives who are working or who have worked outside the home have more power and will derive more authority than wives who have not worked.

Putting Hypothesis 2 somewhat differently, more wives in Husband Dominant homes will have never worked outside the home, and fewer will be working now than in any other group. Wives who are now working will be more likely to belong to families with a balance of power and authority or with the relative power in favor of the wife. The results in Table 2 strongly support this prediction. Significantly more wives in Husband Dominant homes than in all others have never worked. Wives who are now working tend to participate in Syncratic or Autonomic authority relationships.

Control of Family Money and Bills

The control of financial resources in the family presents some theoretical problems. On the one hand, the person who controls the purse strings has a

TABLE 2

EMPLOYMENT EXPERIENCE OF WIFE BY AUTHORITY TYPE

	Authority Type				
Employment Experience	Husband Dominant	Syncratic	Autonomic	Wife Dominant	All Groups
Wife never employed............	40%	25%	21%	27%	27%
Wife previously employed........	48	48	55	46	51
Wife now employed.............	10	25	22	18	20
Not Ascertained	2	2	2	9	2
Total	100%	100%	100%	100%	100%
N	166	201	267	22	656

resource which may be a basis for power in the home. But it is equally likely that the person who has the greater power and authority, from whatever source, will be able to gain and maintain control over this important resource. As Lasswell and Kaplan (5) hypothesize: "Forms of power and influence are agglutinative: those with some forms tend to acquire other forms also" (p. 97). Since many of the decisions which must be made in carrying out the affairs of the family involve money, it is likely that the norms which determine who will make the major decisions will also establish that spouse as the controller of family finances. Perhaps differential control of other-than-financial resources lies behind the authority relationship in this area.

Hypothesis 3: Control of financial resources will be in the hands of the dominant authority figure in the family.

Although Hypothesis 3 predicts that the person in greater authority will also control the financial matters of the family, the direction of causation is dubious. Correlational data, as we have here, can shed little light on this problem. However, Table 3 presents the results of this cross-tabulation. As was predicted, in Husband Dominant homes the husband is much more apt to handle the money and bills, and in Wife Dominant homes the wife is likely to control these resources. In Syncratic homes this responsibility is more often shared than handled by either spouse alone, but the wife often handles this function.

These results confirm Hypothesis 3. Although the relationship is not perfect, the authority figure is much more apt to maintain control over family financial resources than the nondominant spouse. This seems to be one of the sources of power by which the authority figure can enforce his decisions. Since in Autonomic families each member is apt to carry out his own decisions, it is likely that the wife has the authority and is active in those regions which call for handling most of the financial matters.

TABLE 3

PATTERN OF HANDLING MONEY AND BILLS BY AUTHORITY TYPE

Spouse Controlling Financial Resources	Authority Type				Total Sample
	Husband Dominant	Syncratic	Autonomic	Wife Dominant	
Husband more than wife.........	43%	20%	20%	18%	26%
Husband and wife equal..........	36	41	30	5	34
Wife more than husband.........	21	39	50	77	40
Total	100%	100%	100%	100%	100%
N	166	201	267	22	656

Some Emotional Factors in Family Authority Structure

In the theoretical discussion of sources of power, two conditions were specified for the power of O over P: O must have resources of utility to P, and P must have needs or goals which can be satisfied through the utilization of O's resources. So far, we have been looking primarily at possible resources which may be a basis for power, and therefore authority, in the family. Now we shall turn to the second condition and look at some of the needs (especially of the wife) which may be a source of power and authority for the other spouse.

The respondents were asked to rank in importance to them several aspects of marriage: companionship, chance to have children, husband's understanding, love and affection, and standard of living. The average ranking for the total sample was in the order given. In every group, companionship was ranked first, on the average. Standard of living had the lowest mean rank in every group except Wife Dominant, in which case it was ranked second from the bottom.

It is assumed that those wives who rank love and affection first or second have a high need for love and affection. It is also assumed that it is usually up to the husband to satisfy this need. This would be indicative of a situation in which the wife has a strong need and the husband has certain resources, emotional in nature, which can be utilized for the satisfaction of that need. From this situation the husband should derive power which may bring about a change in the authority relationship, especially if his expression of affection is in any way contingent upon her compliant behavior.

Hypothesis 4: Wives who have a strong need for love and affection will have relatively less power, and will have less relative authority, than wives with a weaker need.

Table 4 gives the percentage of wives in each authority type who have a strong need for love and affection (who rank love and affection either first or second). Although there is a slight trend in the predicted direction, the proportion of Husband Dominant wives who are high in this need is not significantly above that of the total population. On the other hand, Wife Dominant wives tend to be very low in their need for love and affection. While the data are consistent with Hypothesis 4, it appears that other factors also need to be considered. Perhaps a strong need for affection is a source of power for the other spouse only under special circumstances, but a weak need enables the person to develop and exercise his own power. That is, a wife who is not seeking emotional support from her husband may feel quite free to exercise her power stemming from other need-resource bases, while a wife who needs continual affectional gratification may fear that this gratification will be threatened if she over-extends her authority. Any such attempt to refine Hypothesis 4 of course needs subsequent empirical validation which cannot be supplied in the present study.

What of the other aspects of marriage which were ranked by the wife? It is assumed that each of them represents a need or goal. Ranking any of them first or second would indicate that it is an important need or goal for the wife. Companionship is an important need to 68 per cent of the wives in the total sample, and all four groups fluctuate within six percentage points of this figure. This seems to be an important need for most wives, but is not an important source of power or authority. This need, unlike many others, may be best satisfied under conditions of equal power. Therefore, a strong imbalance of power might tend to deprive one of satisfaction. If this is true, it would be unlikely that the husband could derive much power from his wife's need for companionship.

Having children is a primary goal for 54 per cent of the wives in the sample, but 68 per cent of the wives in Wife Dominant authority relationships

TABLE 4

WIFE'S NEED FOR LOVE AND AFFECTION BY AUTHORITY TYPE

Wife's Need For Love and Affection	Authority Type				
	Husband Dominant	Syncratic	Autonomic	Wife Dominant	Total Sample
High need	37%	34%	30%	9%	32%
Low need	61	64	69	86	66
Not ascertained	2	2	1	5	2
Total	100%	100%	100%	100%	100%
N	166	201	267	22	656

rank this as first or second in importance. Since they play the most active part in having and rearing children, it may be that wives derive more power for themsleves from this than do their husbands: they are more capable of attaining this goal without continual help from their husbands than is true for other goals. Wife's need for her husband's understanding is moderate in all groups, and no group deviates from the average for the total population by more than seven percentage points. A high standard of living is stated as an important goal for only 13 per cent of the wives in this sample, with no group differing from this significantly. Thus, a desire for a high standard of living is a seldom expressed need.

Age of Wife and Authority Structure

When children first come to a young couple, the responsibilities of the wife increase and at first she is quite dependent upon her husband for help and for emotional support. However, the husband usually cannot be present in the home during much of the day, and the wife must satisfy her needs and those of her children (this being a goal of hers) without the resources he might contribute. She must develop resources of her own to cope with the exigencies of child care and development. Therefore, the power of the husband should be high at first, but the wife's relative power should increase as she becomes more and more competent. By the time the children are grown and about to leave the home, the wife's power (from this source) should be at a peak.

The presence of growing children can contribute to the relative power of the wife in another way as well. As we have seen, emotional resources are important to the wife. Since the husband is not always present to actualize his resources in this direction, many mothers turn to their children for partial satisfaction of this need. Love and affection from her children replaces some of that which formerly came from her husband. The wife's need for her husband's emotional resources decreases for a time.

When a wife passes the age of fifty, and her children are about to leave the home or have already left, she has developed her resources to their highest peak. She may have become accustomed to the security and satisfaction of relatively high power and authority in the home. With the maturation of her children, she has lost what is perhaps her most important function, child rearing, as well as a source of her own need-gratification. At this time, we might expect two contrary trends: first, a return to dependency on her husband for the satisfaction of her emotional needs, and, second, an effort to find a replace-

TABLE 5

AGE OF WIFE BY AUTHORITY TYPE

	Authority Type				
Age of Wife	Husband Dominant	Syncratic	Autonomic	Wife Dominant	Total Sample
Under 30 years.................	32%	20%	27%	9%	26%
30 to 39 years.................	33	46	30	18	35
40 to 49 years.................	18	15	24	23	20
50 years and over.............	17	20	19	50	20
Total	100%	101%	100%	100%	101%
N	166	201	267	22	656

ment for her lost function and to redirect her resources, and thus power, toward other family regions. The former trend will be successful only if the husband is able and willing to fill her needs. (If not, she may seek satisfaction in her mother-in-law and grandmother roles.) With reference again to the Lasswell and Kaplan hypothesis, we should expect that the wife will have gained power and authority in most family regions and therefore that the second trend will be predominant. Most wives should tend to maintain and increase their authority at least up to the time of their husbands' retirement.

These two changes—an increase in the wife's own resources, and a decrease in her need for those of her husband—should bring an increase in the relative power of the wife. Since this increase in power should in turn bring an increase in her relative authority, we should expect fewer Husband Dominant wives and more Wife Dominant wives in the older age categories.

Hypothesis 5: The relative power of the wife will increase with age, leading to an increase in her authority relative to her husband.

Table 5 shows the age distribution for wives in the various authority groups. The Husband Dominant type shows a predominance of wives under thirty years of age and between thirty and thirty-nine. Syncratic wives are typically in the thirty to thirty-nine category. Autonomic family wives are more evenly distributed with respect to age, with a tendency toward the forty to forty-nine category. And half of the Wife Dominant wives are over fifty years of age.

Authority Patterns and Marital Satisfaction

In predicting the marital satisfaction of the wife, several factors must be taken into account—her ability to satisfy her needs and attain her goals, and her adherence to social norms—to mention only two. Both of these factors are involved in the power and authority relationships between husband and wife. Generally speaking, the more power the wife has, the greater her ability to attain her goals, for she can influence others to this effect. Therefore, we might predict that the more power the wife has, the greater her satisfaction in marriage. However, it is also important for her to integrate with society, to behave within the norms of society as a whole, and to have a marital relationship which is advantageous to both herself and her family. Thus, we should expect the wife, if she wishes to be happy, to desire an authority relationship close to that prescribed by the social norms—either a democratic one or one in which the husband is dominant. This need to conform to the social norm might conflict with the prediction suggested above.

An index of marital satisfaction was constructed on a basis of the ranking of the wife's needs and goals and her satisfaction with her need gratification in the family. From this index it is possible to get an estimate of how well the wife's needs and goals are being attained. The index shows the wife's position along a dimension from low to high satisfaction. The respondents are then coded as either above or below the median score for the whole sample. Table 6 gives the percentage in each authority group who are above the median for marital satisfaction.

Syncratic relationships, in which authority is shared by husband and wife, are most conducive to satisfaction for the wife. In these cases, the wife's power is fairly high, but the authority pattern conforms to societal norms. Autonomic wives are less satisfied than the average, perhaps because there is less interaction between husband and wife, and less opportunity for need-gratification. The Wife Dominant authority relationship coincides with low marital satisfaction, perhaps because of societal pressures, but more likely because lack of satisfaction over long periods of time may lead to a striving

TABLE 6

MARITAL SATISFACTION OF WIFE BY AUTHORITY TYPE

Authority Type	Percentage with High Satisfaction	Number of Cases *
Husband Dominant	51%	153
Syncratic	61	186
Autonomic	43	256
Wife Dominant	26	19
Total Sample	50%	614

* Respondents for whom marital satisfaction scores were not ascertained have been excluded from this table so that 60 per cent could be used as a base for comparison. High marital satisfaction is defined here as above the median score for the total sample.

on the part of the wife for more power and authority. Thus in this case, low satisfaction probably came before the increase of authority for the wife. A Husband Dominant relationship may lead to high or low satisfaction for the wife, as this group shows a greater average deviation than any other.

From this we can conclude that power is important but not "all important" in bringing general satisfaction for the wife. Freedom from conflict is also important, as is close adherence to societal norms. Certainly many other factors, not related to power or authority, are also very important in determining satisfaction in marriage for the wife. However, these data suggest an interesting direction for further study.

Summary and Conclusions

The concepts of social power (as based on differential control of resources of value to others for need-satisfaction) and authority (an aspect of role-prescriptions and group norms) were discussed as they pertain to the urban family. Several sources of authority for the husband or wife were explored using questionnaire data from a cross-sectional sample of the Detroit area population. A conceptual scheme for comparing various authority relationships between husband and wife was presented, allowing for a division of the sample into four "types" of family authority structure—Husband Dominant, Syncratic, Autonomic, and Wife Dominant.

1. Husband Dominant families are generally high on mean annual income and on general social status; Wife Dominant families are generally low on these two variables.

2. Wives in Husband Dominant families are less likely ever to have worked or to be currently working outside the home than wives in any other authority type.

3. The spouse who is the dominant authority figure in the home is generally most apt also to handle the family money and bills.

4. A strong need for love and affection on the part of the wife is a source of power and authority for the husband.

5. The authority of the wife increases over the years of marriage so that Husband Dominant wives are apt to be younger, and Wife Dominant wives are older (half are over fifty years of age).

6. Wives in Syncratic families are likely to be well satisfied with their marriage, while Autonomic and especially Wife Dominant wives are more likely to be low on marital satisfaction.

APPENDIX

Decision Questions Upon Which RA and DS Scores Are Based

54. In every family somebody has to decide such things as where the family will live and so on. Many couples talk such things over first, but the *final* decision often has to be made by the husband or the wife. For instance, who usually makes the final decision about what car to get? (SHOW CARD VI)

(CARD VI)	husband always	husband more than wife	husband and wife exactly the same	wife more than husband	wife always
	1	2	3	4	5

55. . . . about whether or not to buy some life insurance

	1	2	3	4	5

56. . . . about what house or apartment to take?

	1	2	3	4	5

57. Who usually makes the final decision about what job your husband should take?

	1	2	3	4	5

58. . . . about whether or not *you* should go to work or quit work?

	1	2	3	4	5

59. . . . about how much money your family can afford to spend per week on food?

	1	2	3	4	5

60. . . . about what doctor to have when someone is sick?

	1	2	3	4	5

61. . . . and, about where to go on a vacation?

	1	2	3	4	5

REFERENCES

1. Cartwright, D., & Zander, A. *Group dynamics: research and theory.* Evanston: Row, Peterson, 1953.

2. Dubin, R. (Ed.) *Human relations in administration.* New York: Prentice-Hall, 1951.

3. Herbst, P. G. The measurement of family relationships. *Hum. Relat.,* 1952, **5,** 3-35.

4. Herbst, P. G., & Middleton, Margaret. The members of a family. In Oeser, O. A., & Hammond, S. B. (Eds.) *Social structure and personality in a city.* New York: MacMillan, 1954.

5. Lasswell, H. D., & Kaplan, A. *Power and society: A framework for political inquiry.* New Haven: Yale Univer. Press, 1950.

6. Lewin, K. *Field theory in social science.* New York: Harper, 1951.

7. Rosen, S., Lippitt, R., & Levinger, G. K. *The development and maintenance of power in children's groups.* A monograph in preparation.

8. Simon, H. A. Authority. In R. Dubin, (Ed.) *Human relations in administration.* New York: Prentice-Hall, 1951.

8

LEADERSHIP AND INTERPERSONAL POWER [1]

JOHN R. P. FRENCH, JR. AND RICHARD SNYDER

Leadership is the subject of much recent research because of its practical importance rather than its conceptual clarity. Though useful as a popular term denoting a broad area of phenomena, "leadership" requires a more limited definition in order to become a useful scientific concept.

We propose a restricted definition of leadership in terms of power: Leadership is *the potential social influence of one part of the group over another.* If one member has power over another, then he has some degree of leadership. Usually every member has some degree of influence over others in an informal group; in other words the leadership is widely distributed throughout the group. Those who are popularly called "followers" are members with less leadership, either because of their personal qualities or because of their subordinate role.

In a formal organization, the influence of the followers and of the leaders is partly determined by the legitimate authority of the positions they occupy. Thus the part of a group which has leadership may be a superordinate position or role regardless of the person who occupies it. In this case the study of leadership involves the study of role relationships as well as interpersonal relations.

This conception implies that leadership is a property of the group rather than a characteristic of an individual—though personality traits may, of course, be determinants of influence. It is the *relationship* which is important, and we must look at both sides of it. We are immediately led to ask, What determines the amount and kind of influence which the leader will attempt to exert? And what determines the extent to which the followers will accept these influence attempts? In answering these questions we will pay

[1] This work was supported under contract with Detachment No. 3 of the Human Resources Research Center, a part of the Technical Training Command of the United States Air Force. The authors wish to acknowledge the help of many members of this unit in collecting and analyzing the data. Particular thanks go to Mr. John V. Moore, for whom the project represented a major responsibility over a period of many months, and to Dr. Arthur Hoehn who did many analyses of the data.

particular attention to the more or less enduring interpersonal and interrole relations existing between the inducer who attempts influence and the recipient toward whom it is directed.

The Hypotheses

Two experiments were designed to test three hypotheses about the determinants of attempted influence and four hypotheses about the effectiveness of these attempts.

The determinants of attempted influence. The basic assumption underlying these hypotheses is that attempts to influence others are instrumental acts whose occurrence is determined by the perceived probability of success in achieving some goal. Therefore influence attempts will occur if the inducer perceives a readiness of the recipient to accept his influence [2] and if he believes that the induced behavior will, in fact, lead him to his goal. Three hypotheses were derived from these assumptions.[3]

Hypothesis I-1: The amount of influence attempted by a leader (or member) over a given recipient increases with increasing acceptance of him by that recipient.

This hypothesis assumes that the amount of influence attempted will be proportional to the perceived probability of success. Presumably the leader will assume that an influence attempt will more probably succeed where the recipient likes him (see Hypothesis II-1 below). At the low end of the scale, where there is dislike between leader and follower, this hypothesis is in line with Newcomb's principles of autistic hostility (11).

Hypothesis I-2: The amount of influence attempted by a leader (or member) increases with increasing certainty in his own opinion.

The measure of the leader's certainty is presumably a measure of his subjective probability that events will prove him correct. Accordingly, the more certain he is, the more strongly he will try to influence others in order to attain either his own goal or a group goal.

Hypothesis I-3: The amount of influence attempted by a leader (or

[2] This assumption is directly in line with Festinger's hypothesis that the strength of the force to communicate to a group member increases with perception that the recipient will change his opinion in the desired direction (4).

[3] These assumptions permit the derivation of several additional hypotheses. In general we would expect that any determinant of the effectiveness of influence attempts will also be a determinant of the amount of influence attempted provided the leader understands this factor and can perceive its operation in his followers. Thus, for example, the preliminary field study found that noncommissioned officers will attempt more influence in areas where it is clear that they have the backing of their superiors.

member) increases with decreasing certainty of opposing opinion in the recipient.

Again this hypothesis stems directly from the assumption that the attempt to exert influence is guided by the perceived probability of success. Where the recipient shows great certainty in his opposing opinions, he will be perceived as strongly resistant to influence, but where he is uncertain he will seem more inducible.

The determinants of the effectiveness of influence attempted. The behavior of the recipient in response to an influence attempt will be determined, among other things, by the nature of his social relations with the inducer. Our problem here is to try to isolate the relevant dimensions of this relationship. Obviously many can be described which seem reasonably likely determinants of influence. Considering both the findings of previous research and the requirements of conceptual clarity, we have chosen three dimensions which promise to be conceptually independent and empirically uncorrelated: (a) the recipient likes the inducer, (b) the recipient accepts the authority of the inducer's role, (c) the recipient accepts the inducer as an expert (9).

Hypothesis II-1: The effectiveness of an attempt by a leader (or member) to influence another member of the group increases with increasing acceptance of the leader by the recipient.

This hypothesis was earlier confirmed by Back (1). Parallel findings show that the influence of the group over the member is determined by the attractiveness of the group for the member (6, 12, 13). Thus both these hypotheses may be subsumed under the more general hypothesis that the influence of an inducing agent (either group or individual), over a person is a function of the attractiveness of the inducing agent for the person.

Hypothesis II-2: The effectiveness of an influence attempt by the leader increases with increasing readiness of the follower to accept the authority conferred by the leader's role.

What is ordinarily called authority in a military organization combines two factors which should be distinguished. (a) The authority of an officer over his men includes *coercive power,* i.e., the ability to punish his subordinates for noncompliance with his orders. (b) It also includes a predisposition on the part of the subordinate willingly to accept the influence of the officer because he perceives it as *legitimate.* Presumably coercive power will lead to overt conformity without covert change of attitude on the part of the subordinate (5). The acceptance of authority as legitimate, on the other hand, should produce covert changes in attitudes and behavior as well as overt conformity. Hypothesis II-2, since it deals only with the acceptance of authority as legitimate, predicts changes in the private opinions and covert behavior of the men.

Hypothesis II-3: The effectiveness of an influence attempt by the leader (or member) increases with increasing perception that he is an expert in the area of the influence attempt.

This common sense hypothesis also has a long research history, whether as the effect of "expert opinion" (10) or "source credibility" (8). Eventually this hypothesis should be refined with respect to the areas of expertness, the interrelations among them, and the relation of this dimension to other dimensions of interpersonal perception. However, our data do not permit such refined analyses.

Hypothesis II-4: The total amount of influence effected by a leader (or member) over a member increases with increases in the amount of influence attempted.

At the low extreme, it seems obvious that one can expect no influence if there is no communication and no attempt at influence. However, the relation between these two variables is not obviously a linear one: it might well be that attempts to influence beyond a certain level, especially if these attempts are not seen as legitimate, might well result in reduced effectiveness. However, within the more usual range of behavior exhibited by a leader, we would expect a monotonically increasing relationship.

The preliminary field study. Before describing the methods used in these two experiments, it will be worth reporting some of the relevant findings from a preliminary field study (2). This study was conducted on the line maintenance personnel of two aircraft maintenance squadrons located at a training base. The relevant data were collected largely through the use of written questionnaires dealing with a number of attitudes toward matters of concern to the men and of importance to the performance of their daily work. The same questionnaire was used to measure the attitudes of the noncommissioned officers who supervised the men. For each attitude, the noncommissioned officer was asked how strongly he attempted to influence his men to believe as he did. Measures of the acceptance of supervisors were supplied largely by ranked sociometric choices made from lists of the personnel in the entire squadron. Our major measures of the influence of the noncommissioned officer over his airmen consisted of measures showing how closely the airman's attitude was related to the attitude of his noncommissioned officer and to the official beliefs and attitudes which the noncommissioned officer is supposed to support.

In analyzing the amount of influence attempted by noncommissioned officers, we found: (a) the closer the noncommissioned officer's own attitude to the officially approved attitudes of the Air Force, the stronger his influence attempts; (b) the noncommissioned officer attempts much stronger influence on attitudes relevant to the work of the group than on attitudes and opinions unrelated to the work; (c) but there is no relation between the acceptance of the leader and the strength of influence he attempts. The surprising lack of clear positive findings on (c) suggested the need for more carefully controlled research, employing less subjective measures of influence attempted.

The effectiveness of the leader tended to be related to his acceptance both as a spare-time companion and as a crew chief. Finally there was some support for the hypothesis that the stronger the influence attempted by the leader, the greater the amount of change he produced in the attitudes of his subordinates. Both of these determinants of effectiveness seemed to require further checking with better measures of effectiveness. The present experiments check these findings (see Hypotheses I-1, II-1 and II-4).

METHODS

Design of the Experiments

The main reason for employing the experimental method in this phase of research was to test more unequivocally our major hypotheses about the influence of the leader as related to interpersonal relations, and in particular, to determine the direction of causation in these relationships. The experimental design involved two parts sufficiently independent to be considered as two separate experiments. The first—the group judgment test— was designed to study the influence of the leader on the opinions and judgments of his followers, while the second—a card-sorting task—was intended to measure his influence on productivity. The first experiment tested the influence of the leader in a free discussion situation where he was permitted to attempt as much influence as he liked using any method he could devise. In the second, both the methods of influence employed and the amount of influence attempted were held constant in order to discover whether there was a *direct* relationship between the effectiveness of attempted influence and the interpersonal relations between leader and follower.

Both experiments employed much more carefully controlled measurement of the effectiveness of influence than was possible in the field study. Instead of inferring the existence of an influence process from the relationship of the airman's opinion to the opinion of his noncommissioned officer, we brought the influence process into the laboratory and measured the actual changes induced by the leader. In the group judgment test this was accomplished by having the airmen record private judgments before discussion with the noncommissioned officer and after the discussion. In the card-sorting experiment the influence of inductions from the leader was measured by the actual change in the quantity and quality of work performed by the group of airmen.

The major independent variables of interpersonal relationship between leader and followers were not manipulated directly because we could find no method for producing sufficiently large changes in these already established relationships. Instead we selected as subjects all noncommissioned officers of a given classification and hoped that the actual interpersonal relationships with the airmen would show enough variation to permit testing of our hypotheses.

The procedure may be summarized briefly:

1. From existing small work groups in the Air Force we selected the supervisor and three members chosen as far as practicable at random. When they arrived at the experimental room, they were told that their cooperation was needed in several research projects, that they were not being tested in any way, and that they would not be identified.

2. Each subject answered privately a written questionnaire measuring the major independent variables of interpersonal relationships.

3. Next, each group participated in the group judgment test. In this experiment each of the members in the group made a number of individual judgments from a set of stimulus figures. Unknown to the subjects these figures were not all the same. Slightly different forms of each figure were distributed in a way designed to produce planned patterns of disagreement within the group. After the members had completed their preliminary judgment, they held a discussion under instructions to try to reach agreement. After the discussion the group members again recorded their private judgments. Observational data provided the measures of attempted influence, and the changes from the preliminary to the final judgment provided a measure of the effectiveness of influence attempted.

4. Finally, the subjects were presented with the card-sorting task as an investigation of different ways of organizing a group. Three airmen were assigned a task of hand-sorting punched cards according to the number of holes in each card. A scoring system, depending upon the total number of cards sorted, the number correctly sorted, and the number of errors, was described and was stated to be the basis for comparing groups of different organization. The noncommissioned officer in charge of the group was as-

signed the task of checking the work of his three airmen, of comparing their results with those of other groups, and giving the group members instructions which would enable them to improve their performance. He was located in an adjoining room and was required to send all communications to his group by written notes. Actually he was asked to copy four standard notes, the first two instructing the group to slow down in order to make fewer errors, the last two instructing them to speed up. This aspect of the design was similar to the experiment of Schachter, Ellertson, McBride, and Gregory **(13)**.

Subjects. Each group consisted of the supervisor and three of his subordinates taken from groups of instructors in the technical training schools at Chanute Air Force Base, Illinois. In our study, we used only noncommissioned officer supervisors and enlisted men serving under them.

We did not request subjects by name, because we hoped to give them as good an assurance of anonymity as possible, in order to increase the validity of their ratings of each other on the "Group Questionnaire," which provided our data on interpersonal relations. In arranging for subjects, we asked the organizations concerned to select men alphabetically by last name to accompany the supervisors. Probably this procedure was followed in most cases, but we know there were some deviations. To the extent that there was any systematic selection of subjects it may have had the effect of reducing the range in our interpersonal variables; but it is hard to see how it could have introduced any bias into the results obtained.

Thirty-six experimental groups were studied during the spring of 1952. From all of these we obtained usable data for the group judgment test. However, in the card-sorting experiment, mainly because of scheduling difficulties, only 26 groups yielded data which could be used in the final analysis.

The Measures of Interpersonal Relations

Personal acceptance. By acceptance we mean essentially personal attractiveness to, or popularity with, another person. We recognize that there may be several different reasons why one person likes another, and also that one person may like another in certain situations more than in others. However, the variable of personal attractiveness or acceptance has considerable generality and can be treated as though it were approximately unidimensional.

The group questionnaire included four items designed as measures of acceptance. The blunt question "How well do you like him?" was from the beginning regarded as the major measure of this variable, with the other three items included as possible refinements. Since this major measure gave a better distribution of responses and apparently higher validity, it was the only measure used in the analysis. This measure of personal acceptance was:

How well do you like him?

A. He's my best friend in the Air Force.
B. He's one of my best friends.
C. He's a good friend of mine.
D. I like him a lot and would like to know him better.
E. I like him fairly well.
F. I don't have much feeling about him one way or the other.
G. I don't like him very much.
H. I dislike him.

Perceived authority. By perceived authority we mean the disposition of a person to perceive as appropriate and to accept the amount of authority possessed by a person who is in a superior role. We are explicitly interested in the authority inherent in the formal roles of an authority structure.

The questionnaire item for measuring the perceived authority of the non-commissioned officer was as follows:

If he wants to use it, how much authority does the typical NCOIC [4] have over the men he supervises?

—— very little authority
—— some authority: but not much
—— a fair amount of authority
—— quite a lot of authority
—— a great deal of authority

Originally this item was intended to be part of a composite measure which also included an item on the airman's attitudes towards whether the non-commissioned officer had too much or too little authority. However, since less than 2 per cent of the subjects reported that he had too much authority, the analysis was performed with only this one item.

Perceived expertness. It is believed that this factor is particularly important in areas where expertness is perceived as necessary, as for example in the technical aspects of aircraft maintenance. In the card-sorting experiment we did not expect expertness to be at all relevant because we had selected activities where practically no skill or ability or intelligence was required. The group judgment test was obviously a task requiring expertness although it was

---

[4] Noncommissioned officer in charge.

not easy to specify the type of ability required. Accordingly our operational measure was the question:

Would you say he was very intelligent, about average, or what?

A. One of the brightest men I know.
B. Very bright—well above average.
C. A little above average.
D. About average.
E. A little below average.
F. A lot below average.

The Group Judgment Test

The central idea of the group judgment test was to create a controlled discussion in which to measure the influence of the leader. We wanted an even division of opinion in the group in order to balance the pressures to change opinions. In addition we wanted the leader to be opposed equally often to each of his three men. In order to control the patterns of disagreement among members in the group, we adopted the techniques used by Back (1). Two subjects were presented with one form and the other two subjects with slightly different versions of geometric figures requiring judgments of the relative length of lines or the relative areas of plane figures (see Figure 1). In Form I, line B is slightly shorter than line A, but in Form II the difference is reversed. Thus there should be a 2–2 division of opinion in the group.

Twelve such items were constructed so that it would be possible to pair each individual with every other individual four times in even opinion splits. Thus, in each group the members received forms as follows:

No. of items	Received Form I	Received Form II
4	Leader & Member 1	Member 2 & Member 3
4	Leader & Member 2	Member 1 & Member 3
4	Leader & Member 3	Member 1 & Member 2

Considerable work was required for the development of the items used. The problem was to get two forms of each item in which the differences between the figures to be compared were sufficiently great to produce the desired judgment fairly consistently, yet not so great that these judgments would be made with a great deal of confidence. We assumed that too high certainty of judgments was undesirable because it would reduce the probability of change of opinion, in line with Hypothesis I-3. In order to get the optimum amount

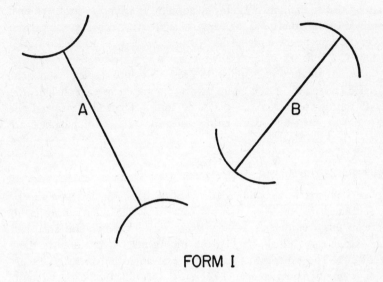

FORM I

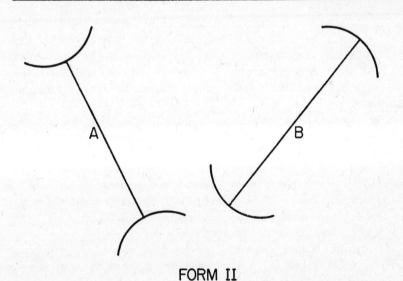

FORM II

FIG. 1. The Two Forms of Item 7 From the Group Judgment Test.

of difference between the two figures of an item, four or five forms of each item were submitted to a group of 61 naive subjects as a "visual comparison test." On the basis of these pre-test data, twelve items were selected designed to produce 2–2 splits in opinion. In the actual experiment 63 per cent of them did in fact produce such splits. In order to reduce suspicion about the amount of disagreement in the group, two additional items were included on which all four subjects received the same form. The test items and the answer booklet containing 5-point rating scales for certainty of judgment are reported in full by Snyder (14).

Administration of the Group Judgment Test

After the subjects had completed the written questionnaires, the experimenter told them that the Air Force was concerned with discrepancies in intelligence reports from agents assigned to the same geographical area, and that it was felt that "discussion between the agents might eliminate these discrepancies." The experiment was justified as an investigation of the accuracy of a group report compared to initial individual reports and post-discussion individual reports.

Seven of the visual comparison items were then presented to the subjects with instructions to make private judgments on the relative magnitude of the two figures in each item, without making any measurements, and to indicate their certainty of each judgment. Subjects were told that they would then discuss their judgments together, and finally would rejudge privately. It was suggested that they might want to jot down a few notes on their answer sheets since they would not have the geometric figures before them during the discussion.

As each subject completed his preliminary judgments the experimenter picked up his test booklet but left the answer sheets for use in the discussion. Subjects then discussed each item in order, with instructions to reach a public group decision as to the "correct" answer. The regular supervisors were designated as group leaders in this decision-making process.

After reaching a group decision on an item, each subject returned to his answer sheet, made another private judgment, and again indicated his degree of certainty before discussing the next item.

After subjects judged, discussed, and rejudged each of the first seven items, the answer sheets were collected and the remaining seven items were administered using the same procedure.

Two attempts were made to increase the pressure toward a change of opinion on the part of the subjects. First, each group was required to reach a decision on a group answer. Second, in giving the instructions, the experimenter commented that "our experience so far has shown that most men are able to improve their answers a lot after the discussion."

On items where there were 2–2 splits the conflict between the two sides frequently was so difficult to resolve that the subjects would appeal to the experimenter for some solution to the dilemma. Evidently they were highly involved and task oriented. There seemed to be no suspicions concerning the validity of the differences in opinion.

Measurement of influence attempts. In order to test our major hypotheses we had to have data on how much—or how hard—each subject attempted to influence the opinions of the others in his group. These measures had to be specific to the content of the test items, since our measures of effectiveness consisted of changes in the test items. After some initial attempts to use more elaborate instruments, we divided all verbal interactions into three observational categories: (a) influence attempts, (b) opinion change, (c) other.

1. *Influence attempts.* In this category were recorded only communications about the content of the item upon which the group was attempting to reach agreement. The following types of attempted influence were included:

    a. an initial statement of the judgment made, *if it was elaborated, defended as correct, or stated with emphasis;*

    b. reiterations of an opinion previously stated;

    c. statements about the stimulus figures of which the intent, as judged by the observers, was to defend the opinion held by the speaker;

    d. communications apparently calculated to reduce the certainty of an opponent's opinion or to question the basis of his judgment;

    e. communications questioning the ability of an opponent to make the required judgments, including joking attacks, such as "I guess you need some glasses;"

    f. statements indicating rejection of influence attempted by others.

2. *Opinion change.* This category might equally well have been designated "acceptance of influence" because it was defined as including all communications indicating overt compliance with an influence attempt. The category "opinion change" was designed quite specifically to provide evidence of overt acceptance of influence, regardless of whether it appeared that the person had actually (covertly) changed his opinion or not. Scored in this category were:

    a. remarks indicating that the individual had actually changed his judgment;

b. statements indicating reduced confidence in an initial judgment;

c. statements conceding the validity of an opponent's reasoning or arguments, unless such statements were clearly "rhetorical" (for example, such responses as, "You may have a point there, but I'm still sure the triangle was bigger," would be scored simply as "influence attempt," but the response, "I'm not so sure you're not right, after all," would be score as "opinion change") ;

d. remarks conceding the group decision to the opposing side, even when qualified by a clear statement that the person had not changed his own opinion.

3. *Other.* The interaction scored under this heading included all communications not recorded in one of the other categories. Much of the interaction so scored could be very easily discriminated, because it consisted of all the communications which did not deal directly with the test material. Thus, it included all "procedural" interaction and all irrelevant or "out-of-field" remarks. It also included remarks aimed at establishing the characteristics of the item under discussion.

The unit in our measure of interaction was the single uninterrupted speech. The temporal sequence of these units within the observation of the single test item was not recorded but the distinction between items was maintained. The observers recorded the person initiating a communication but not the person to whom it was addressed because during the pre-test it became clear that practically all of the interaction categorized as attempted influence was directed toward persons who held the opposite opinion and that it was reaching the two opponents equally.

Computations of the reliability of observation were based upon data from two observers who were both present at 25 of the 29 experimental sessions from which usable observational records were obtained. We selected a sample of about 17 per cent of the data by picking ten groups at random and including, from half of these groups, scores on seven odd-numbered items and, from the remaining half, scores on the seven even-numbered items. An observation "score" was defined as the number of interactions recorded for a single subject in one category on one item. Since there were four subjects in each group, our estimates of reliability are based on 280 scores in each observation category.

We first calculated inter-observer reliability coefficients for "influence attempts" and for "total participation" (the sum of scores in all three categories). The product moment correlation in each case was .92, indicating only fairly good reliability considering the fact that we threw together data from groups and from items which varied greatly in the total volume of interaction recorded.

One further question of reliability was investigated. Could the observers discriminate "influence attempts" from other communications? To answer this question we correlated "influence scores" with the next largest category—"other." The resulting coefficient of .41, while highly significant statistically, is still low enough to prove in conjunction with the high reliability coefficients that the discrimination of influence attempts was meaningful.

Since one of the two regular observers was present at all but one experimental session, his records were used exclusively where possible.

The Card-Sorting Experiment

Experimental task. The card-sorting experiment has already been described as an experiment involving a production task. Several general considerations determined the nature of the task selected. First, the task should be simple and require a minimum of skill or ability so that individual differences would not be a major factor determining performance and so that we could ignore any effects of learning, at least after a very brief familiarization period. Second, the task should permit easy and reliable measurement of both the quantity and quality of performance. Third, the task should be as routine and uninteresting as possible so that the restraining forces of satiation would prevent maximum performance even during the short time of the experiment. If the subjects were already producing as much as possible, there could be no increase in production in response to the influence attempted by the supervisor.

The task selected involved a hand-sorting of machine tabulating cards of the familiar type used in IBM equipment. These cards were punched with holes and had to be classified according to the number of holes. The only way the subjects could sort the cards correctly was to count the holes. The measure of quantity was the number of cards sorted, and the measure of quality was the proportion of cards correctly sorted.

The number of holes in each card ranged from 21 to 25. This number was great enough so that the cards could not be sorted by direct inspection; instead the subjects had to go through the boring procedure of counting each hole. Yet the time required to classify each card was so short that no substantial variation in performance measure would be due to units of production partially completed at the time the cards were collected.

All three sorters in the experiment placed the cards into a single five-compartment tray. Thus from their point of view the task was a group task and the product could be measured only as a group product. We may assume that most of them perceived that the supervisor had no information about what they produced as individuals. Hence, they were to a degree "protected" from the supervisor and at the same time they were prevented from effectively competing with one another for the supervisor's approval. In short, we had created a cooperative group in which the actions of any member had equal consequences for all four.

Administration of the card-sorting experiment. This experiment was presented to the subjects as a study of the best way to *organize* a group to do a job—how the work should be divided up, how it should be supervised, and so on. The experimenter explained the standardized task and the scoring system for comparing different groups. He pointed out that the task, like many routine jobs in the Air Force, would be organized so that the supervisor could not work right with his men. Instead he would be working in another room. In order to prevent too close supervision, the experimenter explained, the man in charge would be required to communicate to his subordinates by written notes. He would be given certain information about the speed and accuracy achieved by other groups, and this information could be used as a basis for sending written instructions to his own group concerning the quantity and quality of their work.

After the leader had been taken from the room and the subjects had worked for several minutes, the experimenter came back, picked up the filled tray, replaced it with an empty one, and carried the sorted cards into the other room, ostensibly to be checked by the supervisor. For the purpose of recording performance, the total sorting time was divided into nine periods of four minutes each. The first three periods were used as a base line against which to measure changes in productivity and errors. For the next three periods the subjects were induced by the supervisor to work slowly; they received the first message at the beginning of Period 5. The last three periods were fast periods with the subjects receiving messages to speed up at the beginning of Period 7 and again at the beginning of Period 8.

Influence attempts by the supervisor. As soon as he had been separated from the other members of the group, each supervisor was given a brief explanation of the experiment and asked to copy off in his own handwriting each of the four messages on a separate slip of paper. The messages, in order of delivery to the sorters, were the following:

1. "Too many mistakes. Take it slower."
2. "Slow down a lot. It will give us a better score in the end."
3. "It's going fine. Forget about mistakes and try for speed."

4. "Sort as fast as you can. Never mind about mistakes. Let's try for a record."

It was hoped that the apparent inconsistency between the first two and the last two notes would appear plausible to the subjects because of the elaborate scoring system and the detailed description of the supervisor's job given by the experimenter. As it turned out, this effort at plausibility may not have been entirely successful, as indicated by the informal group interviews conducted with subjects at the end of each experimental session. Comments by some of these subjects did suggest that there was some suspicion about the content of the notes, but how frequently there was enough suspicion to have an important effect on the responses is impossible to judge accurately.

Nevertheless these highly controlled, experimental, influence attempts by the supervisor did have an effect on the performance of the sorters.

The regular trend in Table 1 indicates that the messages influenced the behavior of the sorters. Despite considerable variation in over-all performance, every group worked faster in the "fast periods" than in the "base periods." All but four of the groups worked more slowly in the "slow periods" than in the "base periods." We can conclude that the experimentally controlled influence was successful.

TABLE 1

GROUP MEAN PRODUCTION AND ERRORS FOR EACH PERIOD OF THE CARD
SORTING EXPERIMENT *

		Mean Number of Cards Sorted	Mean Percentage of Errors
Base Periods:	1	54.2	12.1%
	2	54.3	8.1
	3	56.3	8.4
Slow Periods:	4	48.1	5.8
	5	44.7	5.8
	6	49.4	5.2
Fast Periods:	7	60.4	6.2
	8	64.8	9.7
	9	69.5	7.9

* Based on 25 rather than 26 groups, since for one group an error in collecting the cards prevents separating periods 5 and 6.

RESULTS OF THE GROUP JUDGMENT EXPERIMENT

Determinants of Attempted Influence

Acceptance. Hypothesis I-1 predicts that the amount of influence attempted by a leader (or member) will increase with increasing acceptance of him. Comparing leaders of different groups, we should find that the more accepted leaders attempt more influence. Within a group we should find that the leader (or member) directs more influence toward those who accept him.

The correlations for testing the predictions comparing different groups are presented in Table 2.

As predicted, those leaders who are more accepted by their subordinates tend to attempt more influence ($r = .28$, $p = .08$). Likewise, members attempt more influence when they are more accepted by the leader ($r = .54$, $p < .01$). These two confirmations of the hypothesis are not independent since the amount of influence attempted by the leader correlates .55 with the amount attempted by the members of the same group. However, if we partial out the amount of influence attempted by the leader, the correlation between influence attempted by members and acceptance of the members by the leader drops only to .50.

All the other correlations in Table 2 are not significant, so we can rule out the alternative hypothesis that the amount of influence attempted by an inducer is determined by how much he likes the inducee.

Considering all the correlations in Table 2, it is clear that the amount of influence attempted in the group is determined by a process of interaction

TABLE 2

CORRELATIONS RELEVANT TO ACCEPTANCE AND ATTEMPTED INFLUENCE

	1	2	3	4
1. Acceptance of leader by members.......... ..		.18	.28	.12
2. Acceptance of members by the leader..... ..		..	.20	.54
3. Influence attempted by the leader........ ..		..	..	.55
4. Influence attempted by members........ ..		..	..	..

Notes:

1. N for all correlations is 29, the number of groups from which we have observation data.

2. The measure of acceptance of leader by members is the sum of all the ratings of the leader by the members. The measure of acceptance of members is the sum of the ratings of those members by the leader.

3. The measure of influence attempted is the mean frequency per item (and per person) for all items where an initial 2-2 split occurred.

in which the behavior of all persons is highly interdependent. Though it cannot be inferred with certainty, the results suggest that the leader is able to set the tone for his group to a high degree, even in a situation where his official position seems largely irrelevant. This interpretation is supported by a multiple correlation of .69 between the amount of influence attempted by members and the amount attempted by their leader together with the extent to which they are accepted by their leader. That is, the amount of influence attempted by a member is determined by the amount attempted by his leader and how much the leader likes him. This may be considered quite a high correlation since certainty of initial opinion (the other known determinant of attempted influence) is not taken into account here.

In order to test the prediction from Hypothesis I-1 that a person *within* a group will direct more influence toward those who like him, two additional analyses were made—one for leaders and one for members. Within a group any inducer, for example the leader, will on various items attempt influence toward three *pairs* of opponents: members 1 and 2, members 1 and 3, and members 2 and 3. For each group, the mean number of influence attempts made to the pair of opponents with lowest acceptance of the leader was subtracted from the mean number made to the pair with highest acceptance of the leader. This turned out to be a relatively crude analysis because of the number of tied scores for acceptance and because of the overlapping membership in the high and low pairs. In both analyses, the differences were in the predicted direction but not significantly different from zero.

A third method of analyzing the data combines the effects of variations within and among groups. Treating each item separately, we tabulated the acceptance scores for the particular opponents on that item and the amount of influence attempted by the leader on the same item. The mean influence score, when both opponents accepted the leader highly, was 5.12; when the acceptance by one was high but by the other was low, the mean influence score was 4.01; when acceptance by both opponents was low, the influence attempted was 2.67. In short, almost twice as much influence is attempted toward high- as toward low-accepting opponents.

Certainty. Our remaining hypotheses in Group I relate the strength of attempted influence to the degree of certainty characterizing the opinions of the participants in a discussion. The analysis has been restricted to the data relating to leaders, not only because we are mainly concerned with the influence attempts of leaders, but also because the interdependence of all the factors operating in the group leads to difficulties in interpreting findings from an analysis in which each of the several members is considered separately as providing an independent test.

Our measures of certainty were the certainty ratings which accompanied the judgments made by the subjects on each of the test figures. These ratings were assigned values from 1, "completely certain" to 5, "very uncertain." In this analysis, we shall be concerned only with the ratings accompanying the preliminary judgments. As a subject's certainty changed, it undoubtedly had an effect upon his readiness to attempt influence, but to take this into account would require not only the final certainty ratings but also a continuous record of changes during the discussion, which could not be obtained.

Hypothesis I-2 states: The amount of influence attempted by a leader (or member) increases with increasing certainty in his own opinion. The first two analyses made to test this hypothesis parallel the "among groups" and "within groups" analyses used in the study of the acceptance variable. First, for each leader the mean initial certainty rating and the mean number of influence attempts made by the leader on the 2-2 split items were calculated. A Pearson r was then computed between these 29 pairs of means. The obtained r was $-.31$ which is in the expected direction and is statistically significant at the .05 level. Thus, in accordance with the hypothesis, leaders with relatively high initial certainty tended to make more influence attempts than leaders with relatively low initial certainty.

Hypothesis I-2 also predicts that a leader will tend to make more influence attempts on those items on which he is relatively certain than on those on which he is relatively uncertain. The test of this prediction was done as follows: for each leader, items with certainty ratings of 1 ("completely certain") and 2 ("quite certain") were placed in one set and those with certainty ratings 3 ("fairly certain"), 4 ("rather uncertain"), and 5 ("very uncertain") were placed in another. Eight of the leaders made initial certainty ratings which were all in the "high-certainty" set, and two made all their ratings at the low-certainty level. An analysis for the remaining 19 leaders showed an average of 1.27 more influence attempts per item for the "high-" than for the "low-certainty" items. A t-test for correlated measures indicates this is statistically significant at the .08 level ($t = 1.88$, $df = 18$, two-tailed test).

The magnitude of the relationship stated in Hypothesis I-2 can be best demonstrated by an analysis which combines the two effects reported above. We categorized all of the items from all of the leaders according to the leader's initial certainty on the particular item. For each category, Table 3 shows the mean number of influence attempts per item made by the leader.

From the three analyses together, we may conclude that there is a substantial and significant relationship confirming Hypothesis I-2.

TABLE 3

LEADER'S CERTAINTY AS A DETERMINANT OF HIS INFLUENCE ATTEMPTS

	Leader's Initial Certainty	Mean Leader Influence Attempts	Number of Items
High	1................	4.60	62
	2................	4.95	92
	3................	3.14	49
Low	4 and 5 *...........	2.06	16

* These categories were combined because category 5 was used only a few times on initial judgment.

The final hypothesis in this group is Hypothesis I-3: The amount of influence attempted by a leader (or member) increases with decreasing certainty of opposing opinion in the recipient. Here, if data on recipiency of influence attempts were more complete, leader influence could be related to the certainty of each opponent separately. Since these data could not be obtained reliably, the certainty of both opponents must be considered jointly, and the test of this hypothesis is perhaps somewhat less powerful as a consequence.

The method of analysis used was similar to that for Hypothesis I-2. Both "among groups" and "within groups" analyses were accomplished. First, the opponents' mean certainty rating per item was determined for each group, and these mean certainty ratings were correlated with the mean numbers of influence attempts of the respective leaders. The obtained Pearson r was .07 ($N=29$). This is far from statistically significant.

In the "within groups" analysis, the mean certainty of the two opponents was computed for each item. Then for each leader the items were divided into those on which the opponents showed high certainty (all items for which the opponents' mean certainty rating was 2.00 or less) and those on which they showed low certainty (all items for which the opponents' mean rating was greater than 2.00). The mean number of leader influence attempts per item was computed separately for each of the two sets of items for each leader. Finally, the algebraic difference in number of influence attempts made on the two sets of items was calculated for each leader, and a t-test was performed on the distribution of differences. For the 24 groups in which there were one or more items in each of the two categories, the mean difference in average number of leader influence attempts was .61. Though in the predicted direction, this difference is significant at only the .15 level.

In order to examine the combined effects of variations within and among leaders, we made a cross-break (similar to Table 3) of the mean influence attempted for items categorized according to the certainty of the opponents. The results showed no relation except for a slight trend at the extremes.

Thus all three analyses are consistent in showing no significant confirmation of Hypothesis I-3. Since most groups started the discussion by sharing their judgments and certainty ratings, the negative results are probably not due to inadequate perception of the opponent's certainty. It seems more likely that a contrary process was operating simultaneously: when the opponent was less certain he changed more quickly and hence the leader could attempt less influence and still obtain his objective.

Determinants of the Effectiveness of the Leader

The remaining hypotheses concern effectiveness of attempted influence. According to these hypotheses, the noncommissioned officer will be more successful in influencing his subordinates to the extent that they like him, they accept the authority of his role, they perceive him as an expert,[5] and he attempts more influence.

The analyses for these hypotheses focus on the covert influence rather than the overt influence of the leader. Thus the opinion changes dealt with are changes from initial private opinion to final private opinion rather than changes from initial private opinion to the group answer. Likewise the changes in certainty of opinion reflect private, covert influence. However, a few comments about the leaders' overt influence seem appropriate. Each test situation provided by the group judgment test was an equilibrium situation, i.e., the subjects found themselves in a decision situation in which—for the group to accomplish its task of submitting a group answer—it was necessary for one side or the other to give way. Usually as soon as any one person had indicated a change of opinion, the discussion moved rapidly to a close, either with or without the expressed agreement of the remaining member. Despite the fact that the experimental activity was far removed from the usual role of the noncommissioned officer, the final group answer more frequently agreed with the initial private opinion of the leader and his partner than with the initial opinions of the leader's opponents ($p = .02$ by chi^2). Also, there was a tendency (not statistically significant) for the noncommissioned officer's influence on the group answer to be related to his acceptance by his opponents.

[5] The three interpersonal variables were found to have little relationship to each other. The highest intercorrelation among them was .27 ($N = 36$) between members' acceptance of the leader and the degree of expertness they perceived the leader to have.

As already indicated, our chief interest is in the covert opinion changes. In 161 (or 59 per cent) of the 273 2-2 split situations for which data were obtained, at least one group member made such a change. The leader showed less tendency to change opinion than did the leader's partner and the leader's partner less than the leader's opponents, but the differences were small.

Opinion changes in relation to acceptance. Hypothesis II-1 says the more the group leader is accepted by another member of the group, the more effective will be his attempts to influence this member. One can, on the basis of this hypothesis, predict that the leaders who are highly accepted by their subordinates will be more effective in producing opinion changes than will leaders who are not so highly accepted. This prediction has been tested by comparing leaders among groups.

For each group we computed two indices: the sum of the three members' acceptance of the leader, and an index of leader effectiveness. In this situation, the success of the leader in influencing his group includes inducing his opponents to change their opinions, preventing his partner from switching to the opposite side, and resisting a change of his own opinion. Accordingly, this index of leader effectiveness scored positively changes by opponents and negatively changes by the leader and by his partner. The analysis utilizing this index yielded a Pearson r of .38 (p is approximately .03), so Hypothesis II-1 is confirmed using this measure of leader effectiveness.[6]

The above test of Hypothesis II-1 is somewhat crude because it neglects: (a) the fact that leaders tended to have most influence over the members who liked them most (as predicted by the hypothesis), and (b) the influence of the opponent on the leader (Hypothesis II-1 would predict that leaders will change most toward opponents whom they like most). Therefore an analysis which includes the two-way influence process should account for more of the variance in leader effectiveness than does the simple index summing acceptance of the leader by the three group members. Using the full scale of answers to the question "How well do you like him?" each leader-opponent pair was classified into one of three categories: (a) the leader is more highly accepted by the subordinate than the subordinate is by the leader, (b) they accept each other equally, and (c) the leader is less highly accepted. For each opponent a tabulation was made of the number of 2-2 split items on which he changed toward the leader and the number of items on which he did not change. Change in opponent opinion occurred in 29 per cent of the

---

[6] An index consisting of only the changes of opinion by the opponents yielded an insignificant trend in the same direction.

235 cases where the leader was more highly accepted, 20 per cent of the 185 cases where the leader was equally accepted, and in only 15 per cent of the 127 cases where the leader was less highly accepted. Thus the leader accomplishes almost twice as much influence when he is better liked than when he is less liked by his opponent.

Changes in certainty in relation to acceptance. The certainty ratings which accompanied the subjects' judgments on each item were obtained to provide an indicator of the effectiveness of influence attempts which would be more sensitive than the all-or-none measures based on opinion change. Two predictions regarding the relation of opponents' certainty ratings and acceptance of the leader were made on the basis of Hypothesis II-1. First, for opponents who changed their opinions from disagreeing with the leader on initial private judgment to agreeing with him on final private judgment, we would predict that high acceptors of the leader would be more confident of their new judgment than low acceptors. In other words, one would anticipate a positive correlation between acceptance of the leader and the certainty which the opponents have in their new judgments. The reasoning is that those who accept the leader more highly will be more dependent upon him for feeling their judgments are correct; having changed from disagreement to agreement with the leader, they will have a relatively greater sense of support for their final judgments. Second, those opponents who do not change will have their opinions shaken somewhat and they will respond by decreasing their certainty ratings.

Analyses were made both among groups and within groups to test the first prediction among opponents who changed toward the leader. The among-groups analysis was based on only 19 groups, some groups being omitted because certainty ratings were not available and some because there was not more than one instance in which an opponent made a change in judgment toward the leader. This analysis yielded an r of .53 ($p<.01$), indicating that those groups in which the members were more accepting of the leader tended to be those whose members were more certain of their new opinions. On the other hand the within-groups analysis failed to confirm the hypothesis although it was in the predicted direction. This analysis involved comparison of the mean certainty scores of the high-accepting and the low-accepting opponent in 16 groups. Since most opponents made only one or two changes from disagreement to agreement with the leader, the mean certainty scores involved are not very reliable. The low reliability and the small number of groups could account for failure to achieve a statistically significant result.

The second prediction about the relation of the opponent's certainty ratings and his acceptance of the leader was tested using only an opponent who did not change his opinion to agree with the leader and who knew (on the basis of the group discussion and public group decision) that his final judgment was different from the leader's final judgment. The prediction was that such opponents who were high acceptors would show more decrease (or less increase) in certainty from initial to final private judgment than would low acceptors. This prediction is based on much the same rationale as the first prediction, namely, that high acceptors are more dependent upon the leader for support for their opinions and thus will be more influenced toward uncertainty by expressions of counter-opinion on the part of the leader.

Examination of the data shows that, under the conditions specified by the second prediction, opponents tended to feel increased confidence in their judgments regardless of the level of their acceptance of the leader. However, the degree of increased confidence in judgments counter to the leader's was less in the case of high than in the case of low acceptors. The correlation was $-.29$ (N$=25$, $p=.08$), meaning that there was a near-significant tendency for the groups with high leader acceptance to be those in which opponents registered relatively small increases in certainty of judgment.

The within-groups analysis for the second prediction involved computing separately for each nonchanging opponent in each group the mean change in certainty ratings on items which met the necessary specifications. Then, in each group, the mean certainty change for the opponent with lowest leader acceptance was subtracted from that for the opponent with highest leader acceptance. The mean of the differences so obtained was $-.82$, showing that, on the average, the high acceptor in a group registered a smaller degree of increase in certainty than did the low acceptor in the same group. The mean difference of $-.82$ on the certainty scale is significantly different from zero at the .03 level of confidence (N$=22$, $t=2.00$, $df=21$).

Summary of the evidence for Hypothesis II-1. All of the evidence supports the hypothesis that the effectiveness of an attempt by a leader (or member) to influence another member of the group increases with increasing acceptance of the leader by the recipient.

1. More accepted leaders have more influence ($r=.38$, $p=.03$).

2. The leader accomplishes more influence when he is better liked by his opponent than when his opponent is better liked by him.

3. Opponents who changed their opinions toward the leader who was better liked were more certain of their new opinions ($r=.53$, $p<.01$). Within groups there was a trend in the same direction.

4. Opponents who did not change their opinions were less certain when

they liked the leader more ($r = -.29$, $p = .08$ among groups; and $p = .03$ within groups).

Perceived authority as a determinant of effectiveness. Hypothesis II-2 states: the effectiveness of an influence attempt by the leader increases with increasing readiness of the follower to accept the authority conferred by the leader's role.

The analyses of changes in opinion (using differences within groups and the Pearson correlation among groups) showed no relation to perceived authority. However, a cross-break of the data suggests a curvilinear relationship between perceived authority of the leader and his effectiveness in changing opponents' opinions. Subjects who said that the typical noncommissioned officer has "a good deal of authority" were influenced by their own supervisors almost twice as much as those who responded with "a great deal of authority" or only "a fair amount."

Perceived expertness as a determinant of effectiveness. Hypothesis II-3 states: the effectiveness of an influence attempt by the leader (or member) increases with increasing perception that he is an expert in the area of the influence attempt. Analyses were made both among groups and within groups to test this hypothesis.

For the among-groups analysis, a Pearson r was computed between group indices for perceived expertness and leader effectiveness (the same measure used in the analysis of acceptance).[7] The obtained correlation was $-.32$ ($N = 36$). Since high scores on the perceived expertness measure represent low perceived expertness, this correlation is in the expected direction and significant beyond the .05 level.

The procedure used for the within-groups analysis was the same as that used in connection with acceptance of the leader. A leader effectiveness index (based only on changes in opponent judgment to conform to leader judgment) was computed separately for each opponent in each group. Then, from each group, two opponents were selected: the one who perceived the most expertness in the leader and the one who perceived the least. The leader effectiveness score for the opponent who perceived the least expertness was, in each group, subtracted from the leader effectiveness score for the opponent who perceived the most expertness, and a t-test was made to determine whether the mean of the distribution of differences in leader effectiveness scores was significantly different from zero. The obtained mean of the differences in leader effectiveness was .10, significant between the .05 and .10

---

[7] An index consisting of only the changes of opinion by the opponents again yielded a lower correlation of $-.19$.

level ($t = 1.59$, $df = 29$).[8] As one would expect, this much cruder analysis yields a less significant relationship.[9]

Effectiveness and attempted influence. The final hypothesis predicts that the total amount of influence effected by a leader over a member will increase with increasing influence attempts by the leader.

Using both previous measures of effectiveness, two analyses of the relation within groups and two analyses among groups were made. None of these four analyses showed a significant relation.

On theoretical grounds, we would expect no relationship where the acceptance of the leader was zero; where the leader was disliked, an inverse relation. Accordingly it seemed wise to try an analysis which controlled on acceptance of the leader. We also know that the amount of influence attempted by the leader correlates .55 with the amount attempted by the members (cf. Table 2). In such an argument between opposing sides, it seems likely that absolute increases in the frequency of influence attempted by the leader were being offset by corresponding increases by his opponents. Thus the analysis should also examine the amount of influence attempted by the leader *relative to* the amount attempted by members.

In the last 29 groups, where observational data were available, there were 218 items on which two members opposed the leader and his partner. Thus there were 436 cases where the change of opinion of one opponent could be related to the amount of influence directed by the leader toward the pair of opponents.

Table 4 shows the percentage of these cases where the opponent changed his final private opinion to agree with the leader. In the upper half of the table, opinion change is related to the absolute frequency of influence attempted by the leader; in the lower half, opinion change is related to the amount of influence attempted by the leader expressed as a percentage of the total amount of influence attempted by all four members of the group. In both halves, Table 4 gives the breakdown for high and low acceptance of the leader by the opponent.

For highly accepted leaders there appears to be a curvilinear relation between effectiveness and absolute frequency of influence attempted, but this curvilinearity disappears when using the relative measure of influence at-

[8] In the within-group analysis, six cases were lost because all three members in these groups made the same response on the item used to measure perceived expertness of the leader.

[9] An analysis which drew on both the variance within groups and the variance among groups confirmed Hypothesis II-3 at the .01 level.

TABLE 4

OPINION CHANGE IN RELATION TO ATTEMPTED INFLUENCE

Absolute Frequency of Influence Attempted by the Leader	Percentage Opinion Change by Opponents Where Acceptance of the Leader was:	
	High	Low
0 to 2	21.1 (109) [1]	17.3 (75)
3 to 5	27.4 (91)	23.6 (55)
6 to 8	43.8 (32)	18.8 (16)
9 or more	13.0 (46)	16.7 (12)
	24.5 (278)	19.6 (158)
Influence Attempted by Leader as a Percentage of Total		
0 to 9%	9.8 (41)	10.5 (19)
10 to 19%	23.8 (63)	15.8 (57)
20 to 29%	17.6 (74)	15.0 (40)
30 to 39%	24.6 (57)	33.3 (21)
40% or more	51.0 (43)	33.3 (21)
	24.5 (278)	19.6 (158)

[1] Figures in parentheses indicate the number of cases on which the percentage in each cell is based.

tempted. A weaker trend of the same kind occurs for leaders who are low on acceptance. Clearly, there is no substantial correspondence between the greatest absolute attempts and the greatest relative attempts, or we should obtain the same type of relationship for both measures. Instead the greatest absolute frequency is associated with the smallest change whereas the greatest relative frequency is associated with the greatest change. Thus it appears to have been the "last word" which was important in producing change—in our conceptualization, it was the extra increment in a balanced system of mounting forces which finally produced a resultant sufficient to overcome the restraining force against change of opinion by one of the members. The highly accepted leaders were prepared to make more frequent attempts (see Table 2) to test the limits of their effectiveness, but they also got the last word more frequently.

In summary, the predicted relation of effectiveness to absolute frequency of influence attempted was not supported, perhaps because of a trend toward a curvilinear relation. Effectiveness was related to the relative frequency of influence attempted, though the significance of this relationship was not tested.

RESULTS OF THE CARD-SORTING EXPERIMENT

The aims of the card-sorting experiment, in contrast to those of the group judgment test, were quite circumscribed: (a) to test Hypothesis II-1 which asserts that the more the leader (or member) is accepted by another member of the group, the more effective will be his attempts to influence this member; and (b) to determine the relation between leader effectiveness and members' acceptance of the authority of the noncommissioned officer role. In addition, the relation between leader effectiveness and group members' acceptance of one another was examined.

The measure of leader effectiveness used in the card-sorting experiment consisted of the ratio: number of cards correctly sorted during the last two speed-up periods, to total number of cards correctly sorted in all periods.

Some of the principal characteristics of this measure of leader effectiveness and the reasons why these characteristics appeared desirable may be listed.

1. The measure reflects the extent to which output during "fast" periods exceeded output during "slow" and "base" periods. Response to "fast" and "slow" instructions are both weighted to some degree in this single measure.

2. The measure involves comparison between output during the last two "fast" periods and total output rather than between all three "fast" periods and total output. In designing the experiment a satiating task was purposely chosen with the hope of maximizing the restraining forces on the sorters. Actually, production continued to mount throughout the last three periods; but observations indicated, and comments in post-experimental interviews confirmed, that the need to relax increased rapidly for the sorters as the experiment drew to a close. If our reasoning is valid, differences in effectiveness should be most evident toward the end of a session. The decision was therefore made to base computations of increase in output upon performance in the last two rather than all three of the "fast" periods.

3. The measure, by counting only correct sorts, considers quality as well as quantity of output. The messages introducing the fast periods of the experiment had instructed the subjects to "forget about mistakes" in the interest of speed, but in the context of the task as it had been defined for the subjects, the instruction could be taken literally only by someone who wanted to defeat the purpose of the attempted influence. The correlation between change in speed and change in percentage error from the slow to the fast periods was found to be $-.31$ ($N=78$, the number of card-sorters) showing that those who increased their output the most tended to be those who increased their errors the least. Apparently, the second set of messages, regardless of their

precise wording, had the effect of establishing a generalized pressure toward improved performance; and, as suspected, subjects who responded least readily to the pressure for speed were most ready to take advantage of the permission to relax on accuracy. On this basis, the conclusion was drawn that quality as well as quantity of performance needed to be taken into account.

Acceptance and Effectiveness of the Leader

The analysis employed for studying the relationship between acceptance of the leader and effectiveness of the leader was an "among-groups" analysis. In other words, an index of effectiveness of the leaders and an index of acceptance of the leader (the sum of the ratings of the leader by the three members) were obtained for each of the 26 groups, and the correlation between the pairs of indices was computed. The correlation was .42, showing that the more effective leaders tended to be those who were most highly accepted by their men. Since the obtained r is in the direction predicted and significant at better than the .05 level, the results of the card-sorting experiment confirm Hypothesis II-1.

Perceived Authority and Effectiveness of the Leader

The among-groups correlation of leader effectiveness and the amount of authority group members perceived as residing in the noncommissioned officer role was only .08. The tendency toward a curvilinear relationship which was found in analysis of the group judgment test failed to show up in the card-sorting experiment.

Cohesiveness and Effectiveness of the Leader

It seems reasonable to expect that a leader will be effective in influencing his men partly through his ability to influence group standards. If this be the case, the leader's effectiveness should be greater in cohesive groups where the members are attracted to one another, for we know that more cohesive groups have more influence over their members (1, 6, 12, 13). In the card-sorting experiment this prediction is supported by an obtained correlation of .31, significant at approximately the .06 level, between intermember acceptance and leader effectiveness.

Finally, a multiple correlation coefficient was computed between leader effectiveness on the one hand and the two variables of acceptance of the leader and intermember acceptance on the other. The multiple correlation coefficient and the correlations involved in its computation were as follows:

	r
Effectiveness (1) vs Acceptance of Leader (2)	.42
Effectiveness (1) vs Intermember Acceptance (3)	.31
Acceptance of Leader (2) vs Intermember Acceptance (3)	.64
Multiple Correlation ($R_{1.23}$)	.54

These results suggest that a sizable portion of the group-to-group variance in leader effectiveness can be accounted for in terms of members' acceptance of the leader and of one another. Also of interest is the strong tendency ($r=.64$) for groups in which members accept one another highly to be groups in which the members express a high degree of acceptance of the leader.

SUMMARY AND CONCLUSIONS

Two experiments were conducted to test seven hypotheses about the exertion of influence on judgments and behavior in small groups.

Determinants of Influence Attempted

In the preliminary field study, the amount of attempted influence reported by the noncommissioned officer was strongly related to organizational factors (the extent to which his own attitudes were officially approved and the relevance of the attitudes to the job), but was not related to interpersonal acceptance. In the first experiment these organizational factors were minimized by using judgments or opinions unrelated to the jobs of the subjects; hence interpersonal factors should account for more of the variance.

Hypothesis I-1: The amount of influence attempted by a leader (or member) over a given recipient increases with increasing acceptance of him by the recipient. Taken together, the several analyses of this relation for leaders and for members both within and among groups gives strong confirmation of the hypothesis. Apparently it is a more important determinant for members ($r=.54$) than for formal leaders ($r=.28$).

Hypothesis I-2: The amount of influence attempted by a leader (or member) increases with increasing certainty in his own opinion. Taken together, the three analyses (for the leaders only) significantly confirm the hypothesis.

Hypothesis I-3: The amount of influence attempted by a leader (or member) increases with decreasing certainty of opposing opinion in the recipient. Three separate analyses are consistent in showing no significant confirmation of the hypothesis. Perhaps there was a contrary process operating simultaneously: when the opponent was less certain he changed more quickly, and hence the leader could attempt less influence and still reach his goal. Both of these opposing processes are consistent with the basic assumption that the occurrence of an influence attempt is determined by the perceived probability of success in achieving some goal.

Determinants of Effectiveness

In the field study there was a tendency for influence on opinions to be correlated with interpersonal relations. The first experiment strongly confirms this finding and demonstrates that the interpersonal relation is the independent variable. The second experiment further confirms the finding and extends it to the ability of the leader to influence the productivity of the group.

Hypothesis II-1: The effectiveness of an attempt by a leader (or member) to influence another member of the group increases with increasing acceptance of the leader by the recipient. This hypothesis was significantly confirmed for leader influence on: opinion changes ($r=.38$), changes in the certainty of these opinions ($r=.53$ and $r=.29$), and the productivity of the group ($r=.42$). In this test, the quantity and quality of influence attempts were exactly controlled. The leader's effectiveness in changing opinion is even more strongly related to *reciprocal* acceptance (how much the leader is accepted *relative to* how much he accepts the recipient) when there is opposition between the two. In the production experiment, where there is no such opposition, the effectiveness of the leader is also related to how much the members accept one another ($r=.31$).

Hypothesis II-2: The effectiveness of an influence attempt by the leader increases with increasing readiness of the follower to accept the authority conferred by the leader's role. The data from both experiments failed to confirm this hypothesis. It is possible that the measure of authority was inadequate or that the experimental situation excluded the operation of formal authority.[10]

Hypothesis II-3: The effectiveness of an influence attempt by the leader (or member) increases with increasing perception that he is an expert in the area of the influence attempt. In the experiment on opinions this hypothesis was supported by the variance among groups ($r=.32$) and by a similar trend within groups ($.05 \ p=.10$).

---

[10] A subsequent experiment by John R. P. French, Jr., and Bertram Raven confirms the hypothesis.

Hypothesis II-4: The total amount of influence effected by a leader over a member increases with increases in the amount of influence attempted. As in the field study, this hypothesis was not supported in the first experiment, perhaps because of a trend toward a curvilinear relation. However, effectiveness was related to the *relative* amount of influence attempted, though the significance of this relation could not be tested.

REFERENCES

1. Back, K. W. Influence through social communication. *J. abnorm. soc. Psychol.,* 1951, 46, 9-23.

2. Biddle, B. J., French, J. R. P., Jr., & Moore, J. W. Some aspects of leadership in the small work group. A report to the U. S. Air Force, 1953.

3. Cartwright, D., & Zander, A. *Group dynamics: research and theory.* Evanston: Row, Peterson, 1953.

4. Festinger, L. Informal social communication. *Psychol. Rev.,* 1950, 57, 271-282.

5. Festinger, L. An analysis of compliant behavior. In M. Sherif & M. O. Wilson (Eds.). *Group relations at the crossroads.* New York: Harper, 1953.

6. Festinger, L., Schachter, S., & Back, K. *Social pressures in informal groups.* New York: Harper, 1950.

7. Havron, M. D., Fay, R. J., & Goodacre, D. M. Research on the effectiveness of small military units, PRS Report No. 885, Washington: Personnel Research Section, Adjutant General's Office, U. S. Army, 1951.

8. Hovland, C. I., & Weiss, W. The influence of source credibility on communication effectiveness. *Publ. Opin. Quart.,* 1951, 15, 635-650.

9. Lippitt, R., Polansky, N., Redl, F., & Rosen, S. The dynamics of power. *Hum. Relat.,* 1952, 5, 37-64.

10. Moore, H. T. The comparative influence of majority and expert opinion. *Amer. J. Psychol.,* 1921, 32, 16-20.

11. Newcomb, T. Autistic hostility and social reality. *Hum. Relat.,* 1947, 1, 69-87.

12. Schachter, S. Deviation, rejection, and communication. *J. abnorm. soc. Psychol.,* 1951, 46, 190-207.

13. Schachter, S., Ellertson, N., McBride, D., & Gregory, D. An experimental study of cohesiveness and productivity. *Hum. Relat.,* 1951, 4, 229-238.

14. Snyder, R. An experimental study of the influence of leaders in small work groups. Unpublished doctor's dissertation, Massachusetts Institute of Technology, 1953.

9

THE BASES OF SOCIAL POWER

JOHN R. P. FRENCH, JR. AND BERTRAM RAVEN

The processes of power are pervasive, complex, and often disguised in our society. Accordingly one finds in political science, in sociology, and in social psychology a variety of distinctions among different types of social power or among qualitatively different processes of social influence (1, 6, 14, 20, 23, 29, 30, 38, 41). Our main purpose is to identify the major types of power and to define them systematically so that we may compare them according to the changes which they produce and the other effects which accompany the use of power. The phenomena of power and influence involve a dyadic relation between two agents which may be viewed from two points of view: (a) What determines the behavior of the agent who exerts power? (b) What determines the reactions of the recipient of this behavior? We take this second point of view and formulate our theory in terms of the life space of P, the person upon whom the power is exerted. In this way we hope to define basic concepts of power which will be adequate to explain many of the phenomena of social influence, including some which have been described in other less genotypic terms.

Recent empirical work, especially on small groups, has demonstrated the necessity of distinguishing different types of power in order to account for the different effects found in studies of social influence. Yet there is no doubt that more empirical knowledge will be needed to make final decisions concerning the necessary differentiations, but this knowledge will be obtained only by research based on some preliminary theoretical distinctions. We present such preliminary concepts and some of the hypotheses they suggest.

POWER, INFLUENCE, AND CHANGE

Psychological Change

Since we shall define power in terms of influence, and influence in terms of psychological change, we begin with a discussion of change. We want to define change at a level of generality which includes changes in behavior, opinions, attitudes, goals, needs, values and all other aspects of the person's psychological field. We shall use the word "system" to refer to any such part of the life space.[1] Following Lewin (26, p. 305) the state of a system at time 1 will be denoted $s_1(a)$.

Psychological change is defined as any alteration of the state of some system a over time. The amount of change is measured by the size of the difference between the states of the system a at time 1 and at time 2: $ch(a) = s_2(a) - s_1(a)$.

Change in any psychological system may be conceptualized in terms of psychological forces. But it is important to note that the change must be coordinated to the resultant force of all the forces operating at the moment. Change in an opinion, for example, may be determined jointly by a driving force induced by another person, a restraining force corresponding to anchorage in a group opinion, and an own force stemming from the person's needs.

Social Influence

Our theory of social influence and power is limited to influence on the person, P, produced by a social agent, O, where O can be either another person, a role, a norm, a group or a part of a group. We do not consider social influence exerted on a group.

The influence of O on system a in the life space of P is defined as the resultant force on system a which has its source in an act of O. This resultant force induced by O consists of two components: a force to change the system in the direction induced by O and an opposing resistance set up by the same act of O.

By this definition the influence of O does not include P's own forces nor the forces induced by other social agents. Accordingly the "influence" of O must be clearly distinguished from O's "control" of P (Chapter 11). O may be able to induce strong forces on P to carry out an activity (i.e., O exerts strong influence on P) ; but if the opposing forces induced by another person or by P's own needs are stronger, then P will locomote in an opposite direction (i.e., O does not have control over P). Thus psychological change in P can be taken as an operational definition of the social influence of O on P only when the effects of other forces have been eliminated.

It is assumed that any system is interdependent with other parts of the life space so that a change in one may produce changes in others. However, this theory focuses on the primary changes in a system which are produced directly

[1] The word "system" is here used to refer to a whole or to a part of the whole.

by social influence; it is less concerned with secondary changes which are indirectly effected in the other systems or with primary changes produced by nonsocial influences.

Commonly social influence takes place through an intentional act on the part of O. However, we do not want to limit our definition of "act" to such conscious behavior. Indeed, influence might result from the passive presence of O, with no evidence of speech or overt movement. A policeman's standing on a corner may be considered an act of an agent for the speeding motorist. Such acts of the inducing agent will vary in strength, for O may not always utilize all of his power. The policeman, for example, may merely stand and watch or act more strongly by blowing his whistle at the motorist.

The influence exerted by an act need not be in the direction intended by O. The direction of the resultant force on P will depend on the relative magnitude of the induced force set up by the act of O and the resisting force in the opposite direction which is generated by that same act. In cases where O intends to influence P in a given direction, a resultant force in the same direction may be termed positive influence whereas a resultant force in the opposite direction may be termed negative influence.

If O produces the intended change, he has exerted positive control; but if he produces a change in the opposite direction, as for example in the negativism of young children or in the phenomena of negative reference groups, he has exerted negative control.

Social Power

The *strength of power* of O/P in some system *a* is defined as the maximum potential ability of O to influence P in *a*.

By this definition influence is kinetic power, just as power is potential influence. It is assumed that O is capable of various acts which, because of some more or less enduring relation to P, are able to exert influence on P.[2] O's power is measured by his maximum possible influence, though he may often choose to exert less than his full power.

An equivalent definition of power may be stated in terms of the resultant of two forces set up by the act of O: one in the direction of O's influence at-

[2] The concept of power has the conceptual property of *potentiality;* but it seems useful to restrict this potential influence to more or less enduring power relations between O and P by excluding from the definition of power those cases where the potential influence is so momentary or so changing that it cannot be predicted from the existing relationship. Power is a useful concept for describing social structure only if it has a certain stability over time; it is useless if every momentary social stimulus is viewed as actualizing social power.

tempt and another resisting force in the opposite direction. Power is the maximum resultant of these two forces:

$$\text{Power of } O/P(a) = (f_{a,x} - f_{\overline{a,x}})^{\max}$$

where the source of both forces is an act of O.

Thus the power of O with respect to system a of P is equal to the maximum resultant force of two forces set up by any possible act of O: (a) the force which O can set up on the system a to change in the direction x, (b) the resisting force [3] in the opposite direction. Whenever the first component force is greater than the second, positive power exists; but if the second component force is greater than the first, then O has negative power over P.

It is necessary to define power with respect to a specified system because the power of O/P may vary greatly from one system to another. O may have great power to control the behavior of P but little power to control his opinions. Of course a high power of O/P does not imply a low power of P/O; the two variables are conceptually independent (Chapter 11).

For certain purposes it is convenient to define the range of power as the set of all systems within which O has power of strength greater than zero. A husband may have a broad range of power over his wife, but a narrow range of power over his employer. We shall use the term "magnitude of power" to denote the summation of O's power over P in all systems of his range.

The dependence of s(a) on O.

Several investigators have been concerned with differences between superficial conformity and "deeper" changes produced by social influence (1, 5, 6, 11, 12, 20, 21, 22, 23, 26, 36, 37). The kinds of systems which are changed and the stability of these changes have been handled by distinctions such as "public vs. private attitudes," "overt vs. covert behavior," "compliance vs. internalization," and "own vs. induced forces." Though stated as dichotomies, all of these distinctions suggest an underlying dimension of the degree of dependence of the state of a system on O.

We assume that any change in the state of a system is produced by a change in some factor upon which it is functionally dependent. The state of an

---

[3] We define resistance to an attempted induction as a force in the opposite direction which is set up by the same act of O. It must be distinguished from opposition which is defined as existing opposing forces which do not have their source in the same act of O. For example, a boy might resist his mother's order to eat spinach because of the manner of the induction attempt, and at the same time he might oppose it because he didn't like spinach.

opinion, for example, may change because of a change either in some internal factor such as a need or in some external factor such as the arguments of O. Likewise the maintenance of the same state of a system is produced by the stability or lack of change in the internal and external factors. In general, then, psychological change and stability can be conceptualized in terms of dynamic dependence. Our interest is focused on the special case of dependence on an external agent, O **(31)**.

In many cases the initial state of the system has the character of a quasi-stationary equilibrium with a central force field around $s_1(a)$ **(26, p. 106)**. In such cases we may derive a tendency toward retrogression to the original state as soon as the force induced by O is removed.[4] Let us suppose that O exerts influence producing a new state of the system, $s_2(a)$. Is $s_2(a)$ now dependent on the continued presence of O? In principle we could answer this question by removing any traces of O from the life space of P and by observing the consequent state of the system at time 3. If $s_3(a)$ retrogresses completely back to $s_1(a)$, then we may conclude that maintenance of $s_2(a)$ was completely dependent on O; but if $s_3(a)$ equals $s_2(a)$, this lack of change shows that $s_2(a)$ has become completely independent of O. In general the degree of dependence of $s_2(a)$ on O, following O's influence, may be defined as equal to the amount of retrogression following the removal of O from the life space of P:

$$\text{Degree of dependence of } s_2(a) \text{ on } O = s_2(a) - s_3(a).$$

A given degree of dependence at time 2 may later change, for example, through the gradual weakening of O's influence. At this later time, the degree of dependence of $s_4(a)$ on O, would still be equal to the amount of retrogression toward the initial state of equilibrium $s_1(a)$. Operational measures of the degree of dependence on O will, of course, have to be taken under conditions where all other factors are held constant.

Consider the example of three separated employees who have been working at the same steady level of production despite normal, small fluctuations in the work environment. The supervisor orders each to increase his production, and the level of each goes up from 100 to 115 pieces per day. After a week of producing at the new rate of 115 pieces per day, the supervisor is removed for a week. The production of employee A immediately returns to 100 but B and C return to only 110 pieces per day. Other things being equal, we can infer that A's new rate was completely dependent on his supervisor whereas

---

[4] Miller **(33)** assumes that all living systems have this character. However, it may be that some systems in the life space do not have this elasticity.

the new rate of B and C was dependent on the supervisor only to the extent of 5 pieces. Let us further assume that when the supervisor returned, the production of B and of C returned to 115 without further orders from the supervisor. Now another month goes by during which B and C maintain a steady 115 pieces per day. However, there is a difference between them: B's level of production still depends on O to the extent of 5 pieces whereas C has come to rely on his own sense of obligation to obey the order of his legitimate supervisor rather than on the supervisor's external pressure for the maintenance of his 115 pieces per day. Accordingly, the next time the supervisor departs, B's production again drops to 110 but C's remains at 115 pieces per day. In cases like employee B, the degree of dependence is contingent on the perceived probability that O will observe the state of the system and note P's conformity (5, 6, 11, 12, 23). The level of observability will in turn depend on both the nature of the system (e.g., the difference between a covert opinion and overt behavior) and on the environmental barriers to observation (e.g., O is too far away from P). In other cases, for example that of employee C, the new behavior pattern is highly dependent on his supervisor, but the degree of dependence of the new state will be related not to the level of observability but rather to factors inside P, in this case a sense of duty to perform an act legitimately prescribed by O. The internalization of social norms is a related process of decreasing degree of dependence of behavior on an external O and increasing dependence on an internal value; it is usually assumed that internalization is accompanied by a decrease in the effects of level of observability (37).

The concepts "dependence of a system on O" and "observability as a basis for dependence" will be useful in understanding the stability of conformity. In the next section we shall discuss various types of power and the types of conformity which they are likely to produce.

THE BASES OF POWER

By the basis of power we mean the relationship between O and P which is the source of that power. It is rare that we can say with certainty that a given empirical case of power is limited to one source. Normally, the relation between O and P will be characterized by several qualitatively different variables which are bases of power (30, Chapter 11). Although there are undoubtedly many possible bases of power which may be distinguished, we shall here define five which seem especially common and important. These five bases of O's power are: (1) reward power, based on P's perception that

O has the ability to mediate rewards for him; (2) coercive power, based on P's perception that O has the ability to mediate punishments for him; (3) legitimate power, based on the perception by P that O has a legitimate right to prescribe behavior for him; (4) referent power, based on P's identification with O; (5) expert power, based on the perception that O has some special knowledge or expertness.

Our first concern is to define the bases which give rise to a given type of power. Next, we describe each type of power according to its strength, range, and the degree of dependence of the new state of the system which is most likely to occur with each type of power. We shall also examine the other effects which the exercise of a given type of power may have upon P and his relationship to O. Finally, we shall point out the interrelationships between different types of power, and the effects of use of one type of power by O upon other bases of power which he might have over P. Thus we shall both define a set of concepts and propose a series of hypotheses. Most of these hypotheses have not been systematically tested, although there is a good deal of evidence in favor of several. No attempt will be made to summarize that evidence here.

Reward Power

Reward power is defined as power whose basis is the ability to reward. The strength of the reward power of O/P increases with the magnitude of the rewards which P perceives that O can mediate for him. Reward power depends on O's ability to administer positive valences and to remove or decrease negative valences. The strength of reward power also depends upon the probability that O can mediate the reward, as perceived by P. A common example of reward power is the addition of a piece-work rate in the factory as an incentive to increase production.

The new state of the system induced by a promise of reward (for example the factory worker's increased level of production) will be highly dependent on O. Since O mediates the reward, he controls the probability that P will receive it. Thus P's new rate of production will be dependent on his subjective probability that O will reward him for conformity minus his subjective probability that O will reward him even if he returns to his old level. Both probabilities will be greatly affected by the level of observability of P's behavior. Incidentally, a piece rate often seems to have more effect on production than a merit rating system because it yields a higher probability of reward for conformity and a much lower probability of reward for nonconformity.

The utilization of actual rewards (instead of promises) by O will tend over time to increase the attraction of P toward O and therefore the referent power of O over P. As we shall note later, such referent power will permit O to induce changes which are relatively independent. Neither rewards nor promises will arouse resistance in P, provided P considers it legitimate for O to offer rewards.

The range of reward power is specific to those regions within which O can reward P for conforming. The use of rewards to change systems within the range of reward power tends to increase reward power by increasing the probability attached to future promises. However, unsuccessful attempts to exert reward power outside the range of power would tend to decrease the power; for example if O offers to reward P for performing an impossible act, this will reduce for P the probability of receiving future rewards promised by O.

Coercive Power

Coercive power is similar to reward power in that it also involves O's ability to manipulate the attainment of valences. Coercive power of O/P stems from the expectation on the part of P that he will be punished by O if he fails to conform to the influence attempt. Thus negative valences will exist in given regions of P's life space, corresponding to the threatened punishment by O. The strength of coercive power depends on the magnitude of the negative valence of the threatened punishment multiplied by the perceived probability that P can avoid the punishment by conformity, i.e., the probability of punishment for nonconformity minus the probability of punishment for conformity (11). Just as an offer of a piece-rate bonus in a factory can serve as a basis for reward power, so the ability to fire a worker if he falls below a given level of production will result in coercive power.

Coercive power leads to dependent change also; and the degree of dependence varies with the level of observability of P's conformity. An excellent illustration of coercive power leading to dependent change is provided by a clothes presser in a factory observed by Coch and French (3). As her efficiency rating climbed above average for the group the other workers began to "scapegoat" her. That the resulting plateau in her production was not independent of the group was evident once she was removed from the presence of the other workers. Her production immediately climbed to new heights.[5]

[5] Though the primary influence of coercive power is dependent, it often produces secondary changes which are independent. Brainwashing, for example, utilizes coercive power to produce many primary changes in the life space of the prisoner, but these dependent changes can lead to identification with the aggressor and hence to secondary changes in ideology which are independent.

At times, there is some difficulty in distinguishing between reward power and coercive power. Is the withholding of a reward really equivalent to a punishment? Is the withdrawal of punishment equivalent to a reward? The answer must be a psychological one—it depends upon the situation as it exists for P. But ordinarily we would answer these questions in the affirmative; for P, receiving a reward is a positive valence as is the relief of suffering. There is some evidence that conformity to group norms in order to gain acceptance (reward power) should be distinguished from conformity as a means of forestalling rejection (coercive power) (5).

The distinction between these two types of power is important because the dynamics are different. The concept of "sanctions" sometimes lumps the two together despite their opposite effects. While reward power may eventually result in an independent system, the effects of coercive power will continue to be dependent. Reward power will tend to increase the attraction of P toward O; coercive power will decrease this attraction (11, 12). The valence of the region of behavior will become more negative, acquiring some negative valence from the threatened punishment. The negative valence of punishment would also spread to other regions of the life space. Lewin (25) has pointed out this distinction between the effects of rewards and punishment. In the case of threatened punishment, there will be a resultant force on P to leave the field entirely. Thus, to achieve conformity, O must not only place a strong negative valence in certain regions through threat of punishment, but O must also introduce restraining forces, or other strong valences, so as to prevent P from withdrawing completely from O's range of coercive power. Otherwise the probability of receiving the punishment, if P does not conform, will be too low to be effective.

Legitimate Power

Legitimate power is probably the most complex of those treated here, embodying notions from the structural sociologist, the group-norm and role oriented social psychologist, and the clinical psychologist.

There has been considerable investigation and speculation about socially prescribed behavior, particularly that which is specific to a given role or position. Linton (29) distinguishes group norms according to whether they are universals for everyone in the culture, alternatives (the individual having a choice as to whether or not to accept them), or specialties (specific to given positions). Whether we speak of internalized norms, role prescriptions and expectations (34), or internalized pressures (15), the fact remains that each individual sees certain regions toward which he should locomote, some regions toward which he should not locomote, and some regions toward which he may locomote if they are generally attractive for him. This applies to specific behaviors in which he may, should, or should not engage; it applies to certain attitudes or beliefs which he may, should, or should not hold. The feeling of "oughtness" may be an internalization from his parents, from his teachers, from his religion, or may have been logically developed from some idiosyncratic system of ethics. He will speak of such behaviors with expressions like "should," "ought to," or "has a right to." In many cases, the original source of the requirement is not recalled.

Though we have oversimplified such evaluations of behavior with a positive-neutral-negative trichotomy, the evaluation of behaviors by the person is really more one of degree. This dimension of evaluation, we shall call "legitimacy." Conceptually, we may think of legitimacy as a valence in a region which is induced by some internalized norm or value. This value has the same conceptual property as power, namely an ability to induce force fields (26, p. 40-41). It may or may not be correct that values (or the superego) are internalized parents, but at least they can set up force fields which have a phenomenal "oughtness" similar to a parent's prescription. Like a value, a need can also induce valences (i.e., force fields) in P's psychological environment, but these valences have more the phenomenal character of noxious or attractive properties of the object or activity. When a need induces a valence in P, for example, when a need makes an object attractive to P, this attraction applies to P but not to other persons. When a value induces a valence, on the other hand, it not only sets up forces on P to engage in the activity, but P may feel that all others ought to behave in the same way. Among other things, this evaluation applies to the legitimate right of some other individual or group to prescribe behavior or beliefs for a person even though the other cannot apply sanctions.

Legitimate power of O/P is here defined as that power which stems from internalized values in P which dictate that O has a legitimate right to influence P and that P has an obligation to accept this influence. We note that legitimate power is very similar to the notion of legitimacy of authority which has long been explored by sociologists, particularly by Weber (42), and more recently by Goldhammer and Shils (14). However, legitimate power is not always a role relation: P may accept an induction from O simply because he had previously promised to help O and he values his word too much to break the promise. In all cases, the notion of legitimacy involves some sort of code or standard, accepted by the individual, by virtue of which the external agent can assert his power. We shall attempt to describe a few of these values here.

Bases for legitimate power. Cultural values constitute one common basis for the legitimate power of one individual over another. O has characteristics which are specified by the culture as giving him the right to prescribe behavior for P, who may not have these characteristics. These bases, which Weber **(42)** has called the authority of the "eternal yesterday," include such things as age, intelligence, caste, and physical characteristics. In some cultures, the aged are granted the right to prescribe behavior for others in practically all behavior areas. In most cultures, there are certain areas of behavior in which a person of one sex is granted the right to prescribe behavior for the other sex.

Acceptance of the social structure is another basis for legitimate power. If P accepts as right the social structure of his group, organization, or society, especially the social structure involving a hierarchy of authority, P will accept the legitimate authority of O who occupies a superior office in the hierarchy. Thus legitimate power in a formal organization is largely a relationship between offices rather than between persons. And the acceptance of an office as *right* is a basis for legitimate power—a judge has a right to levy fines, a foreman should assign work, a priest is justified in prescribing religious beliefs, and it is the management's prerogative to make certain decisions **(10)**. However, legitimate power also involves the perceived right of the person to hold the office.

Designation by a legitimizing agent is a third basis for legitimate power. An influencer O may be seen as legitimate in prescribing behavior for P because he has been granted such power by a legitimizing agent whom P accepts. Thus a department head may accept the authority of his vice-president in a certain area because that authority has been specifically delegated by the president. An election is perhaps the most common example of a group's serving to legitimize the authority of one individual or office for other individuals in the group. The success of such legitimizing depends upon the acceptance of the legitimizing agent and procedure. In this case it depends ultimately on certain democratic values concerning election procedures. The election process is one of legitimizing a person's right to an office which already has a legitimate range of power associated with it.

Range of legitimate power of O/P. The areas in which legitimate power may be exercised are generally specified along with the designation of that power. A job description, for example, usually specifies supervisory activities and also designates the person to whom the job-holder is responsible for the duties described. Some bases for legitimate authority carry with them a very broad range. Culturally derived bases for legitimate power are often especially broad. It is not uncommon to find cultures in which a member of a given caste can legitimately prescribe behavior for all members of lower castes in practically all regions. More common, however, are instances of legitimate power where the range is specifically and narrowly prescribed. A sergeant in the army is given a specific set of regions within which he can legitimately prescribe behavior for his men.

The attempted use of legitimate power which is outside of the range of legitimate power will decrease the legitimate power of the authority figure. Such use of power which is not legitimate will also decrease the attractiveness of O (11, 12, 36).

Legitimate power and influence. The new state of the system which results from legitimate power usually has high dependence on O though it may become independent. Here, however, the degree of dependence is not related to the level of observability. Since legitimate power is based on P's values, the source of the forces induced by O include both these internal values and O. O's induction serves to activate the values and to relate them to the system which is influenced, but thereafter the new state of the system may become directly dependent on the values with no mediation by O. Accordingly this new state will be relatively stable and consistent across varying environmental situations since P's values are more stable than his psychological environment.

We have used the term legitimate not only as a basis for the power of an agent, but also to describe the general behaviors of a person. Thus, the individual P may also consider the legitimacy of the attempts to use other types of power by O. In certain cases, P will consider that O has a legitimate right to threaten punishment for nonconformity; in other cases, such use of coercion would not be seen as legitimate. P might change in response to coercive power of O, but it will make a considerable difference in his attitude and conformity if O is not seen as having a legitimate right to use such coercion. In such cases, the attraction of P for O will be particularly diminished, and the influence attempt will arouse more resistance (11). Similarly the utilization of reward power may vary in legitimacy; the word "bribe," for example, denotes an illegitimate reward.

Referent Power

The referent power of O/P has its basis in the identification of P with O. By identification, we mean a feeling of oneness of P with O, or a desire for such an identity. If O is a person toward whom P is highly attracted, P will have a desire to become closely associated with O. If O is an attractive group, P will have a feeling of membership or a desire to join. If P is already closely associated with O he will want to maintain this relationship (39, 41).

P's identification with O can be established or maintained if P behaves, believes, and perceives as O does. Accordingly O has the ability to influence P, even though P may be unaware of this referent power. A verbalization of such power by P might be, "I am like O, and therefore I shall behave or believe as O does," or "I want to be like O, and I will be more like O if I behave or believe as O does." The stronger the identification of P with O the greater the referent power of O/P.

Similar types of power have already been investigated under a number of different formulations. Festinger (7) points out that in an ambiguous situation, the individual seeks some sort of "social reality" and may adopt the cognitive structure of the individual or group with which he identifies. In such a case, the lack of clear structure may be threatening to the individual and the agreement of his beliefs with those of a reference group will both satisfy his need for structure and give him added security through increased identification with his group (16, 19).

We must try to distinguish between referent power and other types of power which might be operative at the same time. If a member is attracted to a group and he conforms to its norms only because he fears ridicule or expulsion from the group for nonconformity, we would call this coercive power. On the other hand if he conforms in order to obtain praise for conformity, it is a case of reward power. The basic criterion for distinguishing referent power from both coercive and reward power is the mediation of the punishment and the reward by O: to the extent that O mediates the sanctions (i.e., has means control over P) we are dealing with coercive and reward power; but to the extent that P avoids discomfort or gains satisfaction by conformity based on identification, regardless of O's responses, we are dealing with referent power. Conformity with majority opinion is sometimes based on a respect for the collective wisdom of the group, in which case it is expert power. It is important to distinguish these phenomena, all grouped together elsewhere as "pressures toward uniformity," since the type of change which occurs will be different for different bases of power.

The concepts of "reference group" (40) and "prestige suggestion" may be treated as instances of referent power. In this case, O, the prestigeful person or group, is valued by P; because P desires to be associated or identified with O, he will assume attitudes or beliefs held by O. Similarly a negative reference group which O dislikes and evaluates negatively may exert negative influence on P as a result of negative referent power.

It has been demonstrated that the power which we designate as referent power is especially great when P is attracted to O (2, 7, 8, 9, 13, 23, 30).

In our terms, this would mean that the greater the attraction, the greater the identification, and consequently the greater the referent power. In some cases, attraction or prestige may have a specific basis, and the range of referent power will be limited accordingly: a group of campers may have great referent power over a member regarding campcraft, but considerably less effect on other regions (30). However, we hypothesize that the greater the attraction of P toward O, the broader the range of referent power of O/P.

The new state of a system produced by referent power may be dependent on or independent of O; but the degree of dependence is not affected by the level of observability to O (6, 23). In fact, P is often not consciously aware of the referent power which O exerts over him. There is probably a tendency for some of these dependent changes to become independent of O quite rapidly.

Expert Power

The strength of the expert power of O/P varies with the extent of the knowledge or perception which P attributes to O within a given area. Probably P evaluates O's expertness in relation to his own knowledge as well as against an absolute standard. In any case expert power results in primary social influence on P's cognitive structure and probably not on other types of systems. Of course changes in the cognitive structure can change the direction of forces and hence of locomotion, but such a change of behavior is secondary social influence. Expert power has been demonstrated experimentally (8, 33). Accepting an attorney's advice in legal matters is a common example of expert influence; but there are many instances based on much less knowledge, such as the acceptance by a stranger of directions given by a native villager.

Expert power, where O need not be a member of P's group, is called "informational power" by Deutsch and Gerard (4). This type of expert power must be distinguished from influence based on the content of communication as described by Hovland et al. (17, 18, 23, 24). The influence of the content of a communication upon an opinion is presumably a secondary influence produced after the *primary* influence (i.e., the acceptance of the information). Since power is here defined in terms of the primary changes, the influence of the content on a related opinion is not a case of expert power as we have defined it, but the initial acceptance of the validity of the content does seem to be based on expert power or referent power. In other cases, however, so-called facts may be accepted as self-evident because they fit into P's cognitive structure; if this impersonal acceptance of the truth of the fact is independent of the more or less enduring relationship between O and P, then P's acceptance of the fact is not an actualization of expert power. Thus we distinguish between expert power based on the credibility of O and informational influence which is based on charactertistics of the stimulus such as the logic of the argument or the "self-evident facts."

Wherever expert influence occurs it seems to be necessary both for P to think that O knows and for P to trust that O is telling the truth (rather than trying to deceive him).

Expert power will produce a new cognitive structure which is initially relatively dependent on O, but informational influence will produce a more independent structure. The former is likely to become more independent with the passage of time. In both cases the degree of dependence on O is not affected by the level of observability.

The "sleeper effect" (18, 24) is an interesting case of a change in the degree of dependence of an opinion on O. An unreliable O (who probably had negative referent power but some positive expert power) presented "facts" which were accepted by the subjects and which would normally produce secondary influence on their opinions and beliefs. However, the negative referent power aroused resistance and resulted in negative social influence on their beliefs (i.e., set up a force in the direction opposite to the influence attempt), so that there was little change in the subjects' opinions. With the passage of time, however, the subjects tended to forget the identity of the negative communicator faster than they forgot the contents of his communication, so there was a weakening of the negative referent influence and a consequent delayed positive change in the subjects' beliefs in the direction of the influence attempt ("sleeper effect"). Later, when the identity of the negative communicator was experimentally reinstated, these resisting forces were reinstated, and there was another negative change in belief in a direction opposite to the influence attempt (24).

The range of expert power, we assume, is more delimited than that of referent power. Not only is it restricted to cognitive systems but the expert is seen as having superior knowledge or ability in very specific areas, and his power will be limited to these areas, though some "halo effect" might occur. Recently, some of our renowned physical scientists have found quite painfully that their expert power in physical sciences does not extend to regions involving international politics. Indeed, there is some evidence that the attempted exertion of expert power outside of the range of expert power will reduce that expert power. An undermining of confidence seems to take place.

SUMMARY

We have distinguished five types of power: referent power, expert power, reward power, coercive power, and legitimate power. These distinctions led to the following hypotheses.

1. For all five types, the stronger the basis of power the greater the power.

2. For any type of power the size of the range may vary greatly, but in general referent power will have the broadest range.

3. Any attempt to utilize power outside the range of power will tend to reduce the power.

4. A new state of a system produced by reward power or coercive power will be highly dependent on O, and the more observable P's conformity the more dependent the state. For the other three types of power, the new state is usually dependent, at least in the beginning, but in any case the level of observability has no effect on the degree of dependence.

5. Coercion results in decreased attraction of P toward O and high resistance; reward power results in increased attraction and low resistance.

6. The more legitimate the coercion the less it will produce resistance and decreased attraction.

REFERENCES

1. Asch, S. E. *Social psychology*. New York: Prentice-Hall, 1952.

2. Back, K. W. Influence through social communication. *J. abnorm. soc. Psychol.*, 1951, **46**, 9-23.

3. Coch, L., & French, J. R. P., Jr. Overcoming resistance to change. *Hum. Relat.*, 1948, **1**, 512-32.

4. Deutsch, M., & Gerard, H. B. A study of normative and informational influences upon individual judgment. *J. abnorm. soc. Psychol.*, 1955, **51**, 629-36.

5. Dittes, J. E., & Kelley, H. H. Effects of different conditions of acceptance upon conformity to group norms. *J. abnorm. soc. Psychol.*, 1956, **53**, 100-107.

6. Festinger, L. An analysis of compliant behavior. In Sherif, M., & Wilson, M. O., (Eds.). *Group relations at the crossroads*. New York: Harper, 1953, 232-56.

7. Festinger, L. Informal social communication. *Psychol. Rev.*, 1950, **57**, 271-82.

8. Festinger, L., Gerard, H. B., Hymovitch, B. Kelley, H. H., & Raven, B. H. The influence process in the presence of extreme deviates. *Hum. Relat.*, 1952, **5**, 327-346.

9. Festinger, L., Schachter, S., & Back, K. The operation of group standards. In Cartwright, D., & Zander, A. *Group dynamics: research and theory*. Evanston: Row, Peterson, 1953, 204-23.

10. French, J. R. P., Jr., Israel, Joachim & As, Dagfinn "Arbeidernes medvirkning i industribedriften. En eksperimentell undersøkelse." Institute for Social Research, Oslo, Norway, 1957.

11. French, J. R. P., Jr., Levinger, G., & Morrison, H. W. The legitimacy of coercive power. In preparation.

12. French, J. R. P., Jr., & Raven, B. H. An experiment in legitimate and coercive power. In preparation.

13. Gerard, H. B. The anchorage of opinions in face-to-face groups. *Hum. Relat.*, 1954, **7**, 313-325.

14. Goldhammer, H., & Shils, E. A. Types of power and status. *Amer. J. Sociol.*, 1939, **45**, 171-178.

15. Herbst, P. G. Analysis and measurement of a situation. *Hum. Relat.*, 1953, **2**, 113-140.

16. Hochbaum, G. M. Self-confidence and reactions to group pressures. *Amer. soc. Rev.*, 1954, **19**, 678-687.

17. Hovland, C. I., Lumsdaine, A. A., & Sheffield, F. D. *Experiments on mass communication*. Princeton: Princeton Univer. Press, 1949.

18. Hovland, C. I., & Weiss, W. The influence of source credibility on communication effectiveness. *Publ. Opin. Quart.*, 1951, **15**, 635-650.

19. Jackson, J. M., & Saltzstein, H. D. The effect of person-group relationships on conformity processes. *J. abnorm. soc. Psychol.*, 1958, **57**, 17-24.

20. Jahoda, M. Psychological issues in civil liberties. *Amer. Psychologist*, 1956, **11**, 234-240.

21. Katz, D., & Schank, R. L. *Social psychology*. New York: Wiley, 1938.

22. Kelley, H. H., & Volkart, E. H. The resistance to change of group-anchored attitudes. *Amer. soc. Rev.*, 1952, **17**, 453-465.

23. Kelman, H. Three processes of acceptance of social influence: compliance, identification and internalization. Paper read at the meetings of the American Psychological Association, August 1956.

24. Kelman, H., & Hovland, C. I. "Reinstatement" of the communicator in delayed measurement of opinion change. *J. abnorm. soc. Psychol.*, 1953, **48**, 327-335.

25. Lewin, K. *Dynamic theory of personality*. New York: McGraw-Hill, 1935, 114-170.

26. Lewin, K. *Field theory in social science*. New York: Harper, 1951.

27. Lewin, K., Lippitt, R., & White, R. K. Patterns of aggressive behavior in experimentally created social climates. *J. soc. Psychol.*, 1939, **10**, 271-301.

28. Lasswell, H. D., & Kaplan, A. *Power and society: A framework for political inquiry*. New Haven: Yale Univer. Press, 1950.

29. Linton, R. *The cultural background of personality*. New York: Appleton-Century-Crofts, 1945.

30. Lippitt, R., Polansky, N., Redl, F., & Rosen, S. The dynamics of power. *Hum. Relat.*, 1952, **5**, 37-64.

31. March, J. G. An introduction to the theory and measurement of influence. *Amer. polit. Sci. Rev.*, 1955, **49**, 431-451.

32. Miller, J. G. Toward a general theory for the behavioral sciences. *Amer. Psychologist*, 1955, **10**, 513-531.

33. Moore, H. T. The comparative influence of majority and expert opinion. *Amer. J. Psychol.*, 1921, **32**, 16-20.

34. Newcomb, T. M. *Social psychology*. New York: Dryden, 1950.

35. Raven, B. H. The effect of group pressures on opinion, perception, and communication. Unpublished doctoral dissertation, University of Michigan, 1953.

36. Raven, B. H., & French, J. R. P., Jr. Group support, legitimate power, and social influence. *J. Person.*, 1958, **26**, 400-409.

37. Rommetveit, R. *Social norms and roles.* Minneapolis: Univer. Minnesota Press, 1953.

38. Russell, B. *Power: A new social analysis.* New York: Norton, 1938.

39. Stotland, E., Zander, A., Burnstein, E., Wolfe, D., & Natsoulas, T. Studies on the effects of identification. University of Michigan, Institute for Social Research. Forthcoming.

40. Swanson, G. E., Newcomb, T. M., & Hartley, E. L. *Readings in social psychology.* New York: Henry Holt, 1952.

41. Torrance, E. P., & Mason, R. Instructor effort to influence: an experimental evaluation of six approaches. Paper presented at USAF-NRC Symposium on Personnel, Training, and Human Engineering. Washington, D. C., 1956.

42. Weber, M. *The theory of social and economic organization.* Oxford: Oxford Univer. Press, 1947.

10

A CRITERION FOR UNANIMITY IN FRENCH'S THEORY OF SOCIAL POWER

Frank Harary

The purpose of this paper is to contribute to the theoretical investigation initiated by French (3) by providing a necessary and sufficient condition for the attainment of ultimate unanimity of opinions in a power structure. In addition the isomorphism is demonstrated between this theory and the theory of higher transition probabilities in Markov chains, as developed in the book by Feller (2). By exploiting this isomorphism the known theorems on Markov chains are translated into their corresponding theorems on social power. One of the results obtained in this manner is that every power structure regardless of initial opinion distribution necessarily converges to a stable distribution of ultimate opinions.

In the processes of deriving this criterion for unanimity, we employ several concepts of independent interest, including an "automorphic group" and a "power subgroup." We also propose a generalization of French's model, and find that the criterion for unanimity developed in French's model still remains valid in the more general theory.

French conceives of interpersonal power as the ability of one person to influence another by virtue of some more or less enduring basis of power (expertness, ability to punish, etc.) Variations in the strength of the basis of power effect variations in influence if and only if power is exerted, i.e., person A communicates an influence attempt to B, a person over whom he has power. Such a communication sets up a force field on B to agree with A's opinion, but this force field meets an opposing one corresponding to B's tendency to maintain his initial opinion unchanged. In the case of opinions measured along a cardinal scale, both these force fields are assumed to have linear gradients: the more A's opinion differs from B's the stronger force he induces on B; and the greater the change demanded of B, the stronger his opposition to the change.[1] It is assumed that B resolves this conflict by changing his

---

[1] French (3) originally called this "resistance" but more recently he distinguishes this "opposition" (based on own forces) from "resistance" (defined as forces induced by the act of A). The more recent usage is adhered to in this chapter.

opinion to exactly that point on the scale where the two forces (existing at that time unit) are equal and opposite. A corresponding equilibrium point exists for the case where two or more members try to influence B to agree with their different opinions.

This theory is formalized by French (3) in the following postulates:

Postulate 1. For any given discrepancy of opinion between A and B, the strength of the resultant force which an inducer A can exert on an inducee B, in the direction of agreeing with A's opinion, is proportional to the strength of the bases of power of A over B.

Postulate 2. The strength of the force which an inducer A exerts on an inducee B, in the direction of agreeing with A's opinion, is proportional to the size of the discrepancy between their opinions.

Postulate 3. In one unit of time, each person who is being influenced will change his opinion until he reaches the equilibrium point where the resultant force (of the forces induced by other members at the beginning of the unit and the resisting force corresponding to his own resistance to change) is equal to zero.

Using the theory of digraphs, French derives seven theorems about the outcome of the influence process as a function of the power structure. He obtains seven analogous statements on the effect of different communication networks. For completeness we include the definitions given by Harary, Norman, and Cartwright (5) of digraphs and the four degrees of connectedness a digraph may have. A "digraph" is a finite set of points A, B, C, . . . and a subset of the directed lines $\overrightarrow{AB}$, $\overrightarrow{BA}$, $\overrightarrow{AC}$, $\overrightarrow{CA}$, $\overrightarrow{BC}$, $\overrightarrow{CB}$, . . . between distinct points. A digraph is "strongly connected" (or "strong") if for every pair of distinct points, A and B, there exists a directed path from A to B *and* a directed path from B to A. A digraph is "unilaterally connected" (or "unilateral") if for every pair of points, A and $B,$ there is a directed path from A to B or from B to A. A digraph is "weakly connected" (or "weak") if it is impossible to separate the points of the digraph into two disjoint classes such that no line of the digraph has one end point in one class and the other end point in the other class. Finally, a digraph is "disconnected" if it is not weak. An explicit coordination between these concepts from the theory of digraphs to the above model is given by French (3). We note again here that A can exert power on B only if there exists a line from A to B.

Since this article is an immediate sequel to French's paper (3), the seven theorems stated in that paper are quoted here. Results of this study are numbered beginning with Theorem 8.

Theorem 1. For all possible patterns of initial opinion, in a completely connected power structure the opinions of all members will reach a common equilibrium level equal to the arithmetic mean of the initial opinions of all the members, and this final common opinion will be reached in one unit.

Theorem 2. In an N-person cycle (which is a strongly connected group) the members will reach a final common opinion at the arithmetic mean, $\left(\frac{1}{N}\right)(a+b+c+ \ldots)$, in an infinite number of units.

Theorem 3. In a unilaterally connected group the opinions of all members will converge to a final common opinion in an infinite number of steps.

Theorem 4. In a weakly connected group the members will not reach common agreement except under special conditions in the distribution of initial opinions.

Theorem 5. The greater the bases of power of A over B (B's attraction to A, B's acceptance of A as an expert, etc.) the more influence A will have on B and subsequently on any other person P for whom there exists a directed path from B to P.

Theorem 6. In a group where the power structure is a three-person cycle in which A has power over B, B has power over C, and C has power over A, and the communication pattern is $A, BC, A, BC, \ldots$, the final common opinion in the group equals $\frac{1}{5}(2a+b+2c)$.

Theorem 7. The amount of change of the deviate toward the opinions of the majority is proportional to the sum of the deviations of all other members from the deviate.

French's main theorems (excluding 5 and 6) deal with cases where power is exerted wherever it exists and where all existing power relations are of equal strength. We restate this part of French's model in the form of the following three axioms. The primitives, or undefined terms, of this axiom system include a *group* of *members* whose power structure is represented by a directed graph.

Axiom 1. At time $t = O$, each of the n members A_1, A_2, $\ldots$, A_n holds an initial opinion a_1, a_2, $\ldots$, a_n given by a real number.

Axiom 2. Power is exerted only at discrete time units denoted by $t = 1$, $t = 2$, etc.

Axiom 3. If the initial opinions of members A and B are a and b and if only B exerts influence on A, then the opinion of A after one time unit is $\frac{1}{2}(a+b)$. Similarly if A, B, and C hold initial opinions, $a, b,$ and c, and only B and C act to influence A, then the opinion of A after one time unit is the arithmetic mean $\frac{1}{3}(a+b+c)$, etc.

It is understood that from $t = 1$ to $t = 2$, the axioms remain valid in the same way as in going from $t=0$ to $t=1$, etc. The attainment of a final common opinion in an infinite number of steps does not require an infinite amount of time. Rather, after the opinions of the different group members come within some preassigned small threshold value, the members will all automatically be regarded as holding the same final opinion and influence attempts will cease.

AUTOMORPHIC GROUPS

The following definitions from digraph theory (4, 5), here worded in terms of social groups, are necessary for a concise statement of Theorem 8, which is a generalization of Theorems 1 and 2. Two group structures are "isomorphic" if there is a one-to-one correspondence between their members which preserves the group bonds. Thus in Figure 1 the groups G and G_1 are isomorphic, with members A and A_1 corresponding to each other, etc.

An "automorphism" of a group is an isomorphism of the group with itself. Two members A and B of a group are called "similar" if there is an automorphism of the group which sends A onto B. Referring to Figure 1 again, the one-to-one mapping of the points of G onto themselves which leaves B and C fixed while interchanging A and D is an automorphism of G. Therefore, in this group G, the members A and D are similar to each other. Analogously, B and C are similar to each other. However, A and B are not similar to each other for there can be no automorphism of G which sends A onto B, in view of the fact that the member A is adjacent to two members while B is adjacent to three.

An "automorphic group" can now be described as one in which all members are similar to each other. For example, every completely connected group is automorphic, and so is any group whose digraph consists of a single directed cycle. In Figure 2, these two kinds of group structure, that is, complete and

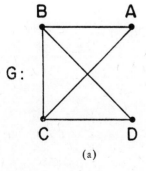

(a)

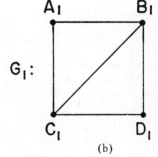

(b)

FIG. 1

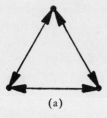

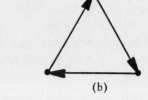

(a)   (b)

FIG. 2

cyclic, are shown. Figure 3 shows that there are other automorphic groups in addition to the complete group and the cyclic group, and indeed the digraph of Figure 3b shows that an automorphic group may be disconnected. It is shown in Harary, Norman, and Cartwright (5) that an automorphic group which is not strong must be disconnected. Thus, there are no strictly unilateral or strictly weak automorphic groups.

By the "complementary group" of a given group is meant that group on the same members in which the line $\overrightarrow{AB}$ occurs if and only if it does not appear in the given group. It is clear that the complementary group to an automorphic group is also automorphic. The two groups of Figure 3 are complementary to each other.

The proofs of the theorems which follow offer no essential difficulties. However, heuristic discussions are provided rather than mathematical details.

Theorem 8. In any strong automorphic group of n persons A_1, A_2, . . . , A_n with initial opinions a_1, a_2, . . . , a_n, the members will reach a final common opinion, z, at the arithmetic mean:

(1) $$z = \frac{1}{n}(a_1 + a_2 + \ldots + a_n).$$

If this group is completely connected, this final common opinion is reached in one time unit (Theorem 1). Otherwise, it takes an infinite number of units. Since a directed cycle constitutes an automorphic group, Theorem 2 is a special case of Theorem 8. Before plausibility considerations for this theorem are

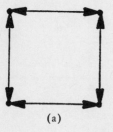

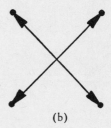

(a)   (b)

FIG. 3

given, the next theorem is stated, which considers the more general situation of any strong group, not necessarily automorphic. Both of these theorems are then discussed together.

Theorem 9. In any strong group (not necessarily automorphic), the members will reach a final common opinion. The converse of Theorem 8 does not hold, that is, there exists a strong group which is not automorphic

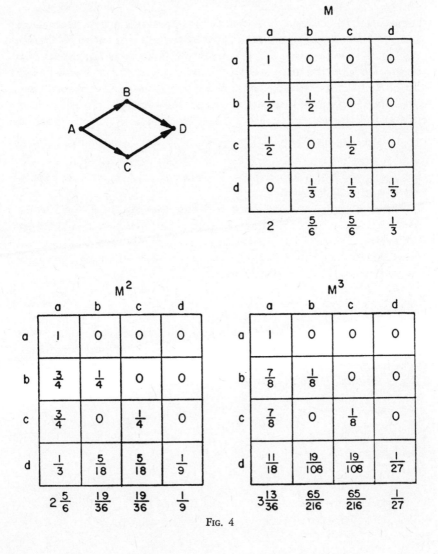

Fig. 4

whose final common opinion is different from the arithmetic mean of the initial opinions.

The last assertion of Theorem 9 may be proved by producing one strong nonautomorphic group whose final common opinion is not equal to the arithmetic mean. Obviously there is only one strong two-member group (up to isomorphism). Therefore, the smallest possible strong nonautomorphic group has three members. Figure 5 provides an example of such a three-member group and a computation of the final common opinion proceeds as follows. Let the members A, B, and C have initial opinions a, b, and c respectively. The procedure is entirely analogous with that shown by French (3, Figure 3). In order that this figure can be available to those readers for whom French's article is not at hand, it is reproduced here as Figure 4.

The computation of the final common opinion of the group in Figure 5 can be indicated in terms of the above mentioned initial opinions a, b, and c. The following matrix M

$$M = \begin{Vmatrix} & a & b & c \\ a & \frac{1}{3} & \frac{1}{3} & \frac{1}{3} \\ b & \frac{1}{2} & \frac{1}{2} & 0 \\ c & \frac{1}{2} & 0 & \frac{1}{2} \end{Vmatrix}$$

shows the modified individual opinions a_1, b_1, and c_1 after one time unit to be:

$$a_1 = \tfrac{1}{3}a + \tfrac{1}{3}b + \tfrac{1}{3}c$$
$$b_1 = \tfrac{1}{2}a + \tfrac{1}{2}b$$
$$c_1 = \tfrac{1}{2}a \qquad + \tfrac{1}{2}c$$

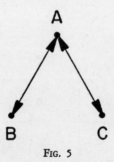

FIG. 5

Computation of the square of this matrix M by ordinary matrix multiplication yields:

$$M^2 = \begin{Vmatrix} \tfrac{4}{9} & \tfrac{5}{18} & \tfrac{5}{18} \\ \tfrac{5}{12} & \tfrac{5}{12} & \tfrac{1}{6} \\ \tfrac{5}{12} & \tfrac{1}{6} & \tfrac{5}{12} \end{Vmatrix}$$

Continuing in this way, one can compute the successive matrix powers M^3, M^4, etc. and verify that to two decimal places one soon arrives at a power $P = M^n$ given by:

$$P = M^n = \begin{Vmatrix} .42 & .29 & .29 \\ .42 & .29 & .29 \\ .42 & .29 & .29 \end{Vmatrix}$$

Then P is an "idempotent matrix," that is, all the positive integral powers of P are equal to each other. This is clearly equivalent to the statement that $P = P^2$. The importance of this concept lies in the fact that idempotence of a matrix is coordinated to stability of the members' opinions. Thus stability (to two decimal points) in the final common opinion of the members of the group of Figure 5 has already been attained after the passage of n time units. The matrix M^n is now translated back to the opinions of the individuals. Let $\bar{a}$, $\bar{b}$, and $\bar{c}$ be the final opinions of A, B, and C. For the case that these three final opinions are equal, this final common opinion is denoted by z. Then reading off the entries of matrix P, we have,

$$z = .42a + .29b + .29c.$$

The coefficients of a, b, and c in the preceding equation may be regarded as an indication of the "relative influence" of A, B, and C respectively as far as the determination of the final common opinion is concerned. We now generalize from this particular strongly connected group to any strong group.

The fact that the sum of the above coefficients is 1 is not a coincidence. In general, in any strong n-member group A_1, A_2, . . . , A_n whose initial opinions are a_1, a_2, . . . , a_n, the *final common opinion*, z, is of the form

(2) $$z = p_1a_1 + p_2a_2 + \ . \ . \ . \ + p_na_n$$

where each of the coefficients p_1, p_2, . . . , p_n is between 0 and 1 exclusive, and

(3) $$p_1 + p_2 + \ . \ . \ . \ + p_n = 1.$$

The result is an immediate corollary of the result from Markov chain theory given below to the effect that the square of a *stochastic matrix* (i.e., a square matrix with nonnegative elements in which each row sum is 1) is a stochastic matrix.

The form given by equation (2) of the final common opinion z can be used to define the "relative influence" of each member A_k as the coefficient p_k of his initial opinion a_k. Theorem 10 collects these observations.

Theorem 10. In a strong group each member has relative influence between 0 and 1 and the sum of the relative influences is 1.

In this form it is intuitively clear that in a strong automorphic group each member has the same relative influence. Expressing this last sentence symbolically with the letter p standing for the relative influence of each member, we obtain on substituting $p_1 = p$, $p_2 = p$, . . . into equation (3),

$$p + p + \ . \ . \ . \ + p = np = 1$$

so that $p = \dfrac{1}{n}$. Substituting $\dfrac{1}{n}$ for each of the coefficients p_k in equation (2), we get

$$z = \frac{1}{n}(a_1 + a_2 + \ . \ . \ . \ + a_n),$$

which is equation (1). This result supports the conclusion of Theorem 8.

In connection with Theorem 10 it is to be noted that all positive integral powers of a stochastic matrix are stochastic matrices. Therefore, at each time unit (on the way to the attainment of final opinions) the sum of the entries in each row of every matrix power is one. Theorem 10 contains the corresponding statement for the limiting case.

POWER SUBGROUPS

For the result of Theorem 9 to be extended to groups which are not necessarily strong, we require the concept of a power subgroup which can be developed from the properties of a point basis of a digraph given in Harary, Norman, and Cartwright (5). A "point basis" of a digraph is a minimal collection of points A, B, . . . , D from which all points are reachable via a directed path. That is, every point of the digraph is reachable from at least one of the points of the set $S = \{A, B, \ . \ . \ . \ , D\}$ but this is no longer the case when one or more points are removed from S. It is assumed that every point is reachable from itself along a path of length 0.

A "strong component" of a digraph is a maximal strong subgraph, that is, a strong subgraph which is no longer strong when even one more point of the digraph is added to it. It is shown in Harary, Norman, and Cartwright (5) that if A is in a point basis S of a digraph and A' is any point in the same strong component with A, then the set of points S' obtained by removing A and adding A' is again a point basis. We may now define a "power subgroup" as a subgroup which forms a strong component and has one of its members in a point basis. In Figures 6 and 7 there are groups with one and two power subgroups respectively. In Figure 6, either A alone or B alone constitutes a

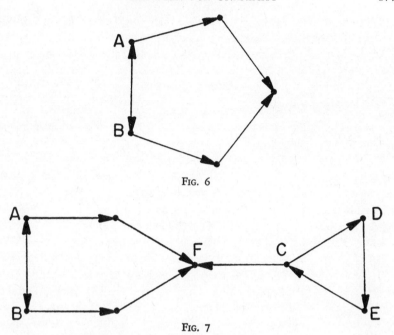

FIG. 6

FIG. 7

point basis, and {A, B} forms the only power subgroup. However, in Figure 7, there are two power subgroups: {A, B} and {C, D, E} and each point basis contains exactly one member from each power subgroup. It is clear that in any group, no member of a power subgroup can be influenced by any group member not in the same power subgroup with him.

Theorem 11. If a group has exactly one power subgroup, then it has a final common opinion which is equal to that of the power subgroup itself.

By definition, the unique power subgroup is strongly connected. Theorem 9 then shows that this subgroup attains a final common opinion. The meaning of Theorem 11 is that the initial opinions of those group members (the "out-members") not in the power subgroup have absolutely no effect on the final common opinion of the group. For regardless of how extreme the initial opinion of a powerless member is, it will eventually be reduced to conformity by the repeated exertion of influence from the power subgroup. In view of this theorem, we define the relative influence of a group member not in the unique power subgroup to be 0. This is consistent with the previous definition of relative influence determined by equation (2). For if $A_1, A_2, \ldots, A_n$ are the members of the power subgroup and $A_{n+1}, A_{n+2}, \ldots, A_m$ are the remaining members, then the final common opinion z of the group of Theorem 11 may be written in the form:

$$z = p_1a_1 + p_2a_2 + \cdots + p_na_n + Oa_{n+1} + Oa_{n+2} + \cdots + Oa_m.$$

It is shown in Harary, Norman, and Cartwright (5) that every unilateral group has a unique power subgroup, but not conversely. When this result is used it is clear that Theorem 11 is a generalization of Theorem 3.

The preceding theorem is now extended to groups having an unrestricted number of power subgroups.

Theorem 12. The final opinions of all members of the same power subgroup of a group are equal. If all the power subgroups of a group have the same final opinion, then all the members attain this final opinion.

The first part of Theorem 12 is a consequence of Theorem 9 and the fact that no member of a power subgroup can be influenced by any group member not in the same power subgroup with him. The second part follows from Theorem 11 and includes all the members who are not in any power subgroup.

In view of Theorem 12, we may use the phrase "the final opinion of a power subgroup" since this final opinion is common to all its members. Combining the last two theorems we see that (a) a group member influenced by only one power subgroup will have a final opinion equal to that of this power subgroup, and (b) a group member influenced by more than one power subgroup (as F in Figure 7) will have a final opinion between the greatest and the smallest final opinions of the power subgroups influencing him.

The above sequence of theorems has already provided a criterion for unanimity, i.e., for the attainment of a final common group opinion. It only remains to state this characterization.

Theorem 13. A group attains unanimity if and only if all its power subgroups have equal final opinions.

This theorem serves to spell out Theorem 4 in the sense that it provides the detailed description of the kind of distribution of initial opinions which is necessary (and sufficient) for the group members to reach common agreement.

MARKOV CHAINS AND SOCIAL POWER

Markov chains constitute a branch of mathematical probability theory which deals with the outcomes of repetitions of an experiment. The simplest probabilistic situation involving several events which does not assume that the probability of each event is time invariant occurs in the study of Markov chains. Here the outcome of the n'th trial or experiment (or in the present context, influence attempt) depends only on the result of the preceding trial and not on any trials before that one.

We make the following coordinations:

1. a member of a power structure
2. a point of a digraph
3. an event in a Markov chain.

The probability at any trial of going from the i'th event to the j'th event is called the (*i, j*)—*transition probability*. The probability of going from the i'th event in a Markov chain to the j'th event in n steps is a *"higher transition probability"* when $n > 1$.

The correspondence between higher transition probabilities in Markov chain theory and the attainment of the final opinions of group members in French's theory of social power will now be discussed. For example, since the four-member group of Figure 4 has a unique power subgroup consisting of A alone, it follows from Theorem 11 that the group reaches a final common opinion by having everyone agree with the original opinion held by A. However, this group still provides an instructive illustration. The matrices M, M^2, and M^3 of Figure 4 are all stochastic. This fact is seen in the following definition from Feller (**2**, p. 309): A square matrix with nonnegative elements and unit row sums is called a "stochastic matrix." Any stochastic matrix can serve as a matrix of transition probabilities. Together with the initial probability distribution, it completely defines a "Markov chain."

It is then shown in Feller (**2**, p. 317) that the powers M^2, M^3, M^4, etc., of any stochastic matrix are not only also stochastic, but give the 2-step, 3-step, 4-step, etc. higher transition probabilities of the given Markov chain. Since it is clear from French's example (see Figure 4) that the process of determining the final opinions of the members of the group is equivalent to the mathematical operation of finding the successive powers of the given stochastic matrix M, the isomorphism between the French theory and higher transition probability matrices in Markov chains may be regarded as established. We now state two important theorems on Markov chains from Feller (**2**) and then translate each of them into the terminology of social power. In this translation process, a "Markov chain" corresponds to a group structure; the "states" or "events" of a Markov chain to the group members. Similarly the initial opinions of the group members are coordinated to the initial probability distribution. Feller (**2**, p. 322), gives the definition: In an "irreducible" chain every state can be reached from every other state. Hence an irreducible Markov chain corresponds to a strongly connected group.

Feller (**2**, p. 327-8) also states that: The matrix M is called "doubly stochastic" if not only the row sums, but also the column sums, are unity. Suppose that the chain contains only a finite number, n, of states. It follows that if a finite irreducible chain has a doubly stochastic matrix M, then in the limit all states become equally probable. When states are coordinated to members, this means that the initial opinion of each member has equal effect in arriving at the final common opinion. It is easily seen that the condition that M be doubly stochastic is not only sufficient but also necessary.

The corresponding result for social power is the content of the next theorem.

Theorem 14. A strong group attains unanimity at the arithmetic mean of the initial opinions if and only if its matrix M is doubly stochastic.

This theorem serves as a complete generalization of Theorem 8 since it gives a characterization of those groups which attain a final common opinion at the arithmetic mean, i.e., groups in which all members have equal influence.

From Feller (2, p. 329), we have: For finite chains there exists a unique stationary distribution and the probability distribution necessarily converges towards it.

This result gives us the theorem which precludes the possibility of continual opinion oscillation.

Theorem 15. In every group, regardless of its power structure or its initial opinion distribution, each member reaches a stable final opinion.

A generalization of the axioms mentioned earlier is obtained by leaving Axioms 1 and 2 invariant and replacing Axiom 3 by the following Axiom 3'. The purpose is to allow for variations in the strength of the bases of power and in strength of opposition of a member to changing his opinion. In this model it is convenient to think of opposition, based on own forces, as the "power" of the person's present opinion over his succeeding opinion. Thus the strength of the basis of power and the strength of opposition can be equated and hence can be represented by the same number. Thus in Axiom 3', the value of r is coordinated to the "strength of the bases of power" of French's Postulate 1 and the equally strong opposition ("resistance") of Postulate 3. With this interpretation, Axiom 3' provides in symbolic manner exactly the same idea as Postulate 1.

Axiom 3'. If the initial opinions of any two members A and B are a and b and if only B exerts influence on A, then the opinion of A after one time unit is

$$ra + (1-r) b,$$

where the real number r is between 0 and 1 exclusive and must be equal for all members of the group. Similarly if A, B, and C have initial opinions a, b, and c, and only B and C act to influence A, then the opinion of A after one time unit is

$$\tfrac{2}{3}ra + (\tfrac{1}{2} - \tfrac{1}{3}r)b + (\tfrac{1}{2} - \tfrac{1}{3}r)c;\ \text{etc.}$$

Obviously, Axiom 3 is the special case of Axiom 3' for the value $r = \tfrac{1}{2}$. One can generalize Axiom 3 still further to obtain the following Axiom 3" in which the strength of the bases of power and the *opposition to change*, r_A, of member A may vary with the group member. This serves to remove the restriction in Axiom 3' that the number r must be equal for all members. To each member A, a number r_A is associated; r_A between 0 and 1. The numbers r_A, r_B, r_C, . . . corresponding to members A, B, C, . . . need not be equal.

Axiom 3". If the initial opinions of any two members A and B are a and b and if only B exerts influence on A, then the opinion of A after one time unit is

$$r_A a + (1 - r_A)b.$$

Similarly if A, B, and C have initial opinions a, b, and c, and only B and C act to influence A, then the opinion of A after one time unit is

$$\tfrac{2}{3}r_A + (\tfrac{1}{2} - \tfrac{1}{3}r_A)b + (\tfrac{1}{2} - \tfrac{1}{3}r_A)c;\ \text{etc.}$$

Axiom 3" is probably closer to reality [2] than either of the Axioms 3 or 3'. Axiom 3' is the special case of Axiom 3" obtained when all the individual values r_A, r_B, r_C, . . . have the same value r. Therefore, any theorem based on Axioms 1, 2, and 3" will also hold in the axiom system: 1, 2, and 3'.

The final theorem shows that even in this individualistically regarded system, the preceding criterion for unanimity (Theorem 13) is still valid.

Theorem 16. In the system determined by Axioms 1, 2, and 3", a group attains unanimity if and only if all its power subgroups have equal final opinions.

---

[2] Many empirical studies show that there are large individual differences in opposition (or conformity) to social influence. It is plausible that an individual's opposition to changing an opinion stems from properties of his cognitive structure and that such opposition will be equally strong against all inducers. On the other hand, resistance to changing an opinion stems from the act of the inducer, and an individual's resistance to different inducers varies with the strength of their coercive power over him (6). Hence this model is more realistic for dealing with opposition than with resistance.

Similar considerations exist for r_A interpreted as the strength of the basis of power. There are large individual differences in the amount of power of group members. For some types of power—for example the legitimate power of a supervisor over his subordinates—a given supervisor's legitimate power over his various subordinates may be approximately equal. For other types, for example power based on interpersonal attraction, a given individual's power varies greatly depending on how much the inducee likes him. Hence this model probably applies better to legitimate power structures than to sociometric structures.

The proof of Theorem 16 is entirely analogous to that of Theorem 13 (the criterion for unanimity in the axiom system: 1, 2, 3). For Theorem 13 is a direct consequence of Theorems 11 and 12, and each of these two theorems remains valid in the axiom system: 1, 2, 3″ even though the numbers r_A are admitted to vary with each group member A.

REFERENCES

1. Cartwright, D., & Harary, F. Structural balance: a generalization of Heider's theory. *Psychol. Rev.*, 1956, **63**, 277-293.

2. Feller, W. *An introduction to probability theory and its applications.* New York: Wiley, 1950.

3. French, J. R. P., Jr. A formal theory of social power. *Psychol. Rev.*, 1956, **63**, 181-194.

4. Harary, F., & Norman, R. Z. *Graph theory as a mathematical model in social science.* Ann Arbor, Mich.: Institute for Social Research, 1953.

5. Harary, F., Norman, R. Z., & Cartwright, D. *Introduction to digraph theory for social scientists.* Ann Arbor, Mich.: Institute for Social Research, in press.

6. Zipf, Sheila G. An experimental study of resistance to influence. Unpublished doctoral dissertation, University of Michigan, 1958.

11

A FIELD THEORETICAL CONCEPTION OF POWER [1]

Dorwin Cartwright

The study of power has long been the prerogative of political scientists and political philosophers. Mere mention of the word makes one think of Machiavelli, Hobbes, Nietzsche, Russell, and a host of others concerned with the philosophy and practice of government. Topics discussed under the heading of power deal typically with the various forms of government, war and diplomacy, operation of the military in government, relations between the economic system and government, such political processes as influencing the vote, exerting pressure, or controlling the disaffected, class and caste, and revolution. Power has traditionally been viewed as an attribute of large social entities or of relations among them.

With this historical perspective it may seem strange to categorize the phenomena studied in this volume under the label of power. Shouldn't essentially different concepts be used to describe matters as diverse as the dealings between General Motors and the United States Government and the interactions between husband and wife? Isn't it merely a careless use of terms to speak of the power structure of both a nation and a summer camp? The basic thesis of this book holds that no categorical distinction between "large" and "small" social entities can be maintained; such concepts as influence, power, and authority (or their equivalents) must be employed in any adequate treatment of social interaction wherever it may take place. We have found that we simply cannot understand the relations among the mental health professions, the behavior of children in summer camps, the making of decisions within the family, or the effectiveness of leadership in work groups without knowing about the power situation.

Although there are undeniably important differences between large, enduring social institutions and more temporary relationships within smaller

[1] The material presented in this chapter is in a real sense the product of a group. It has evolved out of extended and intensive interaction with my colleagues at the Research Center for Group Dynamics, and the great influence of Kurt Lewin will be evident throughout. By assuming sole authorship, I take responsibility for its present formulation, but I must express my debt to all those who have helped shape it.

social entities, it does not follow that a single set of theoretical constructs is inappropriate for treating both. On the contrary, developments within social psychology and within the disciplines concerned with institutions are combining to strengthen the belief that the same concepts should be employed by both. The studies contained in this volume illustrate an increasing awareness of the need for the concept of power on the part of social psychologists. And, certain trends in the study of institutions are making the concept as used there more appropriate for theories of interpersonal relations.

First, there is now considerable agreement among political theorists that power should not be equated with "brute force," "coercion," or "naked power." The popular image of power as involving Machiavellian unscrupulousness is also rejected as too narrow. Thus, Russell (18) asserts that an individual may have power over another as a result of being able to influence him (a) by direct physical power over his body, (b) by rewards and punishments, or (c) by influence of opinion. While there are theorists who would still maintain that power always involves some form of coerciveness, the general trend toward defining it so as to include many forms of social influence ought to reduce substantially the social psychologist's reluctance to employ it in describing social interaction in the family, classroom, camp, neighborhood, workgroup, or other places where brute force may be rarely employed.[2]

Second, power and authority are evolving as central concepts in studies of "middle-sized" institutions such as a business concern, military base, or research laboratory. Problems of administration and of human relations in such organizations are being investigated simultaneously by political scientists, sociologists, and social psychologists, with the result that the same concepts are appearing in theories of all three disciplines. The treatments of administration presented by Dubin (4) and Simon (21) serve as good examples of this trend.

Third, the rise of the "behavioral science" approach has stressed the importance of formulating theories of institutions in terms of behavior of individuals. To the extent that this undertaking succeeds, any categorical distinction between institutions and interaction among people becomes untenable. Perhaps the most relevant example of this approach for the study of power is provided by Lasswell and Kaplan (11) who assert that the fundamental units of the political process are "acts performed by individuals" and that "terms like 'state,' 'government,' 'law,' 'power'—all the traditional vocabulary

---

[2] Indeed, if one accepts the claim of Simon (22) that power means simply "A's behavior causes B's behavior," then it is hard to see how social psychology could possibly do without the term.

of political science—are words of ambiguous reference until it is clear how they are to be used in describing what people say and do" (p. 3). It is not surprising that, starting with such presuppositions, Lasswell and Kaplan develop a conceptualization of influence and power quite congenial to social psychologists.

There are good reasons, then, to aspire to a single conception of power which can be used in the various disciplines of the social sciences, but two requirements will have to be met before a unified conceptual system is actually achieved. First, power will have to be defined so as to have unambiguous logical relations to other concepts both in theories of human behavior and in theories of institutions. Only in this way can the two kinds of theories be unambiguously linked together. Needless to say, such a linkage will be difficult because its achievement will mean bringing into a single, coherent conceptual system component systems deriving from diverse intellectual traditions and concerned with different kinds of phenomena. Furthermore, none of the existing component systems has achieved a high level of conceptual rigor. The second requirement is for close interaction between formalization and empirical work. It is an unfortunate fact that the separation of work into "pure theory" and "brute empiricism" has plagued the study of power perhaps more seriously than any other field of investigation. Work of either extreme sort is no longer of much value.

The studies reported in this volume have been guided by these requirements, though they cannot be said to have met them fully. Concentrating on phenomena traditionally within the field of social psychology, they have drawn freely upon ideas originated in other disciplines. Throughout, a middle course has been steered between ambitious formalization and sheer data gathering. Theoretical conceptions have guided the collection of data in each study, but no effort has been made to test a single formal theory which would encompass them all. Obviously, the task of treating power in a fully satisfactory way has only been started. Appropriate next steps will include conceptual refinement, development of improved indicators and measuring instruments, elaboration of theoretical generalizations and hypotheses, and further collection of empirical data. This chapter will focus on the need for conceptual refinement.

THE PROBLEM OF DEFINITION

Anyone reading the literature on power is bound to be troubled by the absence of a generally accepted definition of power. Most authors have taken pains to provide a definition, but each has felt compelled to invent one of his own. Unfortunately, the differences are not merely semantic; they cannot be eliminated by the invention of a dictionary. The following quotations indicate some of the major varieties.

"Power may be defined as the capacity of an individual, or group of individuals, to modify the conduct of other individuals or groups in the manner which he desires." Tawney (23, p. 230)

"Power may be defined as the production of intended effects." Russell (18, p. 35)

"Power we may define as the realistic capacity of a system-unit to actualize its 'interests' (attain goals, prevent undesired interference, command respect, control possessions, etc.) within the context of system-interaction and in this sense to exert influence on processes in the system." Parsons (17, p. 391)

"Power is a special case of the exercise of influence: it is the process of affecting policies of others with the help of (actual or threatened) severe deprivations for nonconformity with the policies intended." Lasswell and Kaplan (11, p. 76)

"Power is the ability to employ force," i.e., to apply sanctions. Bierstedt (2, p. 733)

"For the assertion, 'A has power over B,' we can substitute the assertion, 'A's behavior causes B's behavior.' " Simon (22, p. 5)

"My intuitive idea of power, then, is something like this: A has power over B to the extent that he can get B to do something that B would not otherwise do." Dahl (3, p. 202)

All of these definitions appear to refer to the same broad class of phenomena, being concerned with the influence or control of behavior. It is impossible, however, to demonstrate their equivalence as formal constructs, for each employs terms or specific conditions not found in the others. Such diversity prevents the insertion of any one of these definitions rigorously into a system making use of any other one.

How can agreement about definitions be achieved? One approach would be to try to persuade everyone to accept a definition proposed by some authority or, more "democratically," a definition resulting from a conference-on-definitions. Such efforts have, in fact, been made in the past but to little avail. While they might succeed in establishing a system of measurement or labels for standard operational indicators, they are certain to fail when concerned with basic constructs of theory. Their futility has been pointed out by Lasswell and Kaplan who maintain that "uniformity of usage cannot be brought about either by fiat or exhortation. Nor is this uniformity of any transcending importance. What does matter is self-consistency, and clarity sufficient to make translation and empirical reference always possible." (11, p. x)

A more indirect approach, then, is required. The history of science suggests that science is essentially a free enterprise system in which conceptual systems compete for acceptance and that they stand or fall, if not as whole systems at least in large interdependent parts, carrying their constructs with them. One must rely in the long run upon a sort of inverse "Gresham's law" which holds that good conceptual systems drive out bad. Applied specifically to the problems at hand, this principle suggests that the achievement of a widely accepted definition of power will best be attained if each theorist (or group of theorists) develops an internally consistent conceptual system and then attempts to discover how well it provides an orderly understanding of the relevant phenomena. The inevitable confusion generated by a multiplicity of conceptual systems can be minimized if all theorists will make as explicit as possible the formal structure of their theories. By doing so, the relative merits of different systems can be more readily determined, and their general acceptability more quickly established.[3]

The definition of power proposed here is stated in the terms of Lewinian field theory. Power thereby becomes explicitly related to other constructs in this general theory of human behavior. As a result, hypotheses can readily be generated concerning the empirical relations of power to motivation, cognition, modification of behavior, and other psychological attributes. Since it is not possible here to present the full Lewinian system, a certain familiarity with it will be assumed.[4]

Construction of a Definition of Power

If our definition of power is to refer to the same broad class of phenomena as other uses of the term, it will be concerned with influences upon the behavior of individuals or groups which arise from some "external" source. If the definition is to have a clear logical position within Lewinian field theory, it will have to be stated in the terms employed by that theory. A definition meeting these requirements was proposed by Lewin (13) in his abstract discussion of "organizational interdependence" at the end of the appendix to his theory of frustration and regression. This definition has served to guide

---

[3] Perhaps an observation concerning tactics should be inserted. Insistence upon working toward formal elegance should not be confused with advocacy of developing formal models apart from empirical research. Social psychology is an empirical science, and its terms must have empirical reference. The fruitfulness of any formal system, and its ultimate acceptability, will depend upon how appropriate the formal properties prove to be for the world of empirical phenomena to which they are coordinated.

[4] The most revelant discussion of the broader system of constructs will be found in two books by Lewin (12, 13).

the work reported in this book. Specifically, Lewin proposed that "we might define power of b over a (pow b/a) as the quotient of the maximum force which b can induce on a ($i^b f_{a,x}^{max}$), and the maximum resistance ($f_{a,x}^{max}$) which a can offer. (x indicates the region into which a should locomote according to the will of b; $f_{\overline{a,x}}$ indicates a force in the direction opposite to $f_{a,x}$)." **(13, p. 336)**

According to this conception, power refers to the induction of (psychological) forces by one entity b upon another a and to the resistance to this induction set up by a. Since the behavior of a is determined by the totality of forces operating upon him at any given time, the power of b over a is concerned only with those influences on a's behavior originating with b. It should be apparent, then, that this definition refers to the same broad class of phenomena dealt with by other definitions. Use of this definition in theoretical and empirical work, moreover, has shown it to be quite satisfactory, for many of its properties are found to be reflected in empirical phenomena. At the same time, certain ambiguities have arisen, particularly with respect to the meaning of "induced force," calling for a refinement and elaboration of certain features of Lewin's definition.

Since this definition of power is stated in terms of psychological forces, the conceptual properties of force determine many of the properties of power. In order to convey the full meaning of the concept "power," it is thus necessary to discuss the more basic concept, psychological force.

Psychological Force

It should be noted at the outset that Lewin's concept of force is rather different from that employed by those writers who equate forces to coercion or to the application of sanctions. For Lewin the concept refers to "a tendency to change in some property of the life space" and is defined in terms of direction, strength, and point of application **(12, p. 83)**. In his elaboration of the concept, Lewin distinguished three "types" of forces: "own" which are based upon some need, or tension system, of the person; "induced" which originate in the will of some other person; and "impersonal" which stem from the impersonal parts of the environment.

In an effort to clarify certain properties of Lewin's concept, it is useful to treat "force" in a somewhat unusual manner. Force is defined by means of seven terms, employed here as undefined terms (primitives).[5] Each will be discussed briefly before a formal definition of force is presented.

---

[5] Several of the terms which are treated here as primitives are themselves constructed from other terms in other field theoretical discussions. We leave open the question of

Agent. This term is conceived broadly as any entity which can produce effects or suffer consequences. Most commonly an agent is a person, and we shall be concerned here primarily with two agents: P, the person being influenced, and O, the person exerting the influence.[6] In addition, however, the term can also refer to distinguishable subparts of a person, to groups, and to subparts of groups.

U1. Agents: a finite set, $\Sigma = \{A, B, C \ldots\}$

Act of an agent. For an agent to exert influences or produce effects it must be "active" in some fashion. The event, associated with the agent, which activates an effect is here termed an "act." Exactly what empirical event will be taken as an act of a particular agent will depend upon the nature of the agent and of the influence in question. Acts may produce effects within the life space of the agent performing the act or in the life space of another agent. In the latter case, the act is usually called an "influence attempt."

U2. Acts of an agent, A: a finite set, $\Delta = \{\alpha_A, \beta_A, \gamma_A \ldots\}$

Locus. Every agent should be "locatable" in some space. Location is specified in terms of a set of loci. A locus usually corresponds to Lewin's concept of region and may, therefore, be coordinated to a goal, means-activity, passive state, or position in a group or organization. However, it may also refer to a position on a scale indicating an attitude, cognitive attribute, rate of performance, level of production, and the like.

U3. Loci: a finite set, $X = \{a, b, c \ldots\}$

Direct joining. Whenever two or more loci are to be considered as existing in the same space, their spatial interrelations must be specified. The essential primitive notion here is "direct joining." The intuitive meaning of this term is the possibility of "going directly from one to the other." Thus, if *a* and *b* are means-activities, we would say that *a* directly joins *b* if it is possible to go from one of the activities to the other without passing through any third one. Or, if *c* and *d* are two offices in an organization (e.g., secretary and

which primitives would provide the best basis for a general theory of behavior, though we are impressed with the breadth of phenomena which can be treated with concepts constructed from the primitives listed here. The formal development of a conceptual system requires, of course, the specification of axioms about the primitives. These are not discussed here since our purpose is to indicate the "components" of force, and thus power, rather than to state a formal system of behavior.

[6] Several theorists have employed the term "actor" in much the same way that "agent" is used here. Since it is here intended to allow the same entity to "act" and to "receive," the term "actor" seems not quite appropriate. Dahl (3), in an interesting conceptual analysis of power, has introduced two terms: "actor" and "respondent." Our conception assumes that the same agent may be both an actor and a respondent. For many purposes, however, our notation, O and P, corresponds to Dahl's terms, actor and respondent.

president), c does not directly join d if it is not possible to be promoted directly from secretary to president. The concept, direct joining, might be thought of as corresponding to Lewin's "common boundary of two regions," but we propose to coordinate the concepts, locus and direct joining, to the graph theoretic concepts, point and directed line (8). If we designate the set, Γ, as the collection of all ordered pairs of loci (x, y) such that x does join y (it is not specified that y also joins x) we may state:

U4. Direct joining: x directly joins y if and only if the ordered couple (x, y) exists in Γ.

Motive base. The term "motive base" is used here to refer to the need, motive, drive, or other "predisposition," which energizes behavior. A given motive base is designated by the type of activity or state which "satisfies" it. Thus, we may speak of such things as the need for achievement, cognition, or affiliation, as motive bases.

U5. Motive bases: a finite set, $M = \{M_a, M_b, M_c \ldots\}$

Magnitude indicator. It is desirable to be able to indicate the magnitude or strength of certain constructs. Although there are many unsolved problems in quantifying psychological attributes, we shall assume that in principle it is possible to employ positive and negative real numbers as magnitude indicators.

U6. Continuous magnitude indicators: the real number system, where m denotes a real number. Notation: if we wish to state that the strength of act a of agent A equals the value m, we write $|a_A| = m$.

Time indicator. Each event or state of affairs described should have an indicator placing it in a time sequence. For certain purposes it may be appropriate to employ units of physical time. It is likely, however, that other units may be necessary for other purposes. We require only that a temporal order be specified.

U7. Discrete time indicators: the nonnegative integers, $t = 0, 1, 2, 3 \ldots$
Notation: we may indicate $t = k$ by t_k.

In the use of these terms and others constructed from them it will always be necessary to specify, at least by context, the particular life space, or field, under consideration. In this chapter the life space of P is always referred to unless indicated otherwise.

Definition of force. The construct "psychological force" is a complex term which employs all of the primitives just listed. A particular force is specified by assigning a definite value to each primitive.

D1. Force is a quintuple consisting of (1) act of an agent, (2) motive base, (3) directly joining pair of loci, (4) magnitude, and (5) time.

If we wish to indicate that force f_1 has act a of agent A as its activator, need for g as its motive base, locus a as its location and ab as its direction, m as its strength, and t_k as its temporal position, we write: $f_1 = (a_A, M_g, ab, m, t_k)$. In the notation usually employed by Lewin, $|f_{ab}| = m$ refers to a force in the direction ab with magnitude equal to m; time and motive base are either not specified or given by context, and act of agent has no explicit meaning. Lewin's simpler notation is retained here where only direction and magnitude of force are of major interest.

Own and induced forces. Since the distinction between "own" and "induced" force plays a central role in Lewin's definition of power, we need now to relate it to our formulation. According to Lewin, an own force "corresponds to a person's own needs" and an induced force "corresponds to the wish of another person." While this distinction obviously refers to phenomena of utmost importance, it has proved to be a difficult one to maintain with clear meaning. By distinguishing between the "motive base" of a force and its "activator" we hope to remove some of the ambiguity. According to our view, a force acting on P may be based upon a need of P and yet be activated by some act of another person (a_0). O might say to P, for example, "Why don't you take the evening off and go to the movies?" If we assume that P had a need for relaxation, we could not say unambiguously whether the activated force corresponds to the person's own needs or to the wish of another person. Nevertheless, the empirical situation is clear and can be represented by means of the primitives of force which we propose. In general, the distinction among types of forces may be replaced by designating in each concrete instance the act of agent, motive base, and direction of the force in question.

To illustrate further the proposed treatment, let us consider a related issue raised by Festinger (5): "When a person or group attempts to influence someone, does that person or group produce a totally new force acting on the person, one which had not been present prior to the attempted influence? Our answer is No—an attempted influence does not produce any new motivation or force. Rather, what an influence attempt involves is the redirection of psychological forces which already exist. That is, a force already acting on the person has its direction changed by the influencer." (p. 237) Regardless of whether Festinger's view proves ultimately to be correct, it can be restated in the terms proposed here. He is concerned with two times: t_0, before the influence attempt, and t_1, immediately thereafter. We interpret him to mean that the same motive base (M_g) is involved at both times but that the direction of the force changes (from ab to ax). Although the activator of the force (χ_X) is not specified for t_0, the "influence attempt" of the inducer (a_0) is clearly the activator at t_1. The situation described by Festinger can, then, be represented in our terms as a change from $f_0 = \chi_X$, M_g, ab, m, t_0) to $f_1 =$ (a_0, M_g, ax, m, t_1). Clearly, f_0 and f_1 are identical in some respects and different in others.

It is important to note that, in general, a single act of an agent may activate forces having various motive bases and that different acts of various agents may activate forces having the same motive base. Thus, when O requests that P do something, tendencies toward compliance may result from the fact that the request has "tapped" any of a number of motivations (the need to be liked, to avoid ridicule, etc.). Similarly, a single need of P may be engaged by a variety of acts produced by a variety of agents. Specification of the component terms of force will allow a characterization of all the logically possible combinations of motive base, activator, and direction without recourse to the ambiguous classification of "types" of forces.

Strength of an Act

The term "act of agent" plays a critical role in our treatment of influence and power. Acts may be characterized in various ways. One is by reference to their "content" (i.e., whether they are such things as promises, threats, suggestions, commands, or statements of fact). Such classifications are essential, as we shall see, in specifying "forms" of power. Another way of characterizing an act is in terms of properties of the forces it activates. We assume that a given act may set up several forces in any of several life spaces at any given time and that the directions of these forces in a particular life space may or may not be that intended by the agent. The content of the act usually indicates a direction, though ambiguous acts may provide "poor" indications of direction.

Suppose that a_0 is a request by O that P change from one activity to another. This may set up a force on P to comply (f_{ab}) and one to resist or to do something else ($f_{\overline{ab}}$). Full specification of the forces would assert: $f_{ab} = (a_0$, M_x, ab, m_1, t_k) and $f_{\overline{ab}} = (a_0$, M_x, $\overline{ab}$, m_2, t_k), where both forces have the same act, agent, locus, and time, but not necessarily the same motive base. Now, we may specify the strength of the act with respect to the direction, ab, in P's life space.

D2. Strength of a_0 with respect to ab in P's life space at a given time, t_k.
$|a_0(\text{ab})| = |f_{ab}| - |f_{\overline{ab}}|$, where both forces are activated by a_0.[7]

---

[7] By allowing a given act of O to tap several motive bases of P, we have the possibility that a given act may set up several forces in P's life space at locus, a. Here, and in related definitions, we assume that all forces set up by a given act at the same locus may be combined into two forces, f_{ab} and $f_{\overline{ab}}$.

In the example cited, the strength of the act with respect to ab equals $m_1 - m_2$. Note that if $m_1 > m_2$, the strength of the act is positive and an influence on P in the direction ab is exerted. It should be noted, however, that even if the strength of the act is positive, P need not necessarily change from a to b because other forces may also be operative. If $m_2 > m_1$, the strength of the act assumes a negative value; the net effect of the act is to resist change in the direction ab.

Power

The power of O over P, as we conceive it, is concerned with O's ability to perform acts which activate forces in P's life space.

Definition in terms of acts. At any given time, O is capable of performing a variety of acts. We refer to these as $\Delta(O, t_k)$, the set of all acts which O can perform at t_k. At that time these acts are "potential." We let χ_0 be any element of this set, i.e., any particular act which O can perform at that time. Power may then be defined in these terms.

D3. Power of O over P with respect to ab at a specified time, t_k. Pow O/P
(ab) $= |\chi_0(ab)|^{max}$, where χ_0 is any element of $\Delta(O, t_k)$.

Stated in words, this definition asserts: the power of O over P with respect to a change from *a* to *b* at a specified time equals the maximum strength of any act which O can perform at that time, where strength is specified for the direction ab in P's life space.

Definition in terms of forces. An equivalent definition may be formed by substituting forces for strength of act, in keeping with D2.

D3a. Pow O/P (ab) $= (|f_{ab}| - |f_{\overline{ab}}|)^{max}$, where f_{ab} and $f_{\overline{ab}}$ are related to
the same potential act of O.

The meaning of this definition may be stated in words: the power of O over P with respect to a given change at a specified time equals the maximum strength of the resultant force which O can set up in that direction at that time. The strength of the resultant force on P is determined by the relative magnitudes of the forces activated by O to "comply" and to "resist."

Certain observations may now be made concerning the relations between this definition and the one proposed by Lewin. Both are stated in terms of psychological forces, and both are concerned with the opposition of two forces acting on the person. In Lewin's formula these opposing forces are treated as a quotient; in ours as a difference. Both formulas are concerned with maximal values of these forces. Lewin defines power as the ratio of the maximal values; we define it as the maximal difference. On one remaining point it is difficult to make a definite comparison. Lewin's formula refers to two terms: the force which O can "induce" on P and the "resistance" which P can offer. These phrases are susceptible to several rather different interpretations. We have chosen to follow one of these in our definition of power by considering only the forces which can be activated by an act of O. Accordingly, both the "induced force" and the "resistance" are activated by an act of O. "Resistance" is generated by the influence attempt and distinguished from "opposition" which stems from other factors (see French and Raven's discussion in Chapter 9).[8]

Later in this chapter a systematic survey of the conceptual properties of power is presented. At this point, we merely note the most important features of the concept. Power is a relation between two agents, O and P. It is concerned with the maximum influence which O can exert on P at a given time to change in a given direction. Since it is defined in terms of psychological forces, specification of a particular instance of power requires assigning values to all component terms of all relevant forces. The power of O over P is concerned only with forces which an act of O can activate within P's life space. In principle, any kind of act of O and any kind of motive base of P may be involved. Power must be specified for particular loci of P's life space (the location and direction of the forces). While power must also be specified for a particular time, we are usually interested only in power which remains reasonably stable over a considerable interval of time. Finally, the magnitude of power is determined by the magnitudes of the forces involved.

Power and control. At any given time there may be any finite number of forces at a given locus in P's life space. These may have various activators, motive bases, directions, and magnitudes. Their patterning generates the familiar "types of conflict," and their combination into a single "combined" or "resultant" force which comes to control the behavior of P reflects a "decision." It is a basic axiom of Lewinian field theory that a change of P's life space (including locomotion of P) is coordinated to the concept "combined force" and not to "component force." Stated more formally, P changes from locus *a* to locus *b* during a given time interval if and only if there exists

[8] Another interpretation of Lewin's definition would equate his term "induced force" to our "strength of act of O" and his term "resistance" to a counter-act of P stimulated by the act of O and setting up forces also in P's life space. Under this interpretation Lewin's meaning might be expressed as the ratio: $|\chi_O(ab_p)|^{max}/|\chi_P(\overline{ab_P})|^{max}$. A quite different interpretation of "resistance" would be to conceive of it as a counter-act of P which sets up forces in O's life space: $\chi_P(\overline{ab_O})$. Such an interpretation calls attention to many important problems best referred to as "relative power" and can be handled in our terminology under the concepts Pow O/P(ab) and Pow P/O($\overline{ab}$).

at that time a combined force in the direction *ab* with a magnitude greater than zero.

It is apparent from this axiom that O may be able to activate a component force (i.e., have power over P) and yet not be able to change the direction of the combined force acting on P; forces activated by other agents (including P himself) may be of overwhelming magnitude. In everyday terms, O may ask P to do something and P may experience a tendency to comply but not actually do so. In this case, we should say that O, by activating a component force, has influenced P in some way (produced conflict, wavering, guilt, or what not) but we could not say that O has "controlled" P's behavior. It is possible, of course, for the act of O to be "decisive" and to change the direction of the combined force and thus the direction of P's behavior. If the direction of P's behavior is modified so as to conform to the direction intended by O, then O controls P's behavior.[9]

D4.   O controls P if and only if an act of O results in a *combined* force in P's life space (and hence a change) having a direction which corresponds to that intended by O.[10]

Several definitions of power and authority make use of this notion of "control." Thus, Russell's definition of power (18, p. 35) as "the production of intended effects" might be restated in the following way: O has power over P if and only if O controls P. Dahl's assertion (3, p. 202) that "A has power over B to the extent that he can get B to do something that B would not otherwise do" seems to refer to what we would call ability to control. The definition of authority given by Simon (21, p. 125) as "the power to make decisions which guide the actions of another" is basically the same. According to Simon, O exercises authority over P when he communicates a decision (in our terms,

---

[9] We must omit here a formal treatment of the concept "intention." The term is essential, however, in any discussion of "effectiveness" or "success" of an influence attempt. The research of Lippitt, Polansky, Redl, and Rosen (14) indicates that, even without a formal definition of intention, reliable empirical indicators can be developed to distinguish between "intended" and "unintended" acts of influence.

[10] Two features of this definition should be noted in that they make it differ from some others which have been proposed. First, the definition includes specification of the intention of O. Some authors would assert that O controls P if O's behavior modifies P's behavior, regardless of O's intentions. Second, this definition states no requirement concerning the magnitude of the combined force other than that it must exceed zero. According to this definition, O controls P's behavior provided P complies, regardless of P's speed of performance, persistence, resistance to distraction, and so forth. Many problems encountered by supervisors with regard to "motivation" of subordinates are concerned more with the magnitude of the combined force resulting from the exercise of their authority than with its direction. It would take us too far afield to discuss this interesting problem here.

performs a particular kind of act) which "guides the actions of" (controls) P.

Although there is no way to enforce a single terminology among these and other writers, it is useful to note explicitly how the concepts referred to by the various labels relate to one another. An essential distinction, we believe, is that between ability to influence, or to activate forces, and ability to control. It is evident that, in our terms, the ability to control is a special instance of power (ability to influence) in that O must have some power over P in order to control P. O's exercise of control depends, however, upon many things in addition to the possession of power. In general, it depends not only upon the strength of the act (with respect to the change of P under consideration) performed by O but also upon the strength (with respect to the same change) of all acts performed by all other agents (including P), where it is necessary to take into account directions of the forces set up by the various acts.

CONCEPTUAL PROPERTIES OF POWER

The definition of power proposed here is constructed from the concept "psychological force" and thus from its constituent primitive terms. For this reason, many of the conceptual properties of "power" derive from these primitives. The contribution of each primitive to the conceptual properties of power may now be examined.

Agent

Power is defined as a relationship between two agents, O and P. One must always speak, implicitly at least, of the power of O over P; it is not permissible to speak of power as some absolute attribute of a single agent. It may appear that this defintion thus rules out Parsons' concept of "economic power" (16, p. 124). The difference between economic and political power, he asserts, is that economic power is "lineal," simply a matter of "more or less," while political power is "hierarchical," a matter of "power over." This difference he believes derives from the nature of property and monetary exchange. The more money one has the more services one can command quite apart from other social relationships. Parsons' point is important, but in our view it does not make economic power a different thing from power as defined here. Even when power is derived from economic resources, its exercise comes down ultimately to the activation of forces by O upon P.

The formal requirement that power always be specified as a relationship between two agents leaves open the question of what empirical entities may properly be coordinated to the term "agent." In a fully developed formal system, axioms would be stated specifying the properties of agents, and these properties would have to be respected in any coordination of the term to empirical entities. Even though such axioms have not yet been formally elaborated, it is clear that anything coordinated to O must be capable of performing "acts" and that anything coordinated to P must be capable of being subjected to psychological forces. Individual people clearly meet these requirements. As a starting point, therefore, it is possible to conceive of power as a relationship between two people. Traditional treatments of power and common sense usage suggest that the term "agent" should also be coordinated to empirical entities other than individuals. It does not seem inappropriate, for example, to refer to an executive committee or a legislature as performing acts when it issues an order or passes a law. Such collectivities can then be treated as agents, and we may consider their power over individuals or over other collectivities. In keeping with the same principle, we shall also speak of the power of an individual over such collective agents as committees, groups, and institutions. Needless to say, many difficult problems of conceptualization are generated by permitting the term "agent" to refer both to individuals and to collectivities, but at the present stage of development, social science would gain little, and lose much, by insisting that it is meaningless to speak of the power of a group over its members or of the power of an individual over group decision-making and action.

Defining power as a relationship raises a question concerning the formal properties of the power relation. Only a limited number of these properties are considered here, although an exhaustive examination is needed.

A nonsymmetric relation. If O has power over P, can P have power over O at the same time? Some writers would give a negative answer; they would define power as necessarily asymmetric. While it is clear that many actual power relationships are asymmetric, there is nothing in our definition of power that makes the relation necessarily so. There is nothing, moreover, to make it necessarily symmetric. We conclude, then, that power is a nonsymmetric relation; knowing that "O has power over P" establishes no requirement concerning the relation "P has power over O."

A thorough analysis of this problem requires careful designation of the nature of the change in terms of which power is being specified. Consider the situation of a husband, H, and a wife, W, where each wants to get the other to go out and buy the evening paper. We may ask, What is the magnitude of pow H/W (ab), where ab exists in W's life space and has the meaning "wife goes out for the paper?" We may also ask, What is the magnitude of pow W/H (ab), where ab is located in H's life space and has the meaning "husband goes out for the paper?" The answer to both questions depends upon the maximum strength of the acts which H or W can perform. It is quite possible, in principle, that both H and W can activate strong forces on the other to go out for the paper. If, however, it has been agreed between them that the task is properly that of H or W, then only one may be able to activate forces on the other. Finally, it is possible that the marriage relation is such that neither can influence the other with respect to getting the paper.

It is clear, then, that power relationships between two given agents, O and P, may display any one of four states: (a) O has power over P with respect to a given change of P's life space *and* P has power over O with respect to the "same" change of O's life space; (b) O has power over P with respect to a given change, but P has no such power over O; (c) O has no power over P, but P has power over O; and (d) neither O nor P has power over the other. These four states may be thought of as "types of interdependence." Since it is often asserted that power is necessarily asymmetric, we point out that mutual interdependence is commonly found among mutual friends and members of cohesive groups. French (7) has analyzed such situations in detail with particular reference to changes of opinion or attitude and the development of group norms.

An irreflexive relation. Is power reflexive? Can one properly speak of the power of P over P? It is clear that in everyday language we do speak of "self-control" and of "having power to make oneself do something." It seems probable, however, that such statements actually refer to two different agents, both sub-parts of the same individual. The point at issue conceptually is whether strictly speaking an agent performs acts which activate forces on itself. We are not prepared to make a final determination of this issue, but it does seem likely that apparent instances of reflexive power can be analyzed more "microscopically" into irreflexive relations between two agents. Notions like those of "self-control" or "ability to influence oneself" would seem to refer to intra-individual relationships between such agents as "ego," "super-ego," and "motorium." Unfortunately, the analysis of intra-individual power relationships has not proceeded very far.

A nontransitive relation. The question remains as to whether power is a transitive relation. In other words, if A has power over B and B has power over C, does it necessarily follow that A has power over C? On the basis of our definition of power the answer is clearly that power is not necessarily transitive or intransitive. A boss may be able to activate strong forces on his secretary who, in turn, may be able to influence her husband without this implying in any way that the boss can activate forces on the secretary's husband.

It should be noted, however, that even when a given power relationship is intransitive, influence may be transmitted from A to C via B without A's being able to influence C directly. It should also be noted that in specific social settings power relationships may display transitivity. Such would be the case in a hierarchical organization where each person at a higher level can directly influence everyone at a lower level.

Since the power relation is nontransitive, it follows that when A has power over C there is no necessary restriction upon the possibility that B also has power over C. Both A and B may activate forces on C at the same time, even when they are in opposite directions and when they set up tendencies toward incompatible changes in C. If such is actually the case, then C experiences conflict. Such cases are obviously quite common.

It is of considerable theoretical interest that the concept "directed line" as employed in the mathematical theory of directed graphs is a binary relation which is nonsymmetric, irreflexive, and nontransitive (8) and that a directed graph may therefore be used to depict a given power structure. It must be noted that the relation "has control over" does not necessarily have the same properties as power and therefore requires a separate formal analysis.

Domain of power. For many purposes we may wish to concentrate attention upon a particular agent, O, and determine the other agents over whom O has power. The concept, domain of power, has been employed by Lasswell and Kaplan (11) and others to refer to those people over whom a given person has power. The following definition, therefore, is consistent with this usage.

D5. At any given time, the domain of O's power with respect to a given change (ab) is the set of agents over whom the power of O with respect to ab exceeds a given magnitude, k.

Usually we may let k = O, but for certain purposes some other critical value may be used in specifying a domain. It follows from this definition that the domain of O's power will depend upon the particular change under consideration and upon the value assigned to k.

Act of Agent

The primitive term "act of agent" may be coordinated, in a general theory of human behavior, to a wide range of empirical phenomena. Since the term "agent" is used here to refer only to such social entities as individuals and collectivities of people, the term "act" is coordinated to certain events associated with these agents. Acts of agents, therefore, refer to such things as "suggestions," "commands," "requests," "hints," "policy decisions," "executive orders," or more generally "influence attempts," and "communications."

Classification of acts. In empirical research on power, classes of acts need to be identified so that they may be related to other phenomena in lawful ways. General schemes for recording behavior or for conducting "content analysis" illustrate efforts to classify acts of agents. A fundamental issue in all such schemes is whether a given act should be characterized according to its meaning to O, to P, or to a meaning shared by O and P. This problem is inevitable, of course, because of the nature of acts: an act is produced by O, has effects on P, and since the life spaces of the two may differ in many ways, its significance to each may diverge. From a conceptual point of view acts must be characterized separately according to their meanings to O and to P, although for many purposes their meanings may be assumed to be identical.

Although a comprehensive discussion of the meaning of an act cannot be undertaken here, it may be noted that a major part of an act's meaning can be specified by use of the primitive terms employed in the constructs "force" and "power." A few examples may illustrate the point.

One aspect of the meaning of an act has to do with its intensity. In keeping with our general procedure, the strength of an act of O is defined in terms of the magnitude of force that it activates in P's life space. A corresponding definition of the intensity of an act could be developed from O's point of view, reflecting O's beliefs about the probable magnitude of force that it will set up. In principle these two characterizations of the same act need not necessarily agree. Thus, for example, O might make what he regards as a "mild suggestion" and P might interpret the act as a "strong order." Despite the possibility of such misunderstanding, it is clear that when O and P share the same culture there is at least an approximate agreement between them about the scaling of "objective intensity" of social acts. When a power structure is well established within a group, all (or most) of the members know, at least approximately, which acts will activate strong forces and which agents are capable of producing such acts.

Another constituent of the meaning of an act refers to O's intentions in performing the act. It is evident that O may produce an act which sets up forces in P's life space even though O had no intention of influencing P. The distinction between intentional and unintentional influence played an important part in the research of Lippitt, Polansky, Redl, and Rosen (14) who distinguished between "behavioral contagion," as the spontaneous pickup or imitation of behavior initiated by one child when he displayed no intention of getting the others to do what he did, and "direct influence," as behavior which had the manifest objective of affecting the behavior of another. Observers were able to code these two kinds of acts at acceptable levels of reliability, and significant empirical differences were found between the two kinds of acts. It would seem that the intentionality of acts is of critical importance in processes of influence and power.

The meaning of an act is also heavily weighted by certain of its "directional" properties. When O makes a deliberate influence attempt he usually fashions it so as to convey that a certain agent, or set of agents, should modify their behavior in specified ways. A simple example would be the statement, "George, stop reading the paper and come to dinner." Here the act is directed toward George and is designed to activate a force having the direction from "reading the paper" toward "dinner." Acts may thus have an intended domain of agents toward which they are directed and an actual domain of agents upon whom they activate forces. Similarly, their associated forces may have intended and actual directions within any given life space.

Meyers (15), in his research upon the effects of "positive" and "negative" commands given by adults to children, presents an interesting analysis of the direction of forces set up by various acts. He proposes that a positive command (e.g., "go play with the truck") specifies a clear direction whereas a negative command (e.g., "don't play with the blocks") does not specify an unambiguous locus toward which the child should move. Consistent with this analysis was his empirical finding that negative commands are particularly disturbing to the child. More generally, it is clear that even positive commands may vary considerably in the specificity of direction of the forces they activate. It is clear, too, that some people are generally more skillful than others in producing acts with clear directions. Since an unclearly directed act probably sets up weak resultant forces in the intended direction, it is likely that skill in formulating clearly directed acts contributes to an individual's power.

Yet another determinant of an act's meaning is its motivational relevance. Acts appear to "fit" certain motive bases and not others. For example, a "friendly" act may set up forces in the life space of an agent in certain directions by tapping his need for affiliation, and a "challenge" may activate particular forces by tapping a need for achievement. A full analysis of the motivational relevance of acts must await a satisfactory means for classifying motivational bases.

Finally, the meaning of an act depends upon certain of its temporal features. We simply note here that acts may vary considerably with respect to the duration of the forces which they activate. The difference between a temporary and a permanent injunction serves to illustrate this property of acts. A systematic analysis of the temporal properties of acts should facilitate understanding of such matters as the differences between short-lived and lasting changes of attitude, the "sleeper effect" as described by Hovland and Weiss (9), regression following training as reported by Fleishman, Harris, and Burtt (6), and obedience or noncompliance with the instructions of authorities when absent from their surveillance.

Potential acts. In defining power, we referred to the set $\Delta(O, t_k)$ as all acts which O can perform at a given time. This "repertory of potential acts" is of critical importance in all matters having to do with power. By definition, at any specified time the power of O over P with respect to a change from a to b equals the maximum strength of any act in O's repertory of potential acts. It is important to note that this definition relates power to potential acts; one must distinguish between the possession of power and the exercise of influence. We now examine some of the areas of empirical investigation suggested by defining power in terms of a repertory of potential acts.

First, what determines the content of O's repertory of potential acts? While research on power has thus far provided little information of value in answering this question, three probable determinants may serve to illustrate the nature of the problem: social skill, possession of resources, and social position. Social skill is required in the performance of social acts; O can perform only those acts which he knows how to perform. The possession of resources is essential in the performance of such acts as a bribe, purchase, or reward. And the importance of social position as a determinant of O's repertory of potential acts may be seen in the observation that an "executive order" can be issued only by an executive. Future research on power could profitably concentrate upon the acts of the individual with power and particularly upon the question of how potential acts become part of one's repertory.

Second, What determines O's "choice" of acts from his repertory? Or, to pose a related question, When will a person use the power that he possesses? Research conducted to date can provide only suggestive answers.

It appears, for example, that if a person possesses power he will be inclined to use it. In the study of professional roles conducted by Zander, Cohen, and Stotland (24), each respondent was asked questions about the possession of authority and the exercise of this authority with regard to several different activities. The correlations between extent of possession and extent of use were all in the .80's or above. Hurwitz, Zander, and Hymovitch (10) found that professional mental health workers with high attributed power talked more frequently in group discussions than did those with less power. Lippitt, Polansky, Redl, and Rosen (14) found correlations ranging from .35 to .66

between the power attributed to a member and the frequency of his attempts to influence others. And French and Snyder (Chapter 8) found in their experiment on the influence of supervisors in a formal organization that when a leader is liked by his men his opinion and commands not only carry more weight but he will exert stronger attempts to influence his subordinates. From these and other studies the not surprising generalization is suggested that when O has strong acts in his repertory he will tend to perform them.

It would clearly be a mistake, however, to conclude from these data that a person always tends to perform his strongest acts, for the observed correlations between the possession and use of power are far from perfect. Many conditions undoubtedly affect the actual performance of the potential acts in O's repertory. From research on children's groups it appears that "underusers" of power may not realize that they possess as much power as they have or they may not wish for some reason to influence others. Another kind of restraint on the use of power is suggested by Biddle, French, and Moore (1) who conclude from an investigation of influence in a formal organization that "the leader who represents the organization will attempt less influence (on the attitudes of his subordinates) the further his own attitude is from the organizational attitude." And on the basis of a historical analysis of "economic dominants" in the political power structure of a community, Schulze (20) finds that over the years there has been withdrawal of the economic dominants from participation in the public life of the community. He concludes that one should not assume the necessity of "any neat, constant, and direct relationship between *power as a potential for determinative action, and power as determinative action, itself*" (p. 9). We might expect, in general, that whenever the use of power involves the giving up of resources or the possible reduction in one's power there might arise restraints against the use of power. A complete analysis of this problem would involve matters of motivation, ideology, and strategy in the use of power.

Third, What consequences are there for P when O's repertory of potential acts contains acts of great strength? If O's repertory contains strong potential acts, it is likely that these might activate forces in P's life space which could outweigh forces activated by P himself. It would follow, then, that O's power presents a potential threat to P, even if O has never used his power to thwart P. The threatening aspects of power have been investigated in several of the studies reported in this volume (see Chapters 2, 3, and 4). From this and other research it appears that there are marked individual differences in the degree to which people experience power as threatening and in the particular reactions they display in responses to experienced threat.

From our analysis of the nature of power certain suggestions may be made concerning ways in which people might attempt to reduce the threat inherent in power. One way for P to reduce O's threat to him would be to modify the nature of O's repertory of potential acts. If P can bring about a state of affairs in which it is impossible for O to perform certain acts, P may reduce his experienced threat. A common manifestation of this tendency to modify the repertory of O's potential acts is the attempt by low-power people to reduce the rights, prerogatives, or sphere of latitude of superiors through legislation, collective bargaining, or other means for redefining the acts which O may legitimately perform. In principle, P might modify O's repertory of potential acts by operating on any of the determinants of the repertory. We suggested above that social skill, possession of resources, and social position were three of the many possible determinants. We might, then, expect to find that when people are threatened by power they would attempt to affect these determinants of the powerful agent's repertory of potential acts.

A second, less revolutionary, way for P to attempt to reduce O's threat to him would be to influence O's performance of acts. Many of the reactions to power described by Zander, Cohen, and Stotland (Chapter 2) fall under this heading. One frequently employed technique for reducing the threat inherent in power is for the subordinate to avoid social situations in which the superior might perform a strong, disagreeable act. Another technique consists of attempting to influence O's motivation so that he is friendly, supportive, or cooperative with P. Forms of subordinate behavior characterized as "apple polishing," obsequiousness, or ingratiating servility may be understood as attempts to influence O's selection of acts from his repertory. Other, more constructive, attempts by P to achieve the same end might include efforts to sensitize O to P's needs, to establish a cooperative relationship between O and P, or more generally to create mutual sympathy and understanding. Some of the observed benefits of involving subordinates in group decision-making probably stem from a reduction in experienced threat by heightening P's confidence that O will perform only those acts of his repertory which are safe to P.

Motive Base

The primitive term "motive base," as employed in our conceptualization of power, permits a linking of theories of power to theories of motivation. In a developed formal system any established generalizations about the nature of motives would enter as axioms concerning motive bases. We shall not attempt here to present any specific theory of motivation. We simply note that "motive base" refers to the sorts of phenomena variously referred to as "need," "motive," "drive," "tension system," or "instinct." The important feature of motive base as it relates to the conception of power is that an act of an agent must "tap" a motive base in order for it to activate a force. Suppose that O and P are engaged in a political discussion and that O attempts to get P to adopt a new attitude. Let us assume that O makes an influence attempt (a_o) intended to change P's attitude from e to f (ef). It is our contention that this act will activate a force on P in the direction, ef, only if it taps some motive base of P. Such a motive base might be P's need for approval (M_a). Under the proper circumstances, then, the act of O might tap this motive and thereby activate a force in P's life space directed from e to f. This force would be written: (a_o, M_a, ef, m, t_k).

This general conception, by relating power to motivation, points to many important empirical questions about motivational influences on power. Thus, one may ask, How does the magnitude of a force set up by a given act depend upon the properties of the motive base? It would appear likely, on the basis of other research on motivation, that the stronger the need the greater the magnitude of the force. In the example just cited, this would mean that O can activate a stronger force on P to change his attitude the stronger P's need for approval. Under these circumstances O's power over P with respect to this change of attitude increases with any heightening of P's need for approval.

In any concrete situation, of course, many things in addition to the strength of need determine the magnitude of the force set up by an act. We noted earlier that an act must in some sense "fit" a motive base in order to activate a force. Although little is known about the properties of acts which determine whether or not they will tap any given motive base, the nature of the process is suggested by those acts which are more or less explicit promises. For example, O may say, "If you adopt this attitude, I'll approve of you." Here, P may believe that his compliance with O's request will increase the probability that his need will be satisfied. In general, an act of O will be more likely to tap a need of P and thus make it serve as a motive base for a force on P the greater P's subjective probability that compliance will result in satisfaction of that need. French and Raven (Chapter 9), in their discussion of reward power, describe some of the conditions which affect the activation of a force through the promise of reward.

One important feature of needs is that their satisfaction requires access to certain resources.[11] This requirement is most evident with respect to such

---

[11] A full development of our formal theory will introduce "resource" as another primitive term. Since we do not make extensive use of the term here, we shall not burden the discussion with the additional formal notation. The term is intended to have the same meaning as given in Wolfe's Definition 2 (Chapter 7).

needs as hunger or thirst where consumption of a physical object produces satisfaction. Here, food, water, or something which can be exchanged for them are readily conceived of as resources. In dealing with more social needs the things providing satisfaction are more intangible, but it seems theoretically promising to employ the concept of resource there, too. Thus, we propose that when O "gives approval" he makes a resource accessible to P with which P can satisfy his need for approval. Levinger (Chapter 6) and Wolfe (Chapter 7) have shown that it is possible to conduct empirical research upon such intangible resources.

This conceptualization of motive base and resource is closely related to the treatment by Lasswell and Kaplan (11) of the "value base" of influence and power. They hold that the ability to influence rests on the possession of certain values: "Whenever X has influence over Y, there is some value with regard to which he can exercise influence over Y. This is the base value of the influence relation." (11, p. 83) They distinguish two broad groups of values (an undefined term in their system): welfare values or "those whose possession to a certain degree is a necessary condition for the maintenance of the physical activity of the person," and deference values or "those that consist in being taken into consideration (in the acts of others and of the self)." Specific welfare values are well-being, wealth, skill, and enlightenment. The major deference values are power, respect, rectitude, and affection. The way in which these values are thought to relate to influence and power may be seen in the following quotation.

"The exercise of influence may rest on well-being, on the physical strength of the person exercising it, as in the forms of influence known as 'intimidation' and 'brute force,' for example. It may depend on wealth, as in the case of bribery; on skill, as in the influence of the expert; or on enlightenment, the influence of the sage or teacher. Influence may rest on power, as exemplified by indoctrination; or on respect, the influence flowing from reputation. Rectitude is an influence base in the case of moral authority; and affection is the influence exercised by friends and loved ones." (11, pp. 83-84)

A detailed analysis of how values (as defined by Lasswell and Kaplan) enter into the process of influence would seem to require use of the two terms "motive base" and "resource." In our formulation, O can activate a force on P only if some act of O can tap a motive base of P. In this sense, P's motive base may be thought of as a basis of O's power. But it is clear that O does not possess power simply because P has a need. In addition, O must be able to affect in some way the satisfaction of P's need, usually by being able to provide P with resources or to deprive him of them. Acts of O which set up forces on P convey a direction, "do this," and a motivational consequence, "you will be paid," "you will be wise," "you will be respected," "you will be loved," or "you will be deprived of things valuable to you." Lasswell and Kaplan's concept of "value base," then, corresponds to our two terms, "motive base" and "resource." Two distinct terms are needed because they refer to things which may be attributed separately to different agents (P may have a need while O has the related resource) and because they may vary independently (O's ability to influence P may change because of an alteration either in P's needs or in O's control over resources).

Lasswell and Kaplan introduce the concept "scope of influence" (and power) to refer to "the values involved in the policies affected." They point out that "in a given case influence may be exercised with regard to some values and not others: its scope is limited in various ways. Thus a friend may have influence with regard to the values of affection and respect—he may affect policies concerning these values—but not, say, the values of wealth or power" (11, p. 73). It might seem that "scope of influence," as thus defined, is best related to our term "motive base." Such an interpretation would have clear meaning and would provide a means for describing the fact that in any given relationship between two agents O can influence P by tapping certain motive bases but not others. The set of P's motive bases which O can tap might then be considered as the scope of O's power over P. We do not propose this as a formal definition at this time because there is reason to doubt that this interpretation of Lasswell and Kaplan's meaning would be entirely correct. They seem to assume a close relation between "values" and "policies" and thus make "scope of influence" refer to both. Since we do not assume any necessary relation between the motive base of a force and its location or direction, it is unlikely that any simple translation of "scope of influence" into the terms of our system is possible.

Locus

The next component of the definition of psychological force to be considered is that of "directly joining pair of loci." It will be recalled that the first locus indicated in such a pair specifies the "point of application" of the force and that the pair, as a whole, specifies the direction of the force. Thus, if locus a is coordinated in P's life space to the activity, eating dinner, and locus b to the activity, attending the movies, then the statement that a force contains the pair ab means that there exists a tendency in P's life space for P to move from eating dinner to attending the movies. Since power is defined in terms of forces, a complete specification of the power of O over P must include an indication of the point of application and direction of the forces involved. In other words, the power of O over P must always be specified with respect to a particular pair of directly joining loci in P's life space.

Classification of loci. The abstract term, locus, can be coordinated to many different empirical phenomena, and it is desirable to be explicit in any given situation concerning the "type" of coordination being employed. When dealing with the influence of attitudes and opinions, for example, locus may be coordinated to a distinguishable part of P's cognitive structure. In this case, one may coordinate locus to a position on an attitude scale and consider forces as applying to P's location on such a scale. For other purposes, one may coordinate loci to distinct behaviors and thus study influences on the overt behavior of P. Or, one may coordinate loci to positions in an organization or a group and examine the ways in which O influences P's mobility in a social structure. No complete analysis of the "types of loci" which may be distinguished has been achieved, but the broad outlines of such a typology of loci are suggested by such Lewinian terms as "cognitive structure," "activity space," "social field," "time perspective," "levels of reality," and "person as a differentiated structure." The important point to recognize in this connection is that forces may be activated at loci of various types and that the power of O over P may extend in various ways over various types of loci; O may have great power over some aspects of P's social mobility, less power over certain of his overt behaviors, and virtually none over most of his attitudes.

Range of power. In view of these properties of power, it is useful to define the range of power of O over P.

D6. At any given time, the range of O's power over P is the set of directly joining pairs of loci of P's life space with respect to which O's power over P exceeds a given magnitude, k.

The range of power, like the domain of power, depends upon the particular value assigned to k. For certain purposes we may wish to designate O's range of power over P so as to include quite weak potential influences. For other purposes we may wish to include only much stronger influences.

Consideration of the range of power is important in many problems. French and Raven (Chapter 9) have shown how the range of O's power over P may vary depending upon the particular basis of O's power. Wolfe (Chapter 7) was able to construct a typology of authority relations in the family by designating the ranges of power of husband and wife. Zander, Cohen, and Stotland (Chapter 2), in their study of power relations among the mental health professions, found it possible to describe ranges of power in terms of such classes of activities as diagnosis, therapy, case assignments, social histories and community contacts, and they were able to show certain systematic differences among these. In studies of the power of a group over its members the range of the group's power is of special significance. For any given group there are certain realms of matters over which the group has more power over its members, and others over which it has less. Many labor unions find, for instance, that they have excellent discipline during a strike but that their influence in getting members out to vote is weak. Schachter (19) experimentally varied the "relevance" of member activities to the group and found corresponding differences in the influence exerted on these activities.

While, in principle, the power of O over P may vary freely from locus to locus, there will in fact be empirical interdependencies among loci of various sorts; the collection of loci making up O's range of power over P is hardly constituted on a random basis. Power with respect to certain loci appears to imply power with respect to other loci. Thus, Wolfe (Chapter 7) found that the spouse having dominant power with respect to family finances tended to have power over a wide range of other matters. Much more research is needed before we shall gain a complete understanding of how the range of power is determined. It is likely that there are certain asymmetrical interdependencies among types of loci; a wide range of power regarding P's social locomotion may engender a wide range of power over P's behavior but not vice versa, and a wide range of power over P's beliefs may produce a wide range of power over many diverse aspects of P's life space. Many of the "classical" theories of power assert that some particular range of power is fundamental in that it determines the power in other types of loci. A general hypothesis, proposed by various authors, asserts that there is a tendency for power to spread; once it is firmly established with respect to certain loci its range will tend to enlarge. Such a hypothesis could readily be tested experimentally.

Visibility of loci. Social psychological research on power has stressed one other feature of loci. This has to do with their "social observability" or the fact that some changes in P's life space are more visible to O than others. The degree of observability of compliance has been taken by French and Raven (Chapter 9) to be of special significance in distinguishing among the several bases of power. Essentially the same empirical phenomena have led Festinger (5) to draw a distinction between public compliance and private acceptance of influence attempts. Observability of compliance appears to be important in all forms of power where P's need satisfaction is contingent upon O's evaluation of P's compliance.

Magnitude

Not much need be said about the primitive term "magnitude." It will be recalled that every force has a magnitude indicator, that the strength of an act is defined in terms of the magnitudes of its associated forces, and that power is defined in terms of the maximum strength of potential acts. The magnitude of O's power over P with respect to ab equals the maximum strength (with respect to ab) of any act which O can perform, or equivalently, the maximum combined force which O can set up on P in the direction ab. It is assumed that the magnitude of a force may vary, in principle, with variation in any of the other primitives—act, agent, motive base, loci, and time. In designating the magnitude of O's power, therefore, it is essential to specify it with respect to stated values of these other primitives. We have noted particularly the importance of considering the domain and range of power in quantifying O's power. In comparing the power of any two agents, it is clear that no single, unidimensional scale of magnitude will be adequate. The power of O_1 may differ from that of O_2 with respect to domain, range, motive bases involved, types of acts employed, and various temporal features. While it is undoubtedly useful to order agents with respect to any one of these features, it must be recognized that a different ordering may hold for the other features. Dahl (3) has provided a clear discussion of some of the basic difficulties in rigorously comparing the power of agents. Much further work will be required before an entirely satisfactory solution to this problem has been achieved.

One further feature of the magnitude of power deserves mention. It will be recalled that the strength of an act, and therefore the magnitude of power, may assume negative values. What does it mean to say that the power of O over P with respect to ab has a negative magnitude? In terms of our definitions, the answer is clear: any act which O can perform will result in a combined force on P in a direction away from ab. If O's power over P with respect to ab is negative, no matter how hard O tries to influence P toward ab his net influence will be to stimulate a change in some other direction. Negative power should prove to be a useful concept in treating situations characterized by hostility or warfare.

Time

The primitive term "time" serves two principal purposes in treatments of power. The requirement that a time indicator always be specified constantly reminds us that power may change and helps counteract a natural tendency to think of power structures as static. And, by placing power in a time series it is possible to describe such important aspects of any concrete power relationship as its degree of stability or its tendency to assume certain "preferred" states. Russell (18) and other theorists have advanced various hypotheses about regularities in the modification of power structures and conditions producing change or stability in power relationships. Little empirical research of a social psychological nature, however, has been conducted on problems of this sort. Beginnings in this direction are reported by Rosen (Chapter 5) and by Levinger (Chapter 6). Longitudinal studies of power are needed to remedy certain serious deficiencies in our understanding of the dynamics of power.

REMAINING PROBLEMS

In the foregoing discussion we have attempted to illuminate the essential nature of certain phenomena usually referred to under the labels of social influence and power. The procedure has been to ask what power is and to consider only incidentally hypotheses about the determinants and consequences of power. Our concern has been conceptual rather than operational. This is not to suggest that the empirical aspects of the problem are unimportant or that we have developed the formalization without regard for known empirical findings. But empirical research on power has suffered from a confusion and vagueness of concepts and has provided a poor basis for relating theories of social power to other systematic conceptualizations of human behavior.

There has been no lack of definitions of power. Most of these, however, have merely attached a label to a class of phenomena and have therefore contributed little to the conceptual linking of power to other features of behavior. Only a meager basis for conceptual integration is provided by such definitions as "the capacity to modify the conduct of others in the manner desired," "the ability to apply sanctions," or "the ability to get someone to do something he would not otherwise do." Definitions like these do not possess conceptual properties which place them unambiguously in a general theory of the determinants of behavior. Quite separate concepts are required to describe the way in which conduct is modified, the processes by which sanctions affect behavior, or the events by means of which a person comes to do something he would not otherwise do.

By constructing the definition of power from terms which are currently used in a more extensive theory of behavior, we have hoped to make it possible to incorporate, with some degree of rigor, theoretical treatments of power into this more general theory. But if we have succeeded only in introducing new definitions and distinctions, we have contributed little. The critical test of the conceptualization will be in its usefulness in subsequent empirical research. We turn, then, to some questions which appear to be most pertinent in considering next steps in research on power.

Concept and Phenomena

The objection may be raised that our definition of power does not refer to what power "really" is. Such an objection is, in a sense, meaningless; one can choose to make words mean whatever one wishes, especially since there is no uniformly acceptable definition of power. However, it would create unnecessary confusion to introduce an entirely different definition for a commonly used word. In what respects, then, does our treatment of power refer to empirical phenomena usually discussed under this heading?

In attempting to answer this question, one must distinguish between our *definition* of power and the system of concepts in terms of which the definition is made (i.e., agent, act, motive base, loci, magnitude, and time). Power is defined as a certain combination of these concepts having certain associated values. Of course, other definitions of power could be achieved by selecting other combinations and values of these same concepts without modifying in any way the essential nature of the conceptual system. In a sense, the choice of label for any particular set of terms and values is an arbitrary matter; some other set could just as well be given the label "power." Since the literature, including the chapters of this volume, contains many essentially different definitions of power, it is clear that our definition cannot be made to conform to all of these. Nevertheless, we believe that virtually all of these definitions can be encompassed in our system of concepts.

Consider a few examples. Some authors restrict power to those influences based on coercion or the threat of sanctions. We conceive of the ability to threaten sanctions as one basis of power—threat of sanctions is one kind of act which, when combined with the proper motive base, may activate forces. By examining more closely the nature of such acts and the particular motive bases to which they may relate, we achieve a means for stating systematic relations between threat of sanctions and the magnitude and direction of forces activated by them. Further, by examining how these forces interact with other forces acting on the agent in question, we can describe how the threat of sanctions combines with other influences to modify behavior. It is evident, therefore, that our system of concepts can handle influences based on the threat of sanctions even though we do not choose to *define* power in terms of sanctions.

Other authors make the ability to control behavior (regardless of the technique employed) the essential attribute of power. In fact, this is so prevalent that we have provided a separate definition of "control." It is important to note, however, that this definition is constructed from the same terms that enter into the definition of power. Ability to control another's behavior is, in our terms, a specific instance of the possession of power, and the same conceptual system can be employed in analyzing instances of influence which result in actual control and those which do not.

Still other writers hold that power is an attribute only of groups or institutions and not of individuals. It should be evident that, in terms of our system, this restriction consists in requiring that the term "agent" be coordinated to groups or institutions. While this restriction appears to us to be unwise, it is clear that the system can accommodate such a restriction without damage. To the extent that different empirical phenomena are observed when power is held by a group and by an individual, our system of concepts permits the needed distinctions.

The particular definition of power proposed here, then, is only one of many possible ones which might have been constructed from the primitive terms of our conceptual system. This definition has, we believe, many merits, but we place greater value on the system of concepts than upon the specific definition of power. However one chooses to define power, one must deal explicitly with the kinds of distinctions discussed above as "conceptual properties of power." It may be well, therefore, in summary, to list these inescapable features of power.

1. Power is a relationship between two agents; it is not an absolute attribute of a single agent.

2. The power relationship may be conceived as a relation on an ordered pair of agents. The relation is not necessarily either symmetric or asymmetric; it is irreflexive, though one can speak loosely of the power of an agent over itself; and it is not necessarily either transitive or intransitive.

3. The power relationships between two agents, A and B, may in principle assume any value for the power of A over B and for B over A, resulting in various patterns of interdependence between A and B. It is likely, however, that certain of these patterns are empirically more prevalent than others.

4. The description of an agent's power should specify the domain of agents over whom power exists.

5. Since the power of an agent is defined in terms of his "repertory of potential acts," the nature of this repertory and of its determinants requires investigation.

6. Since the power of O over P indicates O's ability to influence P, it may constitute a threat to P.

7. The exercise of power consists in performing acts. The conditions which determine the choice of acts to be performed thus become an important topic of investigation.

8. Since an act of O must tap a motive base of P in order to activate a force on P, the power of O over P depends in part upon the motivational state of P.

9. Since the satisfaction of a need of P requires access to appropriate resources, the possession of such resources is an important feature of the power situation.

10. The power of O over P always refers to a particular pair of directly joining loci in P's life space (i.e., some definite change). The description of O's power over P therefore must specify the range of loci in P's life space over which power exists.

11. The magnitude of O's power over P with respect to a particular pair of directly joining loci in P's life space equals the maximum resultant psychological force which O can set up on P in the specified direction.

12. Any attempt to compare the power of A and B must refer to specific types of acts, the domains of power, the motive bases involved, the ranges in question, and definite time periods.

Problems of operationalization

The general significance of these implications of the definition of power would seem to be that any operational treatment of power will be prohibitively complicated. How can we hope ever to arrive at an adequate quantitative specification of power? It is clear that we do have to be on guard in developing operational indicators of power; power is not a simple phenomenon. But the task is not insurmountable, for certain empirical facts come to our rescue. Even though in principle the power of O may have a unique value for each P and for each pair of loci in each life space, social systems tend to render equivalent whole classes of loci and of agents. Thus, O will tend to have uniform power over agents P_1, P_2, P_3 . . . with respect to pairs of loci, ab, cd, ef. . . . In well established groups these uniformities make it possible to obtain significant research findings through the use of instruments which do not make all the differentiations implied in the definition of power.

The study of Zander, Cohen, and Stotland (24) of relations among psychiatrists, clinical psychologists, and psychiatric social workers illustrates one way in which this may be done. Here work-related activities were classed under such headings as "diagnosis," "therapy," "writing social histories," and "making community contacts." For each class of activity the power relations between each pair of professional roles were reported by a sample of occupants of the roles. The resulting findings seem to show two things: first, meaningful data are obtained upon the assumption that these classes can be treated as relatively homogeneous units; and second, making the distinction among classes produces significant differences. For example, the power scores for psychiatrists over social workers yielded high intercorrelations among all four classes of activities—in other words the range of power is broad. The power scores for the clinical psychologists over the social workers, however, did not show such correlations—power in one class of activity does not assure power in another. In examining the power of psychiatrists over clinical psychologists it was possible to show that "therapy" is the "center" of the range —the situation there has profound effects on other areas.

In a related study, Hurwitz, Zander, and Hymovitch (10) asked each of forty-two professional mental health workers to rate each of the others according to the amount of weight he would give the other's opinions about matters of mental health. In terms of our definition of power, each P was asked to indicate the power of an O over him in the class of activities broadly labeled as "matters having to do with mental health." An average rating of attributed power was then constructed for each person. When these ratings were compared with a dichotomous classification of prestige made by two community informants, there were only three disagreements for the forty-two people. In a subsequent experiment these people discussed problems of mental health in small groups composed half and half of high- and low-power individuals. Here it was found that those with low power talked significantly less than highs, that when they did talk they addressed their remarks to highs, and that the amount of their participation was exaggerated by the others in postmeeting ratings.

Lippitt, Polansky, Redl, and Rosen (14) were able to obtain stable and meaningful results in their research on the power structure of summer camps by using an instrument which does not specify explicitly any activities at all. They asked each of these children the simple question, "Who is best at getting the others to do what he wants them to do?" Note that each child is asked to average up in his own head the power of each other child over all the other children and over all relevant activities! It seems that children can carry out this task rather easily, for remarkably consistent results were obtained. Thus, it was regularly found that a member with high attributed power is more likely in actual interactions with others to have his behavior imitated by others (he is more contagious), to have his direct influence attempts succeed, and to initiate more influence attempts. Furthermore, it was found that there is a considerable agreement between each child's ranking of himself and the mean ranking attributed to him by others.

These studies and others make it clear that social power of a rather generalized sort can be a salient attribute of one's perceived social world, and that people can report significant features of power relationships. There is some indication of how the perception of power takes place, but there is much yet to be learned. In some of the summer camps mentioned above it was found that children with low attributed power approached the highs in a nondirective and deferential manner while the highs were more directive. These qualitative features of the interaction might be assumed to stabilize the perception of power among the highs and lows alike and to provide cues to any new members. Similar qualitative differences have been reported by other investigators. Unfortunately for the quick generalization, however, the same differences in interaction have not been found in all camps. It seems that the specific cues provided may differ from one culture to another and that measuring instruments may have to be adapted to the particular culture under study.

On the basis of available evidence, then, we may conclude that the problems of operationalizing our definition of power are not insurmountable. While, in principle, the definition calls for the specification of many features of any given situation, it is possible to employ approximations and to rely upon indirect indicators. But the difficulties should not be minimized; the definition does require that certain essential distinctions be preserved in any empirical research. It is to be hoped that knowledge of these essential features of power may help in the avoidance of unwarranted generalizations from measurements which do not provide for essential distinctions. Especially important in this respect is the need to recognize that power is not a single quantity that can be specified without regard to domain and range. Generalizations, for example, from data related implicitly to one range may be quite incorrect when applied to another range. Perhaps equally important are the distinctions between power and control and between the possession and the exercise of power. Measurements of power which rely upon evidence of control, while undoubtedly useful in certain circumstances, run the risk of blurring important distinctions.

In the long run, the major contribution to research to be derived from this formalization of power may well be in the guidance it provides for the construction of new measuring instruments. The formal properties of power indicate empirical features with which the researcher must cope. While it is true that many of these features can be treated only with great difficulty, this fact can hardly be taken as a basis for rejecting the formalization. Rather, it should spur methodological ingenuity.

Power structure

Power, as defined here, is a relationship between two agents. Yet most of the interesting empirical problems of power deal with social systems containing many more than two people. These problems refer to the "power structure" of groups and institutions. What, for example, are the consequences to a social system of having different numbers of levels in a power hierarchy, of having power concentrated or distributed in various ways, of having an arrangement providing for checks and balances, of having various numbers of subordinates to a given superior, or of having people subordinate to more than one superior? Questions of this sort pose a basic theoretical issue: Can the concept of power, defined as a dyadic relationship, be used in analyzing power structures? We believe that it can, though there has been little work specifically dealing with this problem.

One promising avenue for further theoretical advance is provided by the mathematical theory of directed linear graphs (8). This branch of mathematics provides a suitable method for representing configurations of dyadic relations. If the simplifying assumption is made that the essential structural properties of a power system will not be destroyed by merely specifying the presence or absence of power for each ordered pair of agents, then directed graphs may be employed to represent power structures. The essential coordination between empirical phenomena of power and the theory of directed graphs consist in identifying each agent as a point of a directed graph and each instance where one agent has power over another as a directed line from one point to another. With such a coordination, the properties of directed graphs may be used to characterize such structural features of power networks as whether an influence originating at a point can reach every other point, whether or not conflicting influences can be exerted on a given point, how many levels a structure has, or how strongly connected any given structure is. A pictorial drawing of such directed graphs would resemble the familiar organization chart, but the mathematical theory provides rigorous definitions and a set of theorems. It is evident, however, that in the long run a mathematical model will be needed which assigns quantities to lines which indicate the magnitude of power associated with each line.

French (7) has shown how the theory of directed graphs may be employed, along with certain empirical assumptions, to predict the processes of influence and the resulting distribution of beliefs and attitudes in different power structures. French's model has been generalized by Harary and related to the theory of higher transition probabilities in Markov chains (Chapter 10). This approach suggests many promising leads for further research and theory.

In dealing with power structures it is necessary, of course, to observe the same distinctions required in treating power as a dyadic relationship. For example, different structures will be found among the same collection of agents for different ranges of power—a person in a business organization who can influence many others, directly or indirectly, concerning work related activities may occupy a position of little consequence in a structure defined in terms of ability to influence attitudes toward the union. Similarly, different structures may be generated among the same agents by different motive bases—a power structure based on the granting of rewards may be quite different from one based on expertness or attraction.

A final problem may be mentioned, though no solution is suggested. It is clear that agents may establish relations which result in a pooling of power so that working together they can exert influences not possible by any one of them alone. What are the necessary conditions for the power of two or more agents to add up? When a coalition is formed, should the collectivity thus formed be treated conceptually as a single agent? We can only indicate that analysing such questions provides an interesting line for further investigation.

CONCLUDING COMMENTS

1. The studies reported in this book, together with recent work reported elsewhere, indicate that the concept of power can become a central part of social psychological theory.

2. The field theoretical conception advanced here provides, in principle, a means for treating in a single, coherent, conceptual system both individual and social determinants of behavior.

3. According to this conception, the behavior, attitudes, and beliefs of a person, P, are determined by the totality of psychological forces existing in P's life space at any given time. One important set of determinants of these forces consists of acts of agents other than P.

4. The theory of power is concerned with those psychological forces acting in P's life space which are activated by agents other than P. Its basic building block is the dyadic relation between two agents, O and P.

5. The power of O over P depends, in part, upon (a) the acts which O

can perform, (b) the distribution of resources between O and P (as well as other agents), (c) the motive bases of P, and (d) the "cognitive" content of P's life space (i.e., the specific set of directly joining pairs of loci existing there). Empirical research on power should be concerned with all of these classes of determinants and the conditions which, in turn, determine these determinants.

6. The exercise of power requires its possession; O cannot activate forces in P's life space unless the power of O over P differs from zero. In addition, however, the exercise of power consists of the performance of acts whose strength with regard to P differs from zero. Empirical research is needed to discover the conditions which determine the performance of acts and the strength of acts. Such research will need to investigate, among other things, social perception and ideology concerning the ethics and strategy of social influence.

7. Any given power relation has consequences for both agents. When O has considerable power over P (both in magnitude and range), a condition of threat usually exists for P. This relation must also produce consequences for O (the possession of power is said to generate self-confidence, insensitivity, cruelty, or corruption), but few empirical data have been accumulated concerning these outcomes.

8. Ordinarily a given dyadic power relation is an element of a power system. One should expect it, therefore, to depend upon properties of this system. Research is badly needed on the dynamics of power systems, that is, on tendencies for power systems to assume certain "preferred" states.

9. Advances in our understanding of power should result from work in all of the social sciences. Such advances will depend, however, upon the integration of findings into a single conceptual system. The conceptual formulation presented here has been proposed with the hope that it will facilitate such an integration.

REFERENCES

1. Biddle, B. J., French, J. R. P., Jr., & Moore, J. W. Some aspects of leadership in the small work group. A report to the U. S. Air Force, 1953.

2. Bierstedt, R. An analysis of social power. *Am. sociol. Rev.*, 1950, 15, 730-736.

3. Dahl, R. A. The concept of power. *Behav. Sci.*, 1957, 2, 201-215.

4. Dubin, R. (Ed.). *Human relations in administration.* New York: Prentice-Hall, 1951.

5. Festinger, L. An analysis of compliant behavior. In C. Sherif & M. O. Wilson (Eds.). *Group relations at the crossroads.* New York: Harper, 1953.

6. Fleishman, E. A., Harris, E. F., & Burtt, H. E. *Leadership and supervision in industry.* Columbus: Ohio State Univer., 1955.

7. French, J. R. P., Jr. A formal theory of social power. *Psychol. Rev.*, 1956, **63**, 181-194.

8. Harary, F., Norman, R. Z., & Cartwright, D. *Introduction to digraph theory for social scientists.* Ann Arbor: Institute for Social Research, in press.

9. Hovland, C. I., & Weiss, W. The influence of source credibility on communication effectiveness. *Publ. Opin. Quart.*, 1952, **15**, 635-650.

10. Hurwitz, J. I., Zander, A. F., & Hymovitch, B. Some effects of power on the relations among group members. In D. Cartwright & A. Zander (Eds.). *Group dynamics: research and theory.* Evanston: Row, Peterson, 1953.

11. Lasswell, H. D., & Kaplan, A. *Power and society.* New Haven: Yale Univer. Press, 1950.

12. Lewin, K. *The conceptual representation and the measurement of psychological forces.* Durham: Duke Univer. Press, 1938.

13. Lewin, K. *Field theory in social science.* New York: Harper, 1951.

14. Lippitt, R., Polansky, N., Redl, F., & Rosen, S. The dynamics of power. *Hum. Relat.*, 1952, **5**, 37-64.

15. Meyers, C. E. The effect of conflicting authority on the child. *Univer. Iowa Stud. Child Welf.*, 1944, **20**, 31-98.

16. Parsons, T. *The social system.* Glencoe, Ill.: Free Press, 1951.

17. Parsons, T. *Essays in sociological theory.* (Rev. Ed.). Glencoe, Ill.: Free Press, 1954.

18. Russell, B. *Power.* London: George Allen & Unwin, 1938.

19. Schachter, S. Deviation, rejection, and communication. *J. abnorm. soc. Psychol.*, 1951, **46**, 190-207.

20. Schulze, R. O. The role of economic dominants in community power structure. *Am. sociol. Rev.*, 1958, **23**, 3-9.

21. Simon, H. A. *Administrative behavior.* New York: Macmillan, 1956.

22. Simon, H. A. *Models of man.* New York: Wiley, 1957.

23. Tawney, R. H. *Equality.* New York: Harcourt, Brace, 1931.

24. Zander, A., Cohen, A. R., & Stotland, E. *Role relations in the mental health professions.* Ann Arbor: Institute for Social Research, 1957.

INDEX

221

PUBLICATIONS OF THE
INSTITUTE FOR SOCIAL RESEARCH

These publications may be obtained from the

Librarian
Institute for Social Research
University of Michigan
Ann Arbor, Michigan

Research Center for Group Dynamics Series

RCGD No. 1   Changing Attitudes Through Social Contact
by Leon Festinger, Harold H. Kelley

RCGD No. 2   Graph Theory As A Mathematical Model In Social Science
by Frank Harary, Robert Z. Norman

RCGD No. 3   Measuring Group Cohesiveness
by Lester M. Libo

RCGD No. 4   Learning Across Cultures
by Jeanne Watson, Ronald Lippitt

RCGD No. 5   Role Relations in the Mental Health Professions
by Alvin Zander, Arthur R. Cohen, Ezra Stotland

Survey Research Center Series

SRC No. 1   Public Use of the Library
by Angus Campbell, Charles A. Metzner

SRC No. 2   Productivity, Supervision and Morale In An Office Situation
by Daniel Katz, Nathan Maccoby, Nancy C. Morse

SRC No. 4   Industrial Mobility in Michigan
by George Katona, James N. Morgan

SRC No. 5   Productivity, Supervision and Morale Among Railroad Workers
by Daniel Katz, Nathan Maccoby, Gerald Gurin, Lucretia G. Floor

SRC No. 6   Big Business As the People See It
by Burton R. Fisher, Stephen B. Withey

SRC No. 9   The People Elect a President
by Angus Campbell, Robert L. Kahn

SRC No. 10   Satisfactions In The White-Collar Job
by Nancy Morse

SRC No. 12   Consumer Attitudes and Demands, 1950-1952
by George Katona, Eva Mueller

SRC No. 14   Group Cohesiveness In The Industrial Work Group
by Stanley E. Seashore

SRC No. 15   Group Differences In Attitudes and Votes
by Angus Campbell, Homer C. Cooper

SRC No. 16   Consumer Expectations, 1953-1956
by George Katona, Eva Mueller

SRC No. 17   Processes of Organization
by Robert Weiss

Research Center for Group Dynamics Series
Publication No. 6